CONVERSATIONS ON Faith

Insight Publishing Company
Sevierville, Tennessee

© 2004 by Insight Publishing Company.

Published by Insight Publishing Company
P.O. Box 4189
Sevierville, Tennessee 37864

Printed in the United States of America

ISBN: 1-885640-24-2

Table Of Contents

A Message From The Publisher

Faith is a concept with as many textures and nuances as there are people who profess to have it. It is one of the most profound things known to man, and yet it is deeply personal and often times impossible to describe. Faith has compelled kings and queens to expand their territories and conquer nations. Faith has empowered individuals to stand courageously in the face of tyrants, torture, and death. Faith, though unseen, has supported entire nations in times of uncertainty and crisis.

When we decided to publish *Conversations On Faith*, it was our desire to compile frank, honest, and intimate interviews with men and women who have all walked different paths, come from different cultural and socioeconomic backgrounds, and therefore have seen faith work in many different ways in their lives. We asked them to share their stories, their insights, and their inspiration, so others might be encouraged to grab hold of faith and see it work in their life!

It is our hope that you keep this book with you until you've dog-eared every chapter and made so many notes in the margins that you have trouble seeing the original words on the pages. There is treasure here. Enjoy digging!

Interviews conducted by:

David E. Wright
President, International Speakers Network

Chapter 1

LYNETTA JORDAN

THE INTERVIEW

David E. Wright (Wright)
Today we are talking to Lynetta Jordan. Lynetta is a motivational
speaker, relationship builder, and inspirational writer. A powerful
communicator and a successful college educator, she seems to special-
ize in helping underachieving students both in high school and college
set and reach goals. She motivates educational professionals, too.
Lynetta has presented her workshop for educators, *Water For Your
Journey: Refreshment For Educators Who Feel Burned Out* nationally.
Lynetta is also an evangelist who loves to share the good news on the
radio and in public. She loves working with youth, singles ministries,
women's fellowships, and she's performed creative praise dances and
poetry readings. Lynetta feels that her life's work is not her own, but
a higher calling. She believes that she has been gifted and called by
God to help people improve every area of their lives at home, in the
work place, and in the community. Lynetta Jordan, welcome to *Conversations on Faith.*

Lynetta Jordan (Jordan)
Thank you, David.

1

Wright

Lynetta, people refer to you as a dynamic preacher and teacher, and I read that you believe that you were chosen for such a time as this. Could you explain to our readers the process you experienced to decide you were chosen?

Jordan

Many things can happen in our lifetimes to help us realize that were chosen. I've always loved to encourage people and speak words to help them through tough situations. To some, my story may not seem very dramatic. I was raised in and very involved in church as a youth; however, it was when I went to college that I truly established a committed relationship with Christ. I remember very clearly one day near the end of my first semester at Elizabeth City State University; I drove off campus to my bank, not because I really needed money, but because I felt led to go there. Once I arrived, I saw a car accident across the street. I got out of my vehicle and that is when I realized that my trip was not really about me going to the bank, but actually being there to see what had happened. I began walking across the street toward the accident. I remember hearing a voice inside of me saying, "Go over there. Go across the street." I thought, "I can't just walk up to these people. I don't know what they are going to think." Before I knew it my feet were moving in that direction. I walked up to the vehicle and saw a young female driver, about age sixteen. She was inside crying because she had hit a man on a moped. I touched her and said, "Sister are you a believer?" She had a relative there who said, "I'm a believer," I said, "Can we pray?" I grabbed hands and prayed with them that day. I really do not remember all I the words that I prayed. All I know is that I was not my own. My steps were ordered there. I didn't choose to pray on that accident scene. I didn't even realize my own feet were walking there! But, somebody needed something from God. He used me to deliver it (what they needed). I remember driving back to campus that evening, walking back in to my dorm room and laying on the bed asking, "God, what just happened?" I phoned a friend and shared this awe-inspiring experience. We were amazed. Through this unforgettable incident I realized that God had a greater purpose for my life. It was evident that God wanted to use me for His service in a very special way. Clearly, I recall that situation as the beginning of a new level in Christ for me, of a true commitment. I surrendered all. From the depths of my heart I said, "God, I give you everything—my heart, my mind, my soul and my body. I just don't want to be my own anymore because I realize You have something greater in store for me than I even planned or dreamed of myself." David, I can truly say that moment in time was when I knew I was chosen for such a time as this.

Wright

You have said that you have overcome many obstacles to develop an intimate, satisfying relationship with Christ. Will you tell us a little bit about your background and how you came to be who you are now?

Jordan

Sure. I will begin with my school years. I like to encourage the youth today because when I was in high school I was an academic achiever. I was very focused on education and a leader in community service clubs like 4-H and the Key Club. I played the flute and piccolo in marching band. But, you know, academically successful students are not always considered by their peers as members of the "in" crowd. I wasn't part of the "in" crowd, which happened to be those who everyone considered to be popular for the wrong reasons. I wasn't dating everybody. I wasn't drinking. I wasn't doing everything they were doing. I was basically home or involved in community and church activities. I didn't hang out at all the parties. My parents wouldn't even let me go. I hated it sometimes, because I felt like my parents were just keeping me in. Later on in life, I realized that their protectiveness kept me from a lot of danger. I was academically gifted, nevertheless, I was picked on by other students. Every person wants to be accepted. Everyone wants to feel loved. During those times as a teenager, I did know that God cared for and accepted me. I acknowledged that He had given me a family to take care of me, food, clothing, and shelter—life's necessities. I knew that if the people who were joking and teasing on me were not providing any of life's necessities for me, then I really didn't have to listen to what they said. Not being part of their "in" crowd was an obstacle because every young person wants to be accepted and well liked by their peers. That did not always feel comfortable, but I was constantly assured by adults that I was focusing on the right goals. As I matured, I learned that you have to sacrifice something in order to gain greater things in life. Perhaps I sacrificed popularity with everyone to gain a more prosperous and productive lifestyle later on down the road.

As an adult, I have overcome the obstacles of broken relationships, betrayal by former friends, jealousy and envy, and deceitful lies spoken by others. Even in doing my best, some people will speak negative words and try to influence others not to like you. Because I have realized that people and their attitudes toward you can change, I have grown more to love the consistent, never-changing, all wise Savior of my soul.

In fact, I can not tell you how many times I thought of myself as the story of the ugly ducking that turns into the swan. I really did feel that way when I was picked on in school. When people did not express acceptance of me, I knew that I'd become the beautiful swan one day. By going through those experiences, I drew closer to the Lord.

Wright

Now you're putting me on. I've seen your picture.

Jordan

I'm telling you the truth.

Wright

As a female minister have you encountered difficulties ministering to people that male ministers would seldom face?

Jordan

Surprisingly, I have not openly encountered many difficulties. God has shielded my eyes and ears from naysayers, those who believe and vividly express that women should not preach the gospel of Jesus Christ. Though I know oppression for women in ministry exists, I have not openly experienced it, but I am acquainted with female ministers, especially pastors, that have had a difficult road. It may be that I have dealt with people who have been a little more open. Let me share an example of how God has opened the minds of men. Years ago, a lady told me her elderly father's remarks after I had ministered at his church. She said, "My daddy said he really enjoyed you. He kept telling me that there was something special about you. He really learned from you at church that Sunday." She added, "And my daddy usually does not care for female ministers." Hearing that testimony of how this man, one who was usually not too quick to receive the Word from a female minister, was blessed when I ministered was a good sign that I would be received by more men. The Word of God can transcend gender. The Bible does not present a male, female, black or white gospel. It is THE gospel for ALL people. I have tried to keep my focus too, because with all of our progress, I know that there are still a lot of people that are not receptive to females in ministry. I was raised in the AME Zion Church and am presently an associate minister at Believers' Victory Center, a non-denominational church. Both ministries strongly teach that God is equipping males and females for ministry, so personally, I am confident in my call to minister worldwide. I admire and glean from strong women already ministering internationally, like Joyce Meyer and Paula White. I am also privileged to have an aunt who is an experienced local pastor. My prayer is that the work I do and have done—angelistic and motivational speaking, inspiring youth, the radio ministry, and the inspirational writing—speak for me.

Men and women have heard and complemented my radio ministries and talk shows. Since listeners only hear your voice, they can not judge your appearance. This has worked well. For example, some churches love the Lord but believe that women have to wear long dresses, no pants, and no cosmetics. Unfortunately, for people trained that way, my appearance could be a hindrance to them receiving a message that is straight from heaven. So, think about it. The fact that I may be wearing pants or make-up is not a barrier on the radio. I can be received because again, I am preaching the Word of God and God says that His sheep, male or female, know His voice. The Bible says that in the last days God will pour out His spirit upon His sons and daughters. Irrespective of our doctrinal differences, we must not forget what Paul said in Galatians 3:28, *"There is neither Jew nor Greek, there is neither slave nor free, there is neither male nor female; for you are all one in Christ Jesus."*

Wright
You taught in the public school system.

Jordan
Yes.

Wright
When you consider that the constitution guarantees separation of church of state, did you promote your faith and if so, how did you do it?

5

Jordan

I definitely promoted my faith and I'm going to tell you exactly how I did it. I did not preach in my classroom. I didn't have to. I promoted my faith as an advisor and then director for the Northeastern High School gospel choir. Another God-fearing musically gifted staff person and I worked together to coordinate rehearsals, fund-raisers, trips, and public performances. We could openly pray and share scriptures in our rehearsals. And of course, we had a Hallelujah good time singing songs of praise in three part harmony. The first year was exciting, but the second year was even more challenging for me. At the beginning of the year, we were unable to find a choir director, which is a role that must be filled. Both Ms. Johnson, the other advisor, and I contacted everyone we knew. I kept hearing this voice inside of me saying, " You do it," and after every door was closed, I finally received it as Holy Spirit speaking to me. Although I co-founded my own high school's gospel choir and sang in my church and university gospel choirs, I had never directed a choir before. "God. What? You want me to direct the choir?" I inwardly asked. I kept hearing, "You do it." So, guess what happened? I did it. I directed the choir all the way to victory at national gospel choir competition in New York City. Our choir won first place trophies in almost every category. To add icing to the cake, I was named the best director from all the schools represented! Those students and I were ecstatic. The gospel choir students' attitudes, behavior, and grades improved. Students campus wide, students I did not even teach, came to know me as the gospel choir advisor/director. They often stopped by my room to speak, and of course I would smile and greet them with God's love.

On the contrary, I think it's important to realize that there are "risks" to boldly expressing our faith in the workplace. As a partaker in Christ's sufferings, I did experience a false religious accusation from a classroom student. Carefully planned, it was the student's last day in my class. I believe that her trick was intended as retribution for my enforcement of discipline. It was meant to put out my light for Christ in that school. But, as Isaiah 54:17 promises, *"No weapon formed against us shall prosper."* A weapon might be formed against you, but it will not work. At the conclusion of this situation, the parent apologized to me. Spiritual weapons will be formed against us in the public schools and any other workplace. Some ill-hearted persons who know you are a minister will use "ministry" to entrap you, even when you haven't done anything wrong. I have learned to keep standing for Christ because His truth will prevail. Since I can do all things through Christ, I was able to forgive the student, parent, and the principal, even though the principal had recorded this false accusation on my evaluation.

Wright

Tell our readers about the businesses that you have founded. What are they? And what do you aim to achieve through them?

Jordan

I am the president and founder of Lynetta Jordan Ministries, Spoken Words Communication Group, and Dare To Be Dynamic Motivational Seminars. Lynetta Jordan Ministries is an organization destined to empower women, impact the world, and win a wealth of souls for Christ. As an evangelist, I equip people and teach them to apply the Bible to every area of their lives. John 6:63 says that *"The words I speak. They are spirit and they are life."* I use the spoken and written word to bring refreshment, inspiration, and new life to people by sharing God's word in a practical manner through mass media— books, magazines, the internet, radio, and even television. One niche is applying the Bible to our relationships, so I am a relationship builder, too. I look forward to traveling, evangelizing, and strengthening families worldwide.

Spoken Words Communication Group is a nonprofit corporation. Our motto, *"Promoting The Positive, Proclaiming The Good News,"* expresses the broad vision of the organization. Planning, in today's media, negative news sells. We have all heard the phrase, no news is good news. Well, I strongly believe that we must intentionally and purposefully promote the positive events and achievements. Prior to attending college, I had the dreams of becoming a television anchorwoman and creating and owning a communication corporation. This is the beginning of the fulfillment of part of that dream. I put my anchorwoman aspiration on hold after discovering, in my first journalism class, what the typical young journalist has to endure. I had a picture of myself almost being blown away by hurricane force winds because I was trying to report a story and make a good name for myself as a anchor woman. I wanted to go directly to the camera. No hurricanes for me!

Wright

(laughs) You mean you're a cowardly minister.

Jordan

(laughs) No. Of course not. I'm not a cowardly minister. We have to choose our battles and I just do not want to fight that kind of storm if I can avoid it. I will continue to fight the fierce spiritual storms of life, though. I have God's promise to overcome them all.

So, I still earned a bachelor's degree in English—News Media concentration, but I said that I'll do television a little bit later. I realized that I had to be employed in a position that I felt was making a positive contribution to society. Teaching alone impacts lives, but when I taught a public school, I published a news letter to promote faculty and staff accomplishments outside of school. I published copies for the entire staff and students. I also believe in ministry standards of excellence. Through Spoken Words Communication Group, I also desire to increase the effectiveness of ministries, especially those in rural Northeastern North Carolina, in their media promotions, desktop publishing, and planning for major events. I earned a master of the arts degree in Communication—Corporate Communication and Development from Regent University, so I have also conducted corporate training and needs assessments and planned public relations campaigns. Spoken Words Communication Group also helps ministries develop to a higher level of excellence. Finally, Dare To Be Dynamic Motivational Seminars is just like the title. As a keynote speaker, I refresh, motivate, and inspire audiences in businesses, universities, professional conferences, youth groups and even churches to achieve success in life and love. My goal is to motivate them to achieve more than they ever have before. Winning attitudes and winning actions get results. My website is www.LynettaJordan.org. Those three organizations have been birthed through gifts that God has given to me. Like the refreshing workshop I present for educators, *Water For Your Journey*. I love to refresh people, because we need to be renewed. Sometimes it's your peers that do not truly seem to care if you are doing a great job and giving your best everyday. Employees, even entrepreneurs need to be refreshed and reminded that what we do really does count.

Wright

Right.

Jordan

Then it can be your superiors, your bosses that do not complement and encourage you. Some only care about the bottom line and at times, need help to tell the people how significant they are to the achievement of the bottom line. What workers have to know, whether anybody tells you or not, is that they are valuable. Dare To Be Dynamic wants to help companies with high performing employees continue to keep them efficient, excellent, and motivated.

Wright

Let me debunk this ugly duckling thing you were talking about while ago. I have read that you were a black college queen?

Jordan

Yes. I was Miss Elizabeth City State University 1994-1995. Yes, I did transform from the ugly ducking to a swan.

Wright

Could you tell us about that experience? Were you able to promote your faith in that venue?

Jordan

Serving as Miss Elizabeth City State University (Miss ECSU) was an awesome opportunity to promote, share, and demonstrate my faith. Prior to touching the soil, moving into the dorm, and my first day of classes, I told the Lord that I wanted to be a light for Him at ECSU so that others can see the light that is within me and a true manifestation of Christ. I wanted to be a living witness. I had such joy in Jesus that I wanted others to be filled with joy and experience the peace and satisfaction of knowing Him. Walking with Christ had made a difference in my life. So for four years, I spoke to strangers and friends. I smiled at them, beaming darkness-shattering rays of Christ's love. I shared personal testimonies with students and faculty. For instance, if He made financial provision for an expense when I knew that I could not have done it for myself, I shared the story to a student to say, "This is what God can do for you."

I served as college queen my senior year; however, there was a process to winning the title of Miss ECSU. First, I had to be nominated by my peers in my Junior year. After nomination, I had to apply. Once accepted as an official candidate, I had to campaign against four other ladies. It was a very stiff competition. Then we each had the opportunity to demonstrate our talent, poise, and personality in the Miss ECSU Showcase, a pageant. The next day, student elections were held and I won!!! As Miss ECSU, I let my light radiantly shine for Christ both locally and nationally. I was invited to speak at campus assemblies and convocations, community events, and my photo was published in *Ebony* and *Black Excellence* magazines. I also participated in two national pageants, the National Black Alumni Hall Of Fame and the televised Miss African-American Collegiate. Our campus had over fifty student organizations represented at my coronation. Christians, students of other religious beliefs, and I were able to work together in a common spirit of unity. We saw people as people and not as racially divided, religiously divided, divided by handicaps or anything. That is Christlike.

In addition, my friends and I celebrated when students surrendered their lives to Christ. I remember when a male student accepted Christ. Do you know what we did? We threw him a salvation party in a reserved area in the cafeteria during dinner hours. We even purchased a cake and sang a song to the tune of Happy Birthday. Our song said, "Happy Salvation To You." The Bible records that angels rejoice over one sinner that repents. We rejoiced, too. It is a momentous occasion when a college student repents, turns from the world, and lives for Christ. Salvation is a gift that only Jesus could give. None of us have lived perfect lives. Christ has forgiven and redeemed us from many, many entanglements. When you are at your lowest, when you feel like you have made one too many mistakes, when you feel that there is nothing that you could possibly offer Him, that is when Jesus will take your life and create something so beautiful out of that nothingness. Our heart and our lives in total surrender is our offering to the Lord. I was glad to demonstrate a Christlike lifestyle and encourage others I was the campus queen, Miss Elizabeth City State University.

Wright

You know there are almost as many definitions of faith as people I ask. Will you tell me your definition of faith, and give an example of how you think faith should be used to influence others?

Jordan

It is wise to go directly to the biblical definition of faith in Hebrews 11:1. That verse says, *"Now faith is a substance of things hoped for and the evidence of things not seen."* As Christians we are required to walk by faith and not by sight, which can be quite a challenge at times. Walking by faith is not an impossible task because God has given everyone of us the measure of faith, as declared in Romans 12:3. God has planted faith deep within us, but we have to stir it up and work that faith out of us. I believe that faith is like a muscle that needs to be stretched, strengthened, and developed. That concept leads me into my personal definition of faith. You have to remember that I am a former English teacher, so I taught the parts of speech. Thus, I like to examine faith in the noun and the verb tense. I believe we need to understand both. Faith as a noun is how a lot of people view faith today. When asked about their faith, many people respond with "Oh, I am Christian." Some answer with their church denomination. "I am Apostolic. I am Baptist. I am Methodist. I am Episcopal. I am Pentecostal." That's faith as a noun; however our religious affiliation does not define fully define faith. If I were to use faith as a noun, I would define it as the state of standing firm and without wavering on a promise of God, believing that you will receive the fulfillment of that promise even when all evidence appears contrary to God's word concerning the matter. That's pretty lengthy, but it is important to know that faith works when we are standing on the promises of God because faith moves Him to action. He hastens to perform His own word.

The most active definition of faith for me is faith in the verb tense, because faith is an action word. It requires belief and effort from of us. It requires sacrifice. It requires steps of forward movement toward a promise. Faith also requires that we trust God and believe the very thing that seems impossible. So, I like to define faith as an action word. With the definition stated, let me express this. More believers need to get into the practice of exercising their faith. We need to go on a spiritual diet and do a spiritual workout here. We need to stretch our faith muscles. Similar to beginning a new physical fitness routine, we may feel pain in our faith muscle when we first begin to exercise it. We feel that pain that lets us know that we have stretched beyond our usual comfort zone. The truth is that that pain is actually a good sign. It means that we are making progress. It takes faith to believe for a positive outcome when we are in situations that look dim and hopeless. Sometimes God allows us to hit dead ends so that our faith can grow. For example, I have had a bill that I could not pay. I went to mama and she did not have the money, which meant that daddy did not have it either. I could not obtain a loan and I certainly did not need a new debt. Every door was shut. Finally, I threw my hands up and trusted the Lord. He provided in an unexpected way. If you dare to believe God, then He can make a way that you can not see. It is not required that we know how our blessings are going to arrive. We can not always predict their packaging. We just have to know Who is going to bring the blessing. I have an example of that, too.

Wright

Will you please share it with us?

Jordan

I had planned an event, an end-of-the-year banquet. We were inconvenienced at the last minute and had almost five hundred dollars unexpected expenses. I knew I would fall short on the money. I personally did not have it and I knew I had to pay the expenses at the end of the program. As I stood up to make remarks, I heard the Spirit of the Lord speak to me. His words were so profound that I shared them with the audience. He said "This situation is not about HOW you are going to pay for this. It's about WHO is going to do it." He continued, "The same three letters—H O W are also W H O. How or who? It is up to you. Now you can let go of worrying about how it will be done and let me do it." Guess what happened. At the end, without me asking, the caterer told me that he would charge me less money than we initially agreed. Caterers do not volunteer to charge less money. I know that was God. We may have heard our elders say it, but it is true that God will make a way out of what seems to be no way. So, that's something to teach. Our daily lifestyles will improve. We will definitely have less stress if we roll our cares onto the Lord.

When we get into conflicting situations, we would not give up so quickly. We can go back to the Bible, read one of God's promises, and say, "God, You promised this to me. My faith says I believe in you. So you know what? I am not going to worry about it. I am going to relax and watch you be God and move on my behalf." I will be the first person to say that at times, it is a hard thing to not worry. We are so used to pondering and try to fix life's problems on our own. Faith does require that we relinquish our hold, actively let go and release the results to God. A scripture that inspire me is Luke 1:45. *"Blessed is she that hath believed for there shall be a performance of those things that were told her from the Lord."* God has promised to perform and bless me because I believe. Faith walkers excel to heights unknown when we exercise our faith.

Wright

We've talked about difficulties as a female minister and that they weren't perceived as all that difficult. Are there any hardships caused by the fact that you are single?

Jordan

Yes. Ecclesiastes records that two are better than one. At times I desire companionship, to walk in one accord with God's man for me. Ministry requires work and commitment. I believe that it would help to have someone to share life's joys and disappointments. I read that the road to success is often a lonely one. Within the past few months of my life, as many former friends have forsaken me, I have desired the consistent friendship of my husband, the one God is preparing specifically for me. I emphasize *my husband* because though I am single, not just any man will do. Every male is not a man and every man is not a husband.

Wright

Is that right?

Jordan

Yes. The second chapter of Genesis states that God created Eve and made her suitable or comparable to Adam. I know that I am my husband's missing rib, too. We could share our dreams with one another and walk in ministry together for the fulfillment of God's purpose. But, I am still in my season of singleness and God has a good reason for that. You should not put your life, dreams, or ministry on hold because you are not yet married. Once I became successfully and happily single, I turned that into a ministry, too.

Yes. I did. I began to encourage other singles at events and on a weekly radio broadcast. I think that some married persons assume that a single sister's hardship is not having a man to provide for her, go home to, and sleep beside. Some have dealt with that issue well and are content and functional unmarried. For many single persons, the true hardship is answering all of the questions that you are tired of like, "Why aren't you married?"

Wright

Right.

Jordan

"You are a pretty girl. Why aren't you married yet? What's going on? You should be married by now." In the past, women married and began families earlier in life. Many people mean well, but they must understand that I, like many other single women, do not want to get married just to have another man's last name. And I am not trying to prove my independence either. I am expressing my desire for God's total will for my life—in marriage, too. I believe that having God's choice of a mate is really important. He already knows the characteristics of our mate that we will discover ten years down the road. Since I have been strengthened and am able to wait on God's mate in contentment, I have to share insights with struggling singles. It is easy to mope and get stuck in our singleness. If we are not careful, we will focus too much on not having a mate yet and too little on all the wonderful blessings that we do have at this time, this season of our lives.

Wright

Right.

Jordan

I have learned how to walk alone without being lonely. There have been times that I have not dated anyone for a significant period. Time that God has kept me sexually pure. I know that a lot of singles struggle with those things. These are some issues that are often left un-discussed. I do not have all of the answers, but we can search the Bible and then together we can learn from one another's successes and failures. I began to see, wait a minute if God cheered, contented, and kept me, He does not mind doing that for anybody else. Maybe somebody just needs a little bit of encouragement or an opportunity to ask, "How did you do this? How did you overcome this obstacle? What did you do?" That is what singles ministry strives to do. Believe it or not, there are other misconceptions of singles, including when married women think that the single sisters are checking out their husbands. Even as a single female minister, I have seen that look when some women see you four feet away from their spouses. I have integrity. I do not want someone else's spouse. I want my own husband, the one God has for me, when the fullness of my time arrives.

The right relationship really can be a blessing at the right time. God wants us to have productive, healthy, and blessed relationships. Timing is an essential element. It's very, very important. For his own reasons, the Apostle Paul admonished people to remain unmarried, like himself. The Bible declares that while you are single you have additional freedom, I'll say, to care for the things of the Lord. Beyond a beautiful wedding day, there is a marriage that requires daily effort. Married women have many of the same career responsibilities as single women, plus additional household duties, a husband, and maybe even children to prepare for. My goal is to maximize the remaining time that I have as a single woman. I know that my singleness is for a season and seasons change. Just a few months ago the weather was warmer. Now, the climate is different. The natural season has changed. I have ministered this message, *There Is A Reason For Your Season of Singleness*, at a conference. I founded the singles ministry at my church, Believers' Victory Center. I also hosted an FM radio broadcast, which started as the Encouraging Words broadcast, as part of my outreach ministry to singles. My broadcast highlighted how we can apply scriptures to relationship issues we face or will face in our everyday lives. That radio ministry inspired other churches to initiate singles ministries and it touched married persons, too. I am single because I have never been married, but God has enabled me to share His principles with singles that have been separated, divorced, even widowed. What was even more amazing was that I had married people calling and stopping me in the grocery store to say, "You just don't know how much your singles broadcast is blessing us—and we have been married for years." The Word of God works for you whether you are single or married. When you understand God's design, purpose, and thoughts about the holy institution of marriage, single or married, it helps. I want to continue to teach people how to love God's way.

Wright
    Right.

Jordan
    Jesus himself demonstrated that true love is shown when a person makes a significant sacrifice for your benefit. The cross was not a beautiful scene as it is often painted. Jesus was whipped, mocked, and given vinegar to drink. The crown of thorns was pressed into his skull and nails driven deep into his hands. The real picture of Jesus is that He was a bloody mess. But He endured the cross because of the love He had for us and we were yet to be created. There is a song that says that it was not the nails that kept Him on the cross. It was love that kept him there. When somebody cares enough to willingly

sacrifice comfort in consideration of you, too, that usually is a sign that they love you.

As a single person, I understand the love chapter of the Bible, First Corinthians Thirteen. I have suffered through love. I know what it is like to wait on love. I have been kind when I could have acted otherwise. It has been proven and still is being proven in my life that love conquers all. I am thirty years young and I am waiting until I am married to have children. I have unmarried friends that are older than me, too, and are still believing God has a mate for them. I know what it is like to encourage and I have been encouraged in the midst of my storms. Singles ministry is about encouraging one another in the Lord, fellowshipping, and living this time in service for the Lord. It's about preparation, too.

Wright

You've been a speaker for some time now and you are beginning to write more. What sparked your interest in writing?

Jordan

I wrote a short story, *Jezebel Blues*, for a high school assignment. The story, written in first person, is about a weary female blues night club singer. She stands up to sing as usual, but while she is on stage this particular night, she has a flashback to her younger years when she used to sing in church. Immediately, her spirit was stirred and her life changed. She begins singing a song of joy, not sadness and has the whole club on their feet. I received an "A" for my writing then. I further developed that story in a college literature class. That story got around. My college professor gave me a grade of 98. When he returned it to me he said, "Do you understand what I am telling you? This story is close to perfect." He said, "You really have a writing gift." Later I published *Jezebel Blues* in our campus literary magazine. I performed a monologue of the same story as my talent in the showcase when I was campaigning to become our campus queen. While in college, I also wrote a column and a few feature stories for *The Compass*, our newspaper. I graduated in 1995 and I think my next major writing project was my graduate school thesis. That was 1997 and anyone who has written one knows that academic writing is not a leisure creative writing activity.

Years went by. I continued to develop my speaking career and relationship building ministry. In June 2001, I attended the Smart Marriages Conference in Orlando. After a session, another attendee overheard me verbalize my desire to speak more expansively. He tapped me, then passed me a post-it note with a name, Florence Littauer, on it. I had no clue who this man was or whose name he was passing on to me. He advised me to research this lady on the world wide web because she had an organization for Christian speakers. When I did, I discovered www.classervices.com. In October of 2001, I attended their national speakers training, the *Christian Leaders, Authors, and Speakers Seminar*. It's called CLASS. At this training, the president, Marita Littauer, constantly repeated this statement, "If you have something to speak about, you have something to write about. Writing and speaking go hand in hand." That was my cue. I was destined to speak and publish my writings. I continued my journey with the CLASS Career Coaching Seminar, where I prepared myself and learned about the publishing industry at the Christian Booksellers Association's Expo in January 2002. It was the ideal training for me to learn more about the publishing process. In July 2002, on a very clear command from the Lord, I took a leap of faith. I left my full-time college teaching position to develop my ministry. I seriously heard the Lord say, "You already speak, but you have more writing to do." Obedience is better than sacrifice. I had to trust the Lord all the way. It was like walking in the dark and not knowing when, but believing that eventually the light will come on and everything hidden will be revealed. When things are going well for us, we can get caught up in the comfort of our successes and possessions, not realizing that even though we look glamorous, we may not be achieving what we have been created by God to achieve. God had to snatch me out of my comfort zone to thrust me into my greater purpose. I had been an successful educator for years. I had taught at Old Dominion University and Bryant and Stratton College in Virginia. I had educated students at Northeastern High School, College of the Albemarle, and Elizabeth City State University in North Carolina—all before I was thirty years old. Teaching was very familiar for me, but I had to leave the familiar. I had to step out of the boat. I had to walk on water. Personally, I had to exercise this "faith" I was speaking about and trust God myself.

I had to launch out into the deep as the Bible says. God revealed launching out into the deep to me like this. We may travel to a near or distant ocean to go swimming or fishing. In order to catch fish in the ocean, it is usually best to sail out into the deep of the ocean, which could present a risk. It is not very risky to stay on the shoreline; however, there are no living fish there. The only fish on the shoreline, which is a secure place, are dead and washed up by the tide. If we want our nets to be full of fish, we have to travel so far out that we can no longer see the shore. How many of us are shoreline Christians? I don't know about you, but I want some living fish. If I want to gather an abundant harvest, I have to go where the crop is. God is faithful and He will not lead us astray. As Christians we have to launch out into the deep more. We must step out of the boat in order to find out that we really can walk on water. I am a living witness. Jesus will keep you afloat when you step out of the boat. It is tough sometimes, but we have to trust Him.

Wright
Right.

Jordan
I want to catch a harvest.

Wright
When you consider the hard lessons of life what have you learned?

Jordan
As I have suffered through the pain of hurt and rejection, I have learned that God is consistent. Psalm 118:8, the middle verse in the Bible, states that it is better to put your trust in God than to put confidence in man. I have expected people to live by the Golden Rule and treat me as fairly as I have treated them. My heart has been heavy when I experienced the pain of betrayal and disappointment. I had former friends who became envious enemies, employers that did not support me, people who have mistaken my meekness for weakness and tried to take advantage of my Christian kindness. With my own eyes I have seen the attitudes of some associates who used to be happy for me change when God opened amazing doors of opportunity for me. Despite my faithfulness in friendship to them, I saw their enthusiasm for me decline from rushing waterfalls of joy to the drip drop of a kitchen faucet. These were people I expected much more from—men and women in Christ. I hoped that they would journey to higher heights with me, but I have also learned that when God calls you upward, everyone is not able to go. For everyone that lets you down, God always has people who are willing to help you. He always has a ram in the bush. I have been hurt, but no matter how people have treated me, God has always been consistent in His uncondi-

tional love and care for me. In the end, He brings understanding to them. He also enabled me to forgive and love those who hurt me.

Second, I learned the truth of Isaiah 54:17, *No weapon formed against me shall prosper.* Many Christians expect to live lives without controversy. That simply does not happen. In fact, one of the signs that you are doing the right thing can be controversy and opposition. It's how we handle it that counts. Yesterday I was in a totally unexpected car accident, my first one ever. I was on my way to a meeting at Rejoice 100.9 FM, the Christian radio station where I host a Saturday morning community affairs talk show. The station's shows, music, and ministry bless the nations at *www.rejoice100point9.com.* My mind was set on ministry and boom, I became the victim of a car accident. Shaken up and sandwiched between two vehicles, I managed to cry tears of joy in the midst of my devastation. My car appeared to be a total loss, but I was not seriously injured. I know some people who would have been angry with God for allowing that to occur. I realized that accident could have cost me my life if Satan's attempt to take my life was successful. A weapon was formed—I was in an accident. But that weapon did not prosper. I survived! Romans 8:18 proclaims that the sufferings of this present time are not worthy to be compared to the glory that shall be revealed in us. I love that scripture. When I am going through a trying time, trying to endure hardness as a good soldier, I recall that verse. Because I know that I am in the complete will of God, something better must come out of this. That is faith as a verb, faith in action. Instead of becoming bitter because a weapon was formed against me, I will become better.

Third, I have learned that God will faithfully provide. Someone with no outstanding debts, significant savings and investments, and a salaried position with benefits may not classify this as a hard lesson. For me to reach my destiny, I walked out of a full-time college teaching job with salary and benefits, not knowing how much money I would have and when I would have it. I still had bills—including a car payment—and I did not have sufficient savings. I forsook all for the cause of Christ. I felt tested and tried by fire. When you endure an intense wilderness period, which is the only route to the Promised Land, this lesson of God's faithful provision becomes true revelation. He provided for and led the children of Israel on a daily basis. Everyone wants a testimony, but not everyone is willing to endure to test. T E S T are the first four letters of the word *testimony.* So, it is necessary to experience a test in order to have a testimony.

Finally, I had to learn how to receive from others. I was so accustomed to sharing my assets with others that it was not easy for me to ask for support and assistance. There comes a time in your life when you have to let people in. You have to allow people to share their resources with you. Pride is not pleasing to God. It had to be deleted from my life. I had to learn how to ask and receive.

Wright

You know like most of us you have experienced some degree of disappointment, fear, failure. How did you use your faith to over come or come back from those down times?

Jordan

Strong family support and standing on the promises of God helped me come back from every set back. I must say that as God began to bless me more and more, some of my old friends—people that seemed to be with me while I struggled—disconnected with me. Now I know that God was setting me up to receive a harvest and that those losses were truly gains. My grandparents, Rev. and Mrs. Anthony Hathaway Jr., Mrs. Elizabeth Fain and Evelyn Perry, parents, John and Teresa Jordan, my sister Anita Wallace (Julian), Anitra, Precious and other family were there for me through all of my trying times. They supported me with love, prayer, and actions. In fact, my mom often reminded me that Joyce Meyer, Bishop T.D. Jakes, Paula White, and so many others all have testimonies of how they struggled for seasons in their lives. My family and the remaining faithful friends saw God's great call to ministry on my life and their encouraging words and spirit-filled prayers truly, truly helped me. In addition to the strength of family, the scriptures helped me to stand.

Daily I rehearsed the words of God that were already in my heart, especially Philippians four thirteen—*I can do all things through Christ who strengthens me.* I rehearsed Romans 8:37—*Nay, in all these things, we are more than a conquerors.* I reminded myself of Philippians 4:19: *My God shall supply all of my needs according to his riches and glory by Christ Jesus,* even when I appeared to have unmet needs. I continued to tithe whether I had two hundred, twenty, or two dollars to give. Because I tithe faithfully, God promises to rebuke the devour for my sake. Surviving a car accident is an example of Him doing just that. My car was a total loss, but I could have been, too. Again, God kept His promise. I also meditated on Psalms 84:11, which says that He will not withhold any good thing from those who walk uprightly before him. Even while I was going through my own hardships, I still wanted to walk upright with God and maintain the right attitude. Though tempted to, I did not even want a pity party. I chose to celebrate life and emphasize the good after my accident. Before I got out of bed this morning, I decided to make my boast in the Lord. I am grateful to be alive and not severely injured. No bones were broken and I still have a voice to witness for Christ. As a result of all of life's challenges that I have faced, I have a much stronger testimony that I can share to encourage somebody else.

Wright

Well, what a great conversation. I really do appreciate you taking all this time today to talk to me. I've learned a lot and you've given our readers some powerful ideas to consider.

Jordan

Thank you.

Wright

I really appreciate it.

Jordan

Well, I am available to share the good news all across the country, in speech and in print. God has done so much for me. He is so wonderful. I thank God for a real relationship with Him and I want the world to know that. So I will travel this world to win souls over to the Lord's side. God is real and I love Him. I want to teach others how they can establish a direct connection with God themselves. Right relationship with God is attainable.

Wright

Today we have been talking to Lynetta Jordan, and we have found that she is a powerful communicator, and she really believes that she has been gifted and called by God to help people improve almost every area of their lives, at home, in the work place, and in the community. Thank you so much Lynetta for being with us today on Conversations on Faith.

Jordan

God bless you David. Thank you so much for inviting me to share my story.

About The Author

"The Motivator" Lynetta Jordan has energized audiences at convocations, conferences, business, professional, youth, women's and ministry events. An evangelist, enthusiastic talkshow host, singles ministry founder, relationship builder, and former college queen, Lynetta is an honor graduate of John A. Holmes High, Elizabeth City State University, and Regent University. Named "Prophetic Motivator" by a publisher, Lynetta's writings refresh, motivate, and inspire thousands to achieve success in life and love. Contact Lynetta to speak for your event!

Lynetta Jordan

Spoken Words Communication Group

PO Box 1791

Elizabeth City, North Carolina 27906

Phone: 252.337.7797

Email: spokenwords@lynettajordan.org

www.lynettajordan.org

Chapter 2

DR. ROBERT SCHULLER

THE INTERVIEW

David E. Wright (Wright)

Robert Harold Schuller was born in Alton, Iowa. He was raised on his parent's farm nearby, in a small, close-knit community of Dutch Americans. Robert knew from the early age of four that he wanted to be a minister of the church. After graduating from a tiny high school of nearby Newkirk, Iowa, he entered Hope College, in Holland, Michigan, where he earned a Bachelor of Arts degree. Robert was ready to return to Michigan to pursue his religious studies at Western Theological Seminary. In 1950, he received his Masters of Divinity. The young Reverend Schuller married Arvella DeHann of Newkirk, and the newlyweds moved to Chicago, where the newly ordained minister took up his first assignment as pastor of the Ivanhoe Reformed Church. During his ministry, the congregation grew from 38 to over 400. In 1955, Schuller's denomination, the Reformed Church of America, called on him to build a new congregation in Garden Grove, California. With only $500 in assets, he decided to rent a drive-in movie theater, the Orange Drive-in. On the first Sunday, 100 persons attended services seated in their cars, while Reverend Schuller preached from the tarpaper roof of the snack bar. The Garden Grove congregation continued to grow; when a larger building was needed, Rev. Schuller commissioned the renowned architect Phillip Johnson to build a new building, all of glass: the Crystal Cathedral. After almost insurmountable difficulties, this 2,736-seat architectural marvel was dedicated in 1980, "To the Glory of Man for the Greater Glory of God." Today, one million people visit the Cathedral annually. Dr. Schuller is the author of over 30 books, six of which have found a place on the New York Times and Publisher's Weekly best-seller lists. Dr. Schuller, welcome to *Conversations on Faith*.

Dr. Robert Schuller (Schuller)
Thank you, David.

Wright
Dr. Schuller, you have stated, "I learn from my dad to dream, even when the dream seems impossible." Could you tell us about your parents and what impact they had on your early life?

Schuller
Yes, my father and mother were, by all standards I guess, poor. They owned or were buying a farm and they were farming people. That meant they were always able to live with faith because the farmer always has something to look forward to. He plants his seeds. Depression happens when we don't have anything to live for. That's why farmers are believers in God, because they watch their seed sprout and a new plant grow.

Wright
In 1955, with $500 in your pocket, you and your wife started a church. I understand that it took tremendous faith for both of you. What really impressed me, however, was the fact that you knocked on 3,500 doors to learn what the residents wanted—an enormous task. Do you believe that somewhere within the definition of faith lies a charge to do the work necessary for success?

Schuller
I had a whole year to do it. But, absolutely, that is the heart of what faith must be.

Wright

I've been a salesman most of my life, and I'm 63 now, but I've been selling for years and years and anyone who does that much research and door knocking deserves to be successful.

You have referred to yourself as a "Christian Capitalist." Can you tell our readers what you mean?

Schuller

Well, I believe that people should try to achieve self-esteem and hopefully, independence—and freedom is the core of that. In the United States of America, we are free to achieve financial independence. It's not against the law as it would be in a pure socialist state or a pure communist state. Christian Capitalism is a principle of acquiring your own wealth. Capitalism about the principles that I find in Christianity can be as bad as communism or anything else because it can generate greed, deception, theft, murder, you name it. Capitalism is very dangerous, just as freedom is very dangerous without a set of personal morals and ethics. I say a Christian Capitalist lives on three principles. One, earn all you can. Don't make it by trying to win the lottery. You have no pride of achievement if you go about it that way. Also, invest all you can. Finally, give all you can.

Wright

As I prepared for this interview, I was struck by a prayer that you wrote titled *Success*. In it you write this: *Faith stimulates success. Hope sustains success. Love sanctifies success.* Could you comment on Faith, Hope, and Love as it relates to your success?

Schuller

Well, nobody is going to be a true success, meaning satisfied with his accomplishments and living proud with the way that he did it, unless he lives by this trinity of faith, hope, and love.

Wright

Dr. Schuller, as a pastor of the largest RCA church, you were a part of the United States delegation to the funeral of the universally loved Mother Teresa in Calcutta. You stated that she was the "first lady of the 21st century." When did you first meet Mother Teresa and what impressed you the most about her faith in God?

Schuller

What I think impressed me most about her faith in God was that she was a happy person. She smiled. When I stepped off of the President's plane in Calcutta for the funeral, the first huge billboard we saw was her picture with the line, "Smile. It's the beginning of peace." I think I first met her through the writings of a now-deceased friend in England , who became a Christian through her. Then, of course, I visited her home of the dying in Calcutta 30 years ago.

Wright

The Crystal Cathedral is known worldwide as architectural excellence. Can you tell us about how it came to be and a little about its design?

Schuller

Yes. Well, I started this church, as you mentioned, with no money and couldn't find a hall to rent. I knew I had gifts because I was elected to Phi Beta Kappa in college, and national honor fraternities, so I knew I had talents and gifts, but I needed a place to speak. I couldn't find an empty hall anywhere. Finally, I went to a drive-in theater and the guy there said that I could talk from the snack bar rooftop and that's how I started. That would be my church home for over five years. Every Sunday when I prayed or read the Bible or heard religious music, all I could see were clouds and the sky and trees bending in the wind and birds flying. So, 20 years later when I needed a big church, I was homesick for the sky and said to the architect, "Why not make it out of all glass?" So, the Crystal Cathedral was born. It's where I came from as a child when I lived on the farm in the country and the sky was the most dominant thing.

Wright

When I was out at your church a few years ago, I remember one of the guides there was telling us something about the bricks. How instead of putting them horizontally, you had put them vertically. Is that true?

Schuller

It's not *really* true. It's true that Richard Noints was my first architect and that's the one name I didn't see in your letter or your questions. Richard was probably the greatest architect for part of his life and he did the Tower of Hope and the cross on top of it. He did the

Gallery and the first church that I had here. He said that he had always wanted to set stone vertically, but nobody would go along with it—but I did. So, the stone is set vertically here. It is a historic piece of architecture and we never use random stone, just the vertical stone. So, it's not bricks, it's stone. Another thing that was missing in your questions was that the last building that we've just built, that's the most glorious piece of structure. I think it's outstanding. It's done by Richard Meyer. The Getty Museum is doing the Pope's chapel in Rome. This is the only piece of real estate in the United States of America where the buildings are all done by gold medal, F.A.I.A. world-class architects. Richard Noints Tower of Hope, Phillip Johnson's Crystal Cathedral, and now Richard Meyers International Center for Possibility Thinking. We've gotten a lot of press on it and are going to get a lot more.

Wright

When I visited your church it was at Christmas time, I was fascinated by everything I saw. Some of my most cherished memories were of the sculptures on the grounds. The statues of Pharisees and the adulterous woman spoke volumes to me. I didn't have to read the Bible to figure out what was going on. Can you tell our readers where all the beautiful art came from?

Schuller

It came from me. I've been in charge of this place for 48 years. Since I started with nothing, I have the principle that everything makes a statement. A weed says something. A flower says something. Everything makes a statement. Sidewalks make statements. I put Bible verses in granite in the sidewalks so that people would just be walking and accidentally read a word from scripture that might reach them. Then I chose to take what, in my life and heart, are the most important themes in the Bible and turn them into sculpture. *"Let Him who is without sin cast the first stone,"* that's the woman convicted of adultery. The prodigal son—you know the story?

Wright

Yes.

Schuller

Okay, so that's been done. The lost sheep—that's been done. "Peace be still," so Christ and peace is on the water. I picked what I call the most fundamental, historic, classical, powerful, positive principles taught by Jesus and put them in sculpture forms. They're all done by different sculptors. I've got, I think, seven different artists at work.

Wright

When you were talking a few minutes ago about earning as much as you can and investing as much as you can—of course the *Hour of Power* and all that you're able to do out there in Garden Grove just boggles the mind. I've been on a church staff for forty years and I just can't imagine how much all of that would cost weekly for you to be able to reach the entire world like you do.

Schuller

Well, we're on a 65-million dollar budget.

Wright

Wow.

Schuller

The income is always challenging. We've never had a surplus. If we had a surplus, we'd put it into expanding the business. What staff are you on?

Wright

I've been directing church choral music and I write choral music. Right now, I direct at the Kodak United Methodist Church here in Tennessee.

Schuller

Well, we've got a good choral conductor here.

Wright

I know. I listen all the time.

Schuller

The director of the Mormon Tabernacle Choir came to church here last week and he went to our director and said, "Boy, we would like to sing in that cathedral."

Wright

Well, as a matter of fact, while I was waiting for you to come to the phone, your secretary put me on hold, I got to hear your choir sing there for a minute or two. Dr. Schuller, your *Hour of Power* reaches more than 20-million viewers weekly all over the world. You have the opportunity to have some of the most famous people in the world as guests at your church. Do your permanent members feel that they are really a part of a church that fills the need of your community and do they feel a closeness to each other?

Schuller

Not the way they should and that's why we had to open a new facility. That's the building we just opened. It cost me 40-million, it took 17 years, and you've never seen anything like it. Nobody in church-work has ever built anything like it. The front of it opens wide so that when you are in the courtyard, instead of looking at a back wall with power poles and houses over the fence, you're looking at the front of a gorgeous building. The wall totally opens up and you see the huge living room. It's like the lobby of a five-star hotel. There's a beautiful food court, which is just shocking in its beauty. So, it's a gathering place for the people and it's doing wonders. Their attitude towards the *Hour of Power* is that they're assistant ministers. They meet the tourists that come here, a million a year. They sing in the choir for the *Hour of Power*. So, they feel a part of the community when they become a part of the 400 hospitality people. They feel a part of the community when they join the music in the church. They're a part of the community when they man the 24-hour New Hope Telephone Counseling—the first counseling prevention ministry in the United States of America for 34 years. So, organizations that do the ministry form their own sense of community and that's the way it's got to be. As well as through small groups. I don't know how many small groups we have, but they all look upon the local television ministry as our primary world missionary work, which it is.

Wright

But there's still a feeling of community.

Schuller

Only if they get into a small group or become one of the 3,000 members that form these working ministry groups. If they just come, sit in the pew, and go home, no, they don't feel like part of a community.

Wright

When I called recently, you were out inspecting some of the new construction. Are you saying it's on the same location?

Schuller

Oh, it is on the same location.

Wright

So, it's adjacent to the Cathedral?

Schuller

Yes. The three buildings form a triangle. The new building is reflected in the mirrored Cathedral and it can be viewed from the Tower of Hope. If you go through the new building, it is a museum that motivates. The view—in architecture, the most important thing is the view—we don't have a mountain or a lake or a river view here, but what we've got is a view of two buildings that are world-famed for the art of their architecture. Those two buildings are the stunning view from the new building. Nobody has ever seen it until now because there were houses, power poles, and telephone poles. The west side of the buildings are the most beautiful and now they're seen for the first time.

Wright

I just can't wait to see it.

Schuller

You would never know the place. It is stunning. We won first prize for the state of California for the landscaped gardens.

Wright

I came to Anaheim one time to do a speech on presentation skills for professional speakers and I drove to the Cathedral. It was at Christmas time and angels were flying around in the air—I couldn't believe it—and the orchestra. You are just so fortunate to have so much to work with there.

Schuller

I tell you, it is. I've been so fortunate to get the best people in the world to become my friends and they made it great. Like Mary Martin, did you ever hear of her?

Wright

Oh, yes.

Schuller

Alright, Mary Martin, she was on the cover of *Life Magazine* seven times. She flew as Peter Pan. When I was putting together *The Glory of Christmas*, she said that I should have angels and they should fly. She said she knew how to do that and she took charge of it. She got the guy in here to make it happen and that's why we were the first church with flying angels.

Wright

I had no idea. Of course, Mary Martin, she and people like Ethel Merman, they're the grand ladies of Broadway.

Schuller

She's dead now, of course.

Wright

Yes, of course. Dr. Schuller, you have acknowledged that the Rev. Dr. Norman Vincent Peale was one of your mentors.

Schuller

He was a pastor of our first church in America. That church was founded by 54 Dutch colonists in 1628, who bought the land from the Indians. We are the oldest corporation with an unbroken ministry in the United States, secular or sacred.

Wright

What do you think makes a great mentor? In other words, are there characteristics that mentors seem to have in common?

Schuller

First of all, it's excellence. They excel in their chosen career or field. That's the number one thing. Two, they have to respect and love someone that they think has talent and possibilities. When you've got those two going, then you're on your way.

Wright

If you could have a platform, Dr. Schuller, and give our readers advice on how to develop their faith in God in order to live a richer, fuller, more meaningful life, what would you say?

Schuller

I would tell them that the most important thing is to believe in the cosmic being that the Bible calls God. This God is personal, meaning he can think. He's not just a cosmic force or nothing to be admired at all. You can't admire electricity. You can be thankful for it, but you can't admire it. God is intelligent, He is affectionate, and He is eternal. He is part of eternity. The question is then how to develop an awareness of who He is and what He is like. The answer I give is, Jesus Christ. That's why Jesus Christ is the heart of my faith, whether you are Protestant, Catholic, Jewish, or Muslim, he believes in God. That's why I believe in God. How do I know I'm right? I cannot believe that Jesus Christ was wrong. No way. If I think that I'm smarter than Jesus was when it comes to things like prayer and faith in God, then I'm the world's worst egotist and the most lacking in humility. I think I'm living by Jesus' teachings and His claim to be the son of God, the savior. I'm living by it. I tell you, I'm close to 77 and it's given me a fabulous life. Just look around me. Look what we've done. I know that it has all come from God and from Jesus.

Wright

I certainly can see the fruits of His labor every time I look at the television station and see a beautiful edifice there that just really reaches people all over the world. I really appreciate this time that you have taken with us today. I wish you continued success, of course, in leading people to Christ. I think that you are just one of the great men of God. I appreciate the time that you have spent with me.

Schuller

Thank you very much.

About The Author

In 1968, Dr. Schuller founded New Hope, the world's first live, church-sponsored 24-hour counseling and suicide prevention hotline. Since its inception, it is estimated that over a million people have dialed this hotline and received immediate counseling.

The Garden Grove congregation continued to grow; when a larger building was needed, Rev. Schuller commissioned the renowned architect Philip Johnson to build a new building, all of glass: the Crystal Cathedral. After almost insurmountable difficulties, this 2,736-seat architectural marvel was dedicated in 1980, "To the Glory of Man for the Greater Glory of God." Today, one million people visit the Cathedral annually, for regular Sunday worship, for conferences, seminars, workshops and for two annual pageants, The Glory of Christmas and The Glory of Easter.

Dr. Schuller is the author of over 30 books, six of which have found a place on the New York Times and Publishers Weekly best-seller lists. Robert and Arvella Schuller have five children, all active in Christian ministry.

Dr. Robert Schuller
Crystal Cathedral Ministries
13280 Chapman Avenue
Garden Grove, California 92840
Phone: 714.971.4000

Chapter 3

DR. JOHN R. MYERS

THE INTERVIEW

David E. Wright (Wright)

Today we're talking to Dr. John Myers. Dr. Myers' experience in training is primarily in the humanities values, character, theology, media, interpersonal communications, business ethics, and personalization. He holds degrees from Purdue University, Duke University, and United Theological Seminary. He also has launched several building projects and several entrepreneurial enterprises. John leads seminars and workshops nationwide. He provides keynotes targeted to fit your organization's needs. His extensive personal background provides a rich resource upon which to draw. His general topics include vision, leadership, excellence, motivation, family, spirituality, financial planning, and leaving a legacy. He's also an author of several articles, short stories and a dissertation entitled, *Networking In the Global Village for the 21st Century*. John is currently authoring a book entitled, *Greater Things*. Dr. Myers is a member of the National Speakers Association. He serves on the Board of Directors for several organizations throughout the United States, and he is the pastor of the First United Methodist Church in Fort Lauderdale, Florida. John Myers, welcome to *Conversations on Faith*.

John Myers (Myers)

Well, thank you very much.

Wright

Tell us about your earliest faith experience and recollection of God.

Myers

Well, my earliest faith experience was as a baby when I was baptized. Even though I don't quite remember that, I do believe that God was in the middle of it all! We talk about baptism as an outward sign of an inward and a spiritual grace. So, even though I didn't have much to do with it except to be presented by my parents when I was baptized, God's spirit came in and started working internally in my soul and my spirit. My earliest recollection as a child was when I was five years old, and it was a time in which I started to experience something pretty significant. One night while I was sleeping, I woke up and sensed a presence in my room. I saw what I believed at that point to be God. Of course, this was from the perspective of a little boy. The Figure that I saw appeared in the room in a black robe and looking at me with kind eyes. But, the encounter scared me none the less. After all, I was in my bedroom and someone else was too! I closed my eyes and opened them again, and there he was once again. I shared the bedroom with my sister, so I ran across the room and got in bed with her. I closed my eyes again. I opened them and there he was at the foot of the bed once again. I shut my eyes once again. Then it dawned on me that if I closed my eyes, I didn't see this person. So, I decided not to open them again until the next morning. I went to sleep and woke up the next morning. Sure enough, there I was in bed with my older sister and everything was clear and bright and sunny.

That was my earliest recollection. I think actually, it was a dream or some kind of vision. Perhaps God was giving me an idea that He had placed a special call on my life. I thought and still think about that experience often. Whether or not it was a dream, a vision or simply a young boy's imagination, I'm not sure. But you know, someday, according to the Bible, I'll be able to find out.

Wright

You can ask Him yourself.

Myers

I can ask Him myself, "So, what was that?"

Wright

You're going to be really surprised if He says it was the pizza that you ate.

Myers

Yeah, it was the pizza, the shake and the cheeseburger that your mom and dad brought home at 10:00.

Wright

What was you earliest experience of business?

Myers

Well, I was brought up in a business family, and we owned several restaurants in my home town of Marion, Indiana. As a young boy, my dad gave me my first experience in business by letting me go pick up the trash with a stick that had a nail on the end of it in the restaurant parking lots. Later, I graduated to mowing the properties, and then finally, when I was ten or eleven, I moved into the soda fountain area. At age 13 and 14, I was promoted to the grill. At age 18, dad promoted me to Assistant Manager. That's where I learned how to work with people from a management point of view. His approach in training was very important. He taught me that when you are in business you've got to be willing to do everything from soup to nuts; you have to be willing to roll up your sleeves. He taught me that no job is too important or too menial in order to make the business a success. It was an important lesson that he taught me.

Wright

I've always felt that I was a better salesman than anything else. What was your earliest experience in sales?

Myers

Well, the earliest experience in practical sales was in a high end local clothing store which resourced most of the executives in my hometown. It was owned privately by one of the families in our community. I decided I wanted to branch out from the restaurant business when I was about 16 years old. I knocked on doors and finally the owner of the clothing store hired me. It was called Murrell's Clothing Store. Bob Murrell gave me my first opportunity. He said, "Can't really let you be a salesman. You're too young." He said, "Why don't you wash the windows, clean the toilets, push a broom and keep the glass cases cleaned and dusted." I said, "Isn't that really called being a janitor?" He said, "Yeah, I guess that's what that would be called."

Wright

You had it right immediately, huh?

Myers

I'm a quick learner! So, I started out that way, but one day all of the sales people were gone for lunch. This guy came in and he was dressed very nicely. I found out that he was an executive for one of the GM Plants in our town. We started talking. Pretty soon I sold him three suits and several shirts and ties. The sale was quite large. When the owners came back, they saw that I had made an $800.00 sale. That was back in 1973.

Wright

That would be like three or four thousand today.

Myers

It *would* be three or four thousand today. He said, "You know, I think it's time you became a salesman." So, I traded in my mop for a suit and tie. That's when I really found that I loved selling things and working with people. I learned that the whole process was about building a relationship and building trust. I learned that it was about sending a customer away happy and at the same time benefiting the company! That was fun!

Wright

When did you first know that you were to be a leader, public speaker and practical theologian along with your businesses?

Myers

Well, again, during my early years, my teenage years, those were important times. I was a class leader in junior high and also the senior class president for a class of about 800 students. I learned a lot about the art of delegation, vision and implementation.

Also, when I was 16, I received a call to ministry in a very classical sense, where I felt God was really calling me to be a pastor or a Christian minister of some sort. I started having Bible studies in my house, and we started out with five or six kids, and it grew to 50 people every Wednesday night. We had to move out of the house down to the local church. We created systems of leadership that actually propagated, the Bible study, for another eight years following my graduation from high school, college and seminary.

We basically taught principles of excellence in leadership character development, and how to keep things moving. Those were the early years in which I sensed God's calling to work both in business and leadership and in public speaking as well as in direct ministries.

Wright

I'm always interested in unusual experiences. Have you had any unusual experiences that you've had because of your faith?

Myers

Oh yeah! There have been several. A couple of them that I think are pretty interesting: In 1976, I was at Purdue University, and I was singing with the Purdue Varsity Glee Club as a tenor soloist. We went on a trip to Europe. I befriended a lady named Ida. Ida was 86 years old at the time. We became fast friends. We had great discussions at a dinner in Paris. She asked me a lot of questions and I told her about my beliefs, my passion for business, for sales, for ministry and life in general. When I came home, I asked the girl I was dating, Debbie, if she would be my bride and she accepted. We went out into a field in Logansport, Indiana, at the 4-H Fairgrounds of all places and prayed. We asked God to bless what would be our marriage. We committed ourselves to a lifetime of helping others both in business and in faith. When we concluded our prayer, above us there was a beautiful starlit Indiana summer night. We looked up above us and there was a cloud, one great big cloud, and then three jet streams coming out of it. It was quite an unusual sight. We had never seen anything like it. So, we thought that was a sign that God was blessing our union. The next day we were walking along by a lakeside, and I said, "You know, wouldn't it be wonderful to be able to go to the Holy land, and to study some of the ancient biblical places, and to walk literally in the footsteps of those who have gone before us and trace the footsteps of Jesus and Paul and Peter and others?" I said, "Boy, I'd love to do that." Then I said, "I'd love to go to Europe some time and just study culture and history and the like." She said, "Yeah, that would be great." I said, "I wish we had some money for that."

I went home to Marion, Indiana. There was a letter from my new friend, Ida. She said, "You know, I've been looking for someone for five years that I could send anywhere in the world to train them for their chosen field, and for their endeavor." The next line floored me! She wrote, "So I'm going to send you anywhere in the world that you want to go…"

Wright

WOW!

Myers

"…to study, for research, for reflection so you can be the very best minister and leader on the block." That led to some wonderful, wonderful experiences—the Holy Land, Europe, China—over a period of about four years. That was an unusual experience.

The second unusual experience was in 1992 when I was out in southern California. I was getting ready to go to an institute for successful church leadership and the International School of Christian Communicators out at the Crystal Cathedral in Garden Grove, California with Dr. Robert Schuler. It was one of those times, when I was trying to save a little money. I went to a different hotel and asked to see one of the rooms and the CEO of the Western Rim Management Corporation happened to be there. For some reason they called him and he gave my wife and me a VIP tour of the property. It was a very nice property. We started chatting. He said, "So, what are you doing here?" I told him, and one thing led to another. I mentioned that I was invited to go to a post-doctoral study tour of Russia with 17 clergy from across America and one from Korea. He said, "Oh." He said, "What do you want to do there?" I said, "Well, one of the things we want to do is we want to meet with Mikhail Gorbechev." He said, "Ah, Okay. Well, I'll tell you what. Why don't you meet me for breakfast tomorrow morning?" We met him for breakfast the next morning at the hotel, and he had two Russians there. One was a leader in financing in Russia, and another was the nephew of the former KGB Director. This was right after the fall of communism. We started chatting and talking and telling him about the mission and the vision, and he said, "You know, these two can get you in to meet with Gorbechev without any trouble." So five months later, we were in Moscow and we met on April 26 for an hour and a half with Mikhail Gorbechev.

Wright

Goodness gracious!

Myers

Prior to the meeting, I had urged those who were older in our group to see if former President Gorbechev would like to join us in prayer. They made the invitation. So, we joined hands with Mikhail Gorbechev, prayed with the former communist leader, and asked God to bless him upon his endeavors with his new work. During that time, we were also able to find out that he was baptized Russian Orthodox Christian as a baby. He was raised by his mother and his grandmother in the Christian faith, but at a point in his life he decided to go the way of atheism. Then when we asked him if he had any kind of faith at all, he didn't say no, and when we invited him to pray, he joined hands with us.

That was quite an unusual experience and I've often asked the question mathematically, "What is the likelihood that someone traveling from Indiana to California would meet someone that could actually put them in touch with Mikhail Gorbechev for a meeting in Moscow, Russia only to end up praying with him?" That was an unusual faith experience.

Wright

I couldn't help but think when you were talking about proposing to your wife, with the divorce rate as high as it is, and all things being what they are today, wouldn't it be nice if more young couples that decided to get married would pray together? We'd probably need a lot less premarital counseling.

Myers

Absolutely. The praying together does help, you know. It makes a big difference. When you put God in the middle of your relationship, any relationship, it certainly helps a great deal. You know we happened to look up and see what we interpreted to be a sign. Again, it's kind of like that old story I told you about when I was five-years old. The question is whether it was real or whether it just happened to be a meteorological circumstance? One way or the other, we saw it as an affirmation and that wouldn't have happened if we hadn't taken the time to just spend time in prayer and committing ourselves and our lives to God in His work and service. But, I think you're right. It's the old axiom of people who pray together stay together.

Wright

You got that right. What has your faith taught you about living practically?

Myers

Well, I really believe that practical Christianity is what the world is looking for. What I mean by that is an authenticity. It is something that applies to daily living. A faith that basically results in a "want to" experience of living out your faith every day instead of a "have to" experience. A "want to" faith is a kind of experience that's saying, "I'm expecting that God's going to do greater things to my life, in my business and in my family because God has told me that it is completely possible." The "have to" faith is one that says, "You know I have to do this. I have to do that. I can't do this. I can't do that." A "have to" faith gets all bound up. It's not a joyful experience. So to me, having a practical faith application to life means that you know you're a real person with other real people. And people aren't put off because of your faith. Instead, they're engaged because of it. That, to me, is critically important in living my life, and you know, that then translates to what I do with keynotes and working with other people, and of course, as a pastor.

A lot of times people don't even know I'm a pastor when they first meet me, and it's kind of fun because what I like to do is tell them I'm a manufacturer's representative. I tell them and they say, "What do you do?" I say, "Well, I'm a manufacturer's representative." They say, "Well, what do you mean a manufacturer's representative, what kind of company?" I say, "Biggest company in the world." Then they ask the question, "What do you mean the biggest company in the world?" I said, "Yeah, biggest company in the world and oldest company in the world too." Then they say, "Well, what do you guys make?" I say, "Assurance." They say, "You mean insurance." I say, "No, assurance." I say, "I work for God and I'm just one of His representatives and anyone who knows God is a representative too. We usually let the people know about the great assurance that God's given us and you can have it too if you don't already have it." So that's practical faith.

Wright

Every minister that I've ever known, and I have known a bunch, has always told me, "It's so wonderful to talk to people when they don't know I'm a minister." Everybody clams up when I tell them.

Myers

Sometimes that can work to your advantage! The best place is on the golf course. Often, when playing with a new foursome in a pickup game, the first nine holes are spent focusing on the game itself. Then about the ninth hole, people often will ask questions like, "So, what do you do for a living?" It is fun to let them in on what I do. Often, everybody goes, "Ah gee, what did I say? " And if I'm if I'm losing, it's a real psychological advantage!

Wright

That's right (laughter). You are known for your leadership, vision, and the expertise that you've honed to speak across the disciplines of business, faith, politics, education, your keynote, seminars, workshops, strategic planning, and purposeful travel as well as your innovative approach in turning around churches, businesses, and organizations. Tell me, what are some of the keys to your approach?

Myers

Well, I actually teach twelve Expect Greater Things principles. Principle number one is the power of vision. Principle number two is a passion for excellence. Principle number three is a compassion for people, whether you are a company, or a church, or an individual. You can have all the vision and excellence in the world, but if you don't care about people, it's not going to go very far. Principle number four is the determination to redefine the circle. What that really means is asking the question, "Are you an 'innie' or an 'outie'?" Are you always inwardly focused? If you were to form a circle, would you form it looking in or would you find yourself forming it looking out? Actually redefining the circle creates healthy ways to do both and have a balance. Principle number five is a commitment to making a difference locally and globally. For a church, you'd call that missions. For a business or for an individual you'd call it philanthropy. No business that's a healthy business exists only to serve itself. The same is true with a person or a church or any not for profit organization or a for-profit organization. Principle number six is commitment to excellence in leadership and being willing to do whatever it takes to become excellent in leadership style and leadership integrity. Principle number seven is willingness to embrace change for the sake of the mission or organization. Mark Twain always quipped, and I love it, that the only person who likes change is a wet baby. But, the reality is we do have to change. The only constant we have in this world is change. Principle number eight is a passion for living life according to the five P's and that's a whole other topic. I'm actually working on a separate book with that in mind. The five P's are *prayer, purpose, people, program, and property,* in that order. If you flip those upside down and look at everything from a property or program point of view then you will manage myopically. If you flip it on the right side up with prayer or meditation in the lead, then you will focus on purpose. That attracts people. When people are attracted, they want to be a part of the programs. In fact, they help to define them based on their felt-needs. For a company that might mean the services are or the products are. For a church or organization, it means you know what it is that you want to do programmatically to help meet people's needs. Then the property needs always come about when you are in sync with all these other P's. That's living according to the five P's. Principle number nine is making sure you know how to staff properly and build a team for your organization. Principle number ten is working with wealth management and developing a philosophy of how to manage the wealth that you are accumulating or with which you have been entrusted. Wealth management really includes not only a sense of understanding how to manage finances, but how to look at it from a spiritual point of view, and then how to teach others to manage their wealth that way, knowing that all wealth is entrusted to us by God. All wealth is created by God. There are some tremendous books and materials that are available. Principle number eleven is using every means possible to market what your product and your service is. If it's a church, obviously it's using every means possible to proclaim God's love. If it's a business, using public relations, marketing and media to get the word out about what it is that you are offering. Then principle number twelve is to always work for the greater good. For a church, that's the glory of God. For a company, that's to make an impact not only on the employees but also on the community in which the company exists. If it's a global company, that means to look at how to have projects of philanthropy to make a *substantial* social impact. Those are the twelve principles.

| Greater Things Advisory Team (Ad Council) |
| Dr. Myers |
| Co-leads of: each Greater Things team + Stand-alone Committee Chairs + Staff Leads |

"Expect Greater Things"
Executive Committee
PPR Chair
Church Business Admin.
Senior Pastor
Trustee Chair
Ad Council Chair
Finance Chair
Nominations Chair

Nominations Committee
Providing for Greater Things Finance Committee

Staffing For Greater Things (Personnel)
Building For Greater Things (Trustees)
Preparing For Greater Things Pre-School Board
Music Ministry

Meeting Times
Expect Greater Things Exec.
Committee: 6:00 PM, 2nd Mon.

Admin. Council: 7:30 PM, 2nd Mon
Greater Things on Wed. Nights

3rd Wednesday, 6:00 to 9:00 PM
(Dinner & Meeting)

Expect Greater Things Team	Growing for Greater Things Team	Doing Greater Things Team
Welcome, Communication, and Integration	*Spiritual Growth, Development & Nurture*	*Service and Caring, Community & Internal*
Staff Partner & Lay Partner	**Staff Partner & Lay Partner**	**Staff Partner & Lay Partner**
► Advertising	► Worship	► Habitat for Humanity
► Singage	► Stewardship	► Feeding the Homeless
► Greeters	► Sunday School	► Little Schoolhouse
► Parking Lot Ministry	► Small Groups	► Dominican
► Welcome Kits	► Bible Study	► SHARE
► Spiritual Gifts Inventory	► Classes & Seminars	► Sunshine Visitors
► Computer Database	► Lessburg Events & Retreats	► Hospital Visitation
► Internet	► Youth	► Stephen Ministries
► Newsletter	► Children's Programs	► Quilters
► Boy Scouts	► Camp Out	► Methodist Women
► Café	► Family Nights	► Methodist Men
► Madrigal Dinner	► Library	► Sr. Citizen Luncheon
► TV	► Scholarships	► Advocacy Group
► Radio	► Methodist Men	
► Targeted Contemporary Worship	► Promise Keepers (Body Builders)	
	► Contemporary Praise Band	

45

Conversations On Faith

Conversations On Faith

Wright

Tell me about your greater things philosophy— "Expect Greater Things," Grow in Greater Things and Do Greater Things.

Myers

Well, the "Expect Greater Things" philosophy—actually the whole greater things philosophy, is based on a text in the Bible where Jesus was saying farewell to his disciples. He says, "Ask anything in my name, and I will do it that the Father would be glorified in the Son." Then He says, "I'll tell you, you will do greater things than these." Now, Jesus had just walked on the water, He'd just healed people. He'd done all of these things and he says, "You're going to do greater things than these because I go to the Father." He says, "Ask anything in my name and I will do it."

In 1997, I read that passage and it jumped off the page at me! That's developed into a "Greater Things" philosophy that I've been developing and working on and teaching now. To "Expect Greater Things" basically is to help people live with a transformed mind to think differently, to rise above the mundane, to understand that the possibilities are tremendous for each of our lives, that we can literally "Expect Greater Things." This is an absolute promise that we can expect. We are going to live a greater things lifestyle where we can reach our full potential. You know, Robert Schuler calls it "possibility thinking." Norman Vincent Peale called it "the power of positive thinking." Napoleon Hill calls it "the sixth sense." Expecting greater things is the beginning of realizing that God has created us uniquely to do something well beyond ourselves to impact lives in significant ways. Pragmatically, it applies to expecting greater things organizationally. How do you create an "Expect Greater Things" atmosphere within your organization? What do you do to help people start thinking outside the box, and realizing it's okay to do so? Once people start doing that, they can grow in greater things. Growing in greater things really means to have a hunger and also a disciplined approach to growing spiritually, intellectually, financially and relationally.

If you throw a stone into the water it creates a great big ripple effect. That's how we're created. We're created to be ripple effect people. The only way we can do that is if we learn to expect that we can be ripple effect people and then grow to understand how to do it, and then doing greater things is actually doing greater things. It's reaching out philanthropically. It's learning to give 10% (or more) of everything that we have for a greater good, It's learning that giving philanthropically is critically essential to our own spiritual well-being and health. The Christian is taught that tithing is critically important and that it makes a difference. That also translates to corporate America and to doing greater things beyond the company. That's expecting, growing, and doing greater things. Our portal (www.expectgreaterthings.com) will point the reader to the Expect, Grow and Do Greater Things resources.

Wright

What do you think is the greatest challenge facing our culture today?

Myers

Well, I just alluded to it and that is I believe that there is a lack of balance in mind, body, and spirit because we've not really been taking the time to cultivate our souls. We're all so busy and that's the reason why I've created the expect, grow, and do greater things model to give people a place to focus and to say, "You know what? I can expect something beyond the mundane. I can grow. I can do greater things with my life and impact others positively and powerfully. A side benefit is that I achieve a balance in my life as I do so." The opposite affect of not having a balance is that we're creating what I think in 20 years could a spiritual, social and economic disaster for our nation that will be seen in a growing disparity between the haves and the have-nots. One of the greatest challenges facing our culture today is the economic disparity and a lack of philanthropy. The negative ripple effects include rising debt, illiteracy, substance abuse, deepening levels of poverty, homelessness and the list goes on. Expecting, Growing in and Doing Greater Things can combat these social ills effectively and close the gap.

The other challenge facing our culture is obviously, the threat of terrorism that permeates our culture and society. Not so much the terrorism acts themselves, but the fear and the lack of security that terrorism breeds and the lack of trust that can develop. One of the things that thinking people have to do is to help people find courage and then build trust with their neighbor. And, according to the Bible, our neighbor is the person next door and around the world. It is the shop owner down the street and the gang member on the street. Learning about each others' culture and world gives us insights as to how we can work and live together. Part of that comes from greater things thinking, and working together for the greater good.

Wright

Finally, John, you referenced one of my favorite scriptures a few minutes ago when you talked about the Jesus' farewell speech when Jesus said to his followers "you will do greater things than I," which has always been one of my favorites and one that I believe in.

Myers

Oh, I do too.

Wright

It's kind of strange that all of the people that I know, my friends and church members, I've never thought that they believed it. They've always put Christ on a pedestal and "Well, He was divine. He was this and that. I can't do the things that He did when ..." That's the last thing He said. He wanted us to live by faith!

Myers

Yes! He wanted us to understand that we can expect, grow in and do greater things because He goes to the Father. And the reason we can achieve greater things is that the Father would be glorified. The key is that it is all for God's greater glory and our greater experience in life and faith..

Wright

...I wonder why people forget that? Wonder why that is?

Myers

I think people forget who we are. People get focused on organizations, bureaucracies, careers, house and car payments, rent, school clothes, tuition, retirement funds and the like. I've been a pastor for 27 years. I started preaching in a small church when I was 19 years old and had my first full time appointment when I was 26, and have been in full time ministry since '82. I have been around the church world a lot. The one thing that I see is that people turn things upside down. They manage, they look at life through the eyes of property (Do we have enough money to do this? Well, the roof's leaking. We need to take care of the building) instead of living out of a prayerful and purposeful life that's really committed to helping people. And that comes back to those five P's. It's amazing when I teach and consult in companies and also in churches, and I talk about these five P's. A lot of times, people really say, "You know, you're right. We are managing our life and our church and I manage my business according to what I see at the bottom line instead of what I really started out believing: why I started the company, why I started the business, why I started my family, why I started following God, why I started going to church. You're right. I'm doing everything according to my property and what I see in front of me instead of expecting greater things." I think our nation, our churches and our companies can really expect, grow and do greater things, if we start from the other end of that scale on the five P's. Being a people of prayer, being a people of vision. The scripture in Proverbs chapter 29:18 says, "Where there's no vision, the people perish." Now there's another part of that scripture, or another translation, from the New King James version that says, "Where there is no revelation, the people cast off restraint." "How do you get a revelation? How do you find revelation in your life?" People say, "Well, sometimes I get it through prayer." Others say, "Sometimes I get it through study. Sometimes I get it through talking to other people. Sometimes I get it by exercising and all of a sudden I get an Ah Ha in my brain and then you get these revelations that come and up. You say Ah! There's a revelation!" Well, if a person doesn't have a revelation in their life, if they don't have a sense of vision and purpose, then they cast off restraint, which means they have no focus. They have no power. They're just kind of all over the place and they're casting off restraint. But, if you flip that around where there is revelation, the people have focus. They have power. They have a sense of purpose beyond themselves. If you flip around the original text that I quoted, the text would read that where there is a vision, the people will flourish! That's expecting greater things. It's growing in greater things. It's doing greater things to the glory of God and the betterment of our culture.

Wright

Well, what a great conversation. I really appreciate you spending this much time with me today. I've really enjoyed it.

Myers

Well, thank you! I've enjoyed it too, David.

Wright

Today we've been talking to Dr. John Myers. He is a trainer. He has launched several projects. He's entrepreneurial in spirit, and as we have found out today, really, really knows what he is talking about. John, thank you for being with me today on *Conversations on Faith*.

Myers

Thank you. God bless you.

About The Author

Ever since he was a young man, Dr. John Myers has enjoyed leading, entertaining, inspiring , making people laugh and helping people reach their full potential. These natural inclination and talents, combined with academic training and life's experience, have make it possible for Dr. Myers to travel, speak, consult and study in over twenty-one countries, as well as a large portion of the United States. His "Greater Things" philosophy encourages people to believe the best, train for the best and be the best they can be. The philosophy teaches people how to Expect Greater Things, Grow in Greater Things and Do Greater Things.

Dr. John R. Myers

Greater Things Enterprises

Bank of America City Centre

401 E. Las Olas Blvd #130

Ft. Lauderdale, Florida   33301

Phone: 954.649.7905

Fax: 954.523.2134

Email: drjohn@expectgreaterthings.com

www.expectgreaterthings.com

Chapter 4

DALE COLLIE

David E. Wright (Wright)

Today we are talking to Dale Collie, whose military service as a U.S. Army Ranger included command assignments in Europe and Vietnam. Following a yearlong period of recovery from combat wounds, he spent another 10 years on active duty as an amputee. Among his metals for distinguished service is the Purple Heart awarded for wounds received during wartime.

Customer sales, and distribution management experience in Fortune 500 Chemical and Textile Companies more recently enabled Dale to guide a bankrupt charity into a highly successful $37 million operation in just seven years, sheltering the homeless, feeding the hungry and assisting people in the former Soviet Union by creating jobs, providing orphanage relief and adoption services, offering the first ever privately owned Christian Youth Camp in the Ukraine and facilitating other church outreach programs.

For his work with Lighthouse Ministries and American Hunger relief, Dale was identified by Fast Company Magazine as one of America's Fast 50 innovative business leaders for his entrepreneurial achievements.

Academic achievements include a Murray State University Bachelor of Science degree in chemistry and English, and a Michigan State University Master of Arts in English. He has taught at the United States Military Academy in West Point, New York, the University of Kentucky, and Indiana Wesley University. Dale has also served as a chapter president with the National Speakers Association. As a professional motivational speaker and author on leadership and communications, Dale Collie now works with business leaders who want to get the best from their employees—Corporate keynotes, workshops, seminars, church retreats, and personal coaching. Dale Collie, welcome to *Conversations on Faith*.

Collie

Thank You.

Wright

Dale, you've just completed nine years as president of an international charity, but just before that you were earning well over $100,000 per year in corporate America. Tell us how you made the transition from corporate life into full-time ministry.

Collie

The corporate job was rather chaotic, but I felt compelled to assist in restarting Young Life's ministry to teens in Indianapolis. When I prayed that God would structure some time to get this ministry started, He answered by restructuring corporate management to free me up to do whatever I had in mind. In other words, I was out of a job.

Several job interviews revealed that I just didn't want to continue in that arena, and eventually Lighthouse Ministries requested that I help stabilize their nearly bankrupt ministry. Conversations led to full-time employment with Lighthouse, and I had to trust God in this transition because my annual income with Lighthouse was less than the money I paid in taxes the year before.

Wright

What was the focus of Lighthouse Ministries' efforts when you joined them and how did things develop?

Collie

Since 1953 Lighthouse had operated a shelter for homeless men in downtown Indianapolis, but the ministry was in a bad financial situation. One of our big expenses was an annual food cost of approximately $75,000, so it was natural that we would search out free food. What we found was truck loads of food, more than we could use of these particular items. We accepted the food and then looked for several partner organizations to help use all of the food. We had no trouble finding partners or food and soon had more than 200 partners and more than 7 million pounds of food annually. The program grew to such a size that we had to give it its own name, and it now operates nationally as *American Hunger Relief*.

God demonstrated time and time again that he was in charge. When we lacked money, He caused donations to come in. When we were in need, people called to donate food by the truckload.

This is best illustrated by the example of what happened when our distribution manger declined a truckload of spaghetti sauce. He told me that even poor people didn't sit around eating spaghetti sauce. But he did as I asked and called to acquire this odd shipment from Kentucky. Before it arrived, we received a call from Oklahoma offering us a truckload of pasta. Only God can match up truckload recipes like that!

Wright

Did you see miraculous events at the homeless mission as well?

Collie

We did. When I first arrived at Lighthouse we frequently had only 6-9 men in the rehabilitation program, and the success rate was something like 5%. A change of programs and a more demanding schedule actually increased participation instead of driving people away. In recent years we've had more than 25 men at a time in the rehabilitation program with a waiting list. The success rate has climbed to nearly 40%, three to four times the national average. Salvation decisions also grew to approximately 100 per year, an envious number for many full-time churches. God often let us see how our staff efforts led to these decisions, but there were many where God kept to himself the actual choice these men made.

Ben was one of our more dramatic cases. He arrived at Lighthouse Mission in bad shape from drugs and alcohol. Six weeks later we were on a field trip to Mammoth Cave State Park, and these tough street guys were amazed by God's magnificent creation. Many of them had never slept a night away from concrete.

As we sat around the campfire, the chaplain asked the group if any of them thought a year ago that they would be enjoying something like this. A few of the men shook their heads, and others expressed the thrill they found enjoying nature.

Ben spoke up with a tone that caught everyone's attention. "Just six weeks ago, I didn't think I'd ever be here."

"Why's that," asked the chaplain.

"Because I thought I'd be dead by now," said Ben. "Six weeks ago I was walking down the street looking for a place to die. I'd been trying to kill myself for about a year, but now I had what I needed—a bag of drugs in one pocket; a pistol in my other pocket, and a fifth of whisky."

"What brought you to the Mission, Ben?"

"A friend recognized me on the street and said, 'You look bad; get in the car.'

"Of course, I looked bad, trying to kill myself and all. So, I got in his car, and he drove me to Lighthouse."

The chaplain asked, "Are you still suicidal, Ben?"

"No! I would never kill myself now that I know Christ. I have hope for the future," said Ben.

"Well, Ben, after years on the streets what was the pivotal point in all of this?"

Ben became rather animated with his response and humorously said, "Well, Chaplain, it wasn't anything you did."

Laughter filled the night air around the campfire while everyone waited for Ben to explain his statement.

"It was those teenagers who came to paint the bunk beds blue. I worked with them for two days, and not a one of them ever preached at me or told me that I had to change my ways. Not a one of them mentioned scripture. But sometime on the second day, it dawned on me that these kids were painting those bunk beds because they cared for me, because they loved me. There was nothing I could do for them in return. This was the first time I saw God's love in action. Anytime people helped me before, I figured they wanted something from me, but there was nothing these teens could expect in return. They were just doing this work because they loved the Lord and they loved me."

The campfire conversation became lighter after Ben's monologue, but it was clear that his life was saved for the present and for eternity by a group of volunteer teens who thought they were just painting the bunk beds blue.

Wright

Did the teens ever find out about the impact of their work?

Collie

This church group would never have known about their efforts if we hadn't told them about it. But, I've used the example a number of times since then as I speak with various church groups because there is a lesson in this for all of us. The incident is a vivid illustration of what happens when we are available for Kingdom work. We don't have to know the outcome of our efforts when we are called to do something or even when it is over.

Because people don't understand how God works, they sometimes make critical remarks about the cost of sending teenagers on short-term mission trips. Sure it would be less expensive if the kids stayed home and we sent money to the poor people they go to serve. You can build a lot of small houses in an impoverished area for the amount of money it takes to fly a group around the world. We often don't know the result of these efforts? But God's love is shown best through personal relationships.

Wright

Being available seems to be a theme of yours, Dale. How did you come to realize the importance of this?

Collie

When my oldest son was living in the Blue Ridge Mountains, near Boone, North Carolina, he invited me to go to an old-fashioned church revival meeting. Immediately, my mind pictured the sales meeting I was to attend in another town, and I think he could see in my eyes that I was going to make an excuse. He preempted my feeble excuse when he said, "I just thought you would like to hear David Ring speak." He knew I admired the way David Ring continued his evangelism in spite of his disabling cerebral palsy. Instantly, I attempted decided that I would go with my son to this small mountain church instead of going to the sales meeting.

Within the first few minutes, David told the congregation, "I know some of you cannot stay here for my whole talk. But if you are going to leave, I ask you to go now because we don't want to interrupt this special thing I am going to do at the end of tonight's meeting." No one left, of course, and David quickly moved into his sermon, confidently explaining the gospel message of Jesus Christ. He stressed how much he had been used by God in spite of his handicaps. He made light of his own difficulties.

And at the end of the evening, David offered an alter call. He said, "Everyone who wants to accept Christ as Lord and Savior, come down here to the front where we have seven preachers who will pray with you." Several people moved forward, and David said, "Alright, every-one who wants to rededicate their lives to the Lord, come on down front." Then he made an announcement that I thought would empty the pews. He said, "All of you who want to simply make yourselves more available to Christ, come on down here and pray with one of these preachers."

I gave my son a look that said, "I'll go down front with you if you want to do that." And to my surprise, he gave me the same look. We both stood. How could I get out of an offer like that? I intended to go down front just to accompany my son, but somewhere between the pew and the pulpit, my journey of accompaniment turned into one of commitment. I prayed a prayer that I would be more available to Christ.

And that started what has turned into a full-time ministry, a standard of availability that makes me ready for whatever the Lord puts into my path. If I'm invited to speak to a Christian audience, I go unless there is a prior commitment on my schedule. When the Lord puts into my path an opportunity to serve, I do that. If you're avail-able, you're available all the time, not just when it is convenient. And the same thing goes for your possessions, your money, your time, and your family resources. Later on, I discovered that it also meant that all of my ministry resources were also available and that I was not in control of anything.

Wright

I'm aware that you've also done some work in Eastern Europe Dale, was this a part of your being available?

Collie

After I was restructured out of the textile company, I accompanied a missions director on a trip to Ukraine. During the trip one of the full-time missionaries in Southern Ukraine invited me to go to an or-phanage with him. I was pretty enthusiastic about the opportunity, but I didn't realize what I was getting into. The orphanage was a rundown building with no windows, no furniture, no beds or bedding, no food or kitchen appliances, no electricity or heat, and none of the other items needed to take care of the twenty-five children who would arrive the following Monday.

When asked, how she would run the orphanage without any of the equipment needed, the director said, "We'll run it the way the Communists taught us, with enthusiasm!" She had a great smile on her face as she said this, but the tear in her eye revealed the futility of her remark. The twenty-five orphans would arrive in a couple of days and the Siberian winds were already blowing through the windowless openings. We felt terrible as we drove away from the orphanage that evening. As we faced the setting sun, we did what just about any American would do. We brainstormed ideas on how we could help.

Wright

Were you able to help these kids?

Collie

Every idea I surfaced, my friend shot down with excuses about the difficulties of working with Ukrainian authorities, customs officials, and other obstacles that I could not have thought of with my western mind. Finally, I asked about the possibility of the local villagers helping these children. "They have no jobs," the missionary responded. "They have no money. They barely survive themselves. These people want to help, but it is impossible."

"What if we create a business where these people can be employed," I asked. We calculated that a businesses could make enough profit to fix up the orphanage and take care of these children.

Returning to the states, I went against the advice of business people in the US and Ukraine who said the plan was impossible. We assembled and shipped a semi trailer load of used clothing. We were confident that a second-hand clothing store would work in that area. Before we opened the store, many people had only one set of clothing and could afford no replacement apparel. Unemployment was 90%. Shoes cost as much as a month's wages for those who did have jobs.

The first load of clothing sold very quickly, and the number of employees grew until we had more than a hundred families working in several cities and villages. Thousands of people had access to affordable clothing, and there was a profit left over to make repairs at the orphanage.

Today, that small orphanage is a model for many other state run orphanages in that part of the country. This is truly a rags to riches story. Cast-off American clothing is providing for families and orphans—and the donors get a tax break for their generosity.

Wright
What else grew out of these business efforts?

Collie
The business model led to other interesting opportunities. We soon had an auto and truck repair business, a metal working shop, and a sawmill running in that town. Later, we were able to start a youth camp on the Sea of Azov after we introduced a donor to the opportunities that were before us. The camp is operating today with several hundred kids attending each summer. Most of the children are from churches around the country, but many of those orphans we assisted also get to attend. They don't keep track of the number of conversions at the camp, but the first summer we found that 40% of the kids confessed Christ as Lord and Savior during their two weeks at camp. One group of 250 un-churched children saw 90% of the kids come to know the Lord!

In addition to the businesses and the youth camp, we were involved with ministry to the Tatar people who were the focus of my first trip to Ukraine. As with the camp and the businesses, we were just partners with the local congregation. We just facilitated where we could. In the beginning, Americans had some of the needed resources, but the Ukrainians and the church are very capable. Now, we act as a fundraising partner in the USA and Ukrainians manage all of their own businesses and programs.

Wright
Working with Muslim's is kind of tough sometimes. Did you find resistance in this arena?

Collie
Some unique circumstances permitted the ministry to succeed. One of the associate pastors from the local church had a strong vision for witnessing to the Tatar people and made contact with Elmira, a fine woman who became the first Christian among the Tatar. She was actually the first Tatar evangelist in leading others to the Lord. Elmira was crippled by rheumatoid arthritis and relied upon her twelve

year old daughter to take in laundry for their survival. The towns-people paid for their laundry with produce and food from their gardens.

When Elmira attended one of the youth camps with her daughter, she learned make pencil drawings on wooden plaques and then use a wood burning tool to outline the images. Afterward, she colored in the pictures with crayons and coated them with lacquer to make very nice folk art pictures depicting scenes from the Bible. When I first visited her a year later, Elmira had several of these pictures on the walls of her two room house.

She explained, "I use these pictures to tell people about Christ. They come in here with their laundry, and they ask about these pictures. I start right here with Abraham and the alter. Here's Isaac right here. Do you see the lamb here in the bushes? Everybody likes this story." And she told stories of the next picture and the next. This impoverished, crippled, single mother who depended on Muslim neighbors for her livelihood was bold in her witness, even when it could have meant that the neighbors would no longer bring their laundry and she would no longer have food. Her efforts were blessed by the Lord, and she continues her evangelism even though she now gets some support from the USA.

Wright

In all of your travels, which one incident best describes your theme of being available for Christ?

Collie

The incident that best describes my theme of being available for Christ occurred in a remote village in Crimea—Southern Ukraine—where we traveled to check on the progress of a second-hand clothing operation. Typical of the Ukrainian hospitality, the local pastor invited us for dinner at his home and encouraged us to stay even longer to participate in an evening devotional. The offer was impossible to refuse. He had already told the congregation that he was inviting these Americans, and a *desert table* was planned in our honor. You have to remember that these people were living in extreme poverty and spending precious funds.

As the sun slipped low in the western sky, we moved to the house next door and discovered that the devotionals would be held under a grape arbor in the garden. The scene was idyllic. *National Geographic* would have displayed a picture of this romantic setting as the sun reflected from the huge clusters of grapes hanging above us. All of the worship music was in Russian, Ukrainian, and Tatar, of course, songs of praise.

Immediately noticeable was a young guy, maybe seventeen years old, a very cool teen with his baseball cap on backwards. He looked so American, I thought he was from the US when he first appeared. Dima was even more noticeable because he was doing sign language for Luda, a deaf woman who sat across from him in that arbor. He gestured in a big way during the songs and encouraged Luda to *sing* along with him. Intermittently, she joined in, but otherwise smiled and watched intently as he interpreted the songs for her.

The desert table was a grand affair. Our visit was during the harvest, so there was a lot of fruit along with the beautiful cakes and pastries. During an intermission for us to enjoy the sweets, Dima joined us for some conversation.

"You seem to really enjoy the sign language, Dima. Your eyes are full of joy as you interpret the songs."

"Of course, I enjoy it. It is too much work to do this as a job," explained Dima.

"How long have you been interpreting for the deaf," I asked.

"For about two years. I traveled to St. Petersburg (over a thousand miles) three times to learn sign language because there are four deaf people in our village that I want to witness to."

"Is Luda a believer?" I continued.

Dima's buoyant expression turned serious as he said, "No. I have been witnessing to her for over a year now, and she always says she is not ready to repent. Please pray for her. She cannot speak or hear, and she has a hard life."

As Dima made this request, the worship was beginning, so he hurried back to resume his duties. When the first song began, I saw that his wearing the hat backwards was not an influence from the West, but a necessity. With his first interpretation, he knocked the hat entirely off his head—laughed good naturedly, retrieved the hat and put in on—backwards! A few of the songs were recognizable, and I sang along in English when I knew the words. Otherwise, I was able to watch the people during this impressive service. Luda and Dima often caught my attention as she participated more in signing the songs.

At one point of the service, I had the strong impression that Luda would accept Christ as Lord and Savior if someone would offer to pray with her that night. I don't often say that God told me a specific thing, but if there ever was a message directed right at me, this was it.

As the crowd broke up, the interpreter walked out of the arbor and then called to me.

"Here's Dima and Luda. I told them you wanted to ask Luda a question."

"Go ahead and tell her my thoughts," I said.

"No, Dale, I'm just your interpreter. Tell Dima what you want Luda to hear. I'll make it into Russian. He'll make it into sign language."

"I know how it works, just tell her."

"Tell her what? I'm the interpreter," he said.

"Ok—here goes," I said. "Luda, Dima tells me that you know all about Jesus Christ as the son of God. Would you like to offer a prayer of repentance tonight and ask Jesus to come into your heart as Lord and Savior?"

The interpreter translated into Russian, and Dima did his thing. I waited as the question went around the circle and the answer came back. The answer was apparent before the words made their rounds because of Luda's enthusiastic expression and the energetic nod of her head.

Then the lights went out. Did you ever think about how deaf people communicate in the dark? After some confusion, someone found the trouble and had the lights back on. The prayer continued.

Following her emotion-filled prayer, I asked, "Luda, what do you think of all this?" Through two languages went my question, and even though Luda could not hear or speak, she explained, "I'm very excited. I've wanted to pray this prayer for a long time, but I didn't think God could hear me."

Luda's remark is just about the most saddening and, at the same time, the most revealing statement I've ever heard. While Christ came to this earth, suffered and died for the remission of our sins, Luda thought that God couldn't hear her. It was for the least of these that Christ made the sacrifice, but it didn't do Luda any good until she discovered that she, too, was loved by God. Luda's eighteen words also summarized the condition of so many who go through life thinking that God cannot hear their desperate cry for help. Her remark would be well understood by all of those who think they must meet certain conditions before God can hear them.

Because of the late hour and the long ride facing us, we expressed our appreciation to the pastor and his wife for their hospitality and for including us in the worship service. Everyone was elated with Luda's decision to repent, and arrangements were made to join her the next afternoon for a time of Bible study.

These things filled my mind as we traveled northward through the darkness. The animated conversation about the visit gave way to drowsiness after a day filled with travel, enthusiasm, and emotion. One by one, the passengers in the small car fell silent, and I nodded off to sleep. Jolting bumps woke me frequently, and our driver fixed his eyes on the dirt track ahead. Mental pictures of Luda and Dima and the grape arbor fought with sleepiness.

God was saving one more revelation for me that night as I remembered a prayer that I had prayed more than two weeks before my travel to Ukraine. In my half sleep I realized that I had prayed about Luda and her salvation.

The prayer was about Luda, but not by name, as I asked God to allow me to witness to some person on this trip. I was rather confident that we would achieve our objectives and that I would get to speak to audiences of well over a hundred. My prayer, however, was that I could witness to an individual, one on one. Immediately upon making the prayer, however, I withdrew it, saying, "Oh God, just forget about that. I don't speak Russian." During the prayer I saw the humor in my statement, because I knew that God already knew that I didn't speak the language.

In looking back on the prayer, I can see that my withdrawal of the request was an expression of momentary disbelief. I did not trust God to fulfill my prayer, and rather than have it denied, I simply said, "Forget about that, God. The language barrier makes it impossible for me to witness to an individual." Under the harvest moon, just outside a grape arbor where we had all worshiped God for more than two hours, God answered that prayer, in spite of my momentary disbelief. I was blessed to be present as Luda accepted Jesus Christ as her Lord and Savior.

I was both humiliated and impressed that God allowed me to witness to Luda, and He must have gotten a little chuckle when I realized what He had done through two languages instead of the one that I had found to be an obstacle. Once again I prayed—that God would someday allow me another visit with Luda when we both speak the same heavenly language. With such a blessing, I am confidently available to Christ and use my storytelling ability in keynote presentations, seminars, workshops, and retreats in an effort to motivate others to action.

Luda's remark was such a powerful and motivating example that I am compelled to help anyone who might think, *"I've wanted to pray this prayer for a long time, but I didn't think God could hear me."*

Wright

What a great story! Dale, I really appreciate the time you've taken with me today in *Conversations on Faith.* I've learned a lot and I'm sure my readers will also learn. I just really appreciate you doing this for us.

Collie

Well, thank you, David. I enjoyed being with you and I pray for your success with your work there.

Wright

Thank you so much.

About The Author

Dale Collie—motivational speaker on leadership and communication. Former US Army Ranger, Combat Infantry Commander, Fortune 500 executive, and teacher at the United States Military Academy at West Point, University of Kentucky, and Indiana Wesleyan University. Selected by *Fast Company* as one of America's Fast 50 innovative leaders for guiding a bankrupt ministry into a $37 mm success in just seven years. Author of *Frontline Leadership: From War Room to Boardroom* and *Winning Under Fire: US Army Strategies for Managing Corporate Stress.*

Dale Collie

Courage Builders, Inc.

Phone: 877.826.5543

Email: collie@couragebuilders.com

www.couragebuilders.com

Chapter 5

TRAVIS P. CLARK

THE INTERVIEW

David E. Wright (Wright)
Today we are talking to Travis Clark. Since graduating Texas Bible College, Travis has held several different local church positions. Today he is the children's pastor at The Dacusville Church, in the upstate of South Carolina. Travis also travels evangelistically, sharing the love of Christ with kids around the world. Travis Clark, welcome to *Conversations on Faith*.

Travis Clark (Clark)
Thank you very much, David. I appreciate the opportunity.

Wright
Travis, tell us a little bit about your background personally and professionally.

Clark
Personally, I grew up in Greenville, South Carolina. I have the kind of parents I hope I can be. I grew up playing sports and was very involved in youth group. When I graduated high school, I went off to Bible College, where I continued to grow in my walk with the Lord.

After graduating Bible school, I moved back home and got involved in the ministry. Everything in my life seemed to be going quite well. Then, in 2002, I went through the toughest time of my life. I began to wonder if the book of Job had been written as prophecy for my life, as opposed to a story of someone else's. However, God is faithful, and in 2003, He has revolutionized my life. It is very humbling to look back at where I was as to where I am now.

Professionally, I have been in ministry for almost nine years now. I was ordained as a minister in February 1996, and have been a children's pastor and a youth pastor. Both were great opportunities, and today I am a children's pastor again. I am so excited about what God has in store for this ministry. I have been able to lock arms with a great church and an awesome Pastor. I also travel as a children's evangelist, speaking at kid's camps, and in local church kid's rallies. These local church rallies are dedicated as a time of outreach for the church. In June of 2003, I was invited to be the key speaker at a summer kid's camp in Ireland. What a dream come true!

Wright

What is your greatest passion?

Clark

That's always a tough question. There are several things I love, but my greatest passion is to see children on fire for Jesus. I love to work with adults. I love to work with teenagers, but seeing children being ministered to and seeing that light come on for the first time is a true passion of mine. I love to teach children how to worship Jesus, and then watch them worship Him. I love it when a kid realizes for the very first time that he or she really "can do all things through Christ..."

Wright

I've got a 14 year old daughter and it has really been interesting watching her grow in faith in the last few years through youth work. She just came back from a youth conference with 9,000 Methodist youths in Gatlinburg Tennessee. Boy, I'll tell you, she's hard to live with after one of those rallies. She's been checking out my Christianity every day.

Clark

That's great!

Wright

What is the biggest lesson you've learned about life so far?

Clark

David, there are a lot of lessons that I have learned. Regrettably, many of them have been learned the hard way. I guess the biggest lesson is one that I am still learning, and that is humility. In business, you often hear "humility is the best policy." I have found that when you understand that you owe somebody, that someone else has made this possible for you, that whatever you are living in, or whatever you are doing, you owe the people that went before you. That is when you understand humility. I thank God that I didn't have to do everything on my own. As one person said, "When you see a turtle on a fence post, you know they didn't get there on their own." David, I truly am that turtle on a fence post, and learning humility has a lot to do with that.

Wright

You said that 2002 was a real down year for you. Did you question your faith during these times, and if you did, how do you hold on to your faith during the tough times?

Clark

Well, the year started out with a major blow to me personally, followed by a major blow to me professionally. The church I was in began to fall apart; everything in my life began to fall apart. The thing that I had to hold on to, and the thing that I would encourage others to hold on to, is the big picture. God is faithful when we will back away and let him be God. When you read books about successful people, or talk to people, you learn that everyone goes through hard times. It is those people that are able to look at the big picture and know that they will not always be where they are right now, that will make it through those hard times. During that time, I learned that in order for God to take me to something, I had to allow God to bring me through something. That was the biggest thing that helped me go through those tough times. God is so faithful.

Wright

Tell us a little bit about your ministry.

Clark

David, I am so thankful that God has called me into the ministry for such a time as this! The answer to that question is two fold. The first part I will describe is my role as a children's pastor. This ministry will always thrive on the love of God. We shout, we scream, we dance, we laugh, we play, we worship, and we see kid's get saved! Someone once said of me, "he ain't your mama's preacher." I hope that was a good thing and I hope I always stay on the cutting edge of children's ministry. Everything we do revolves around teamwork; every person has a specific role to play.

The second part of that answer refers to my role as a children's evangelist. Again, I want to bring with me the energy of a rock show. I always encourage the churches to have every kid they can find come to these services. The theme of these rallies is always salvation. I have given altar calls for salvation during these rallies and watched kid's and parents alike respond to the power and love of God. In addition to preaching, our desire is to encourage the children's ministry team that is in that local church. So, my ministry is one that is very motivational to the team in place. My ministry is locking arms, strengthening and building up. It is our prayer as a ministry to always to join hands with the local church. The local church has been very good to me. In my growing up years, the kid's and youth ministries, and even today I'm part of a great local church. The way we lock arms is through kid's ministry. Our goal when we go into a church is not just to blow up and blow out, but to have a party for Jesus where every person gets rocked with the power of God!

Wright

What are some of the challenges for kid's ministry in today's church?

Clark

Kid's Ministry is so much fun, but it can be tough nowadays. Kid's have everything in the world. They have tons of options. They have TV, where the commercials or the shows change camera angles every three to five seconds. They have computers and games, they have it all! This is the world we live in, so as a church, it can be tough. A child's attention span has been taught to hang in with that three to five second change, and then as a kid's pastor, or teacher or even a public school teacher, we have to appeal to that same attention span. So, I think the thing that you really have to be careful with in kid's ministry is just staying fresh, not letting things get old. You've got to stay relevant to the world they live in and you've got to stay fresh. I once heard the gospel message explained like potatoes. The minister said that no matter what, you had to serve kids potatoes (the gospel). He went on to say that in the 1950's and 60's, American families served mashed potatoes and gravy with every meal. In this century we are likely to go to a drive-thru for fries at every meal. He said that Americans were still eating potatoes; they were just being served differently. You must realize that we live in a fast paced, multi-media age, and that flannel graph Suzy is long gone. You should continue to present the gospel as strong, maybe even stronger than ever, just present it in a more relevant way. It is really tough, but you can do it. If we can do it here in Dacusville, S.C., you can do it as well. Through prayer, a little research and just trying to stay fresh and relevant.

Wright
Yeah, I can just imagine a child sitting still in a church service listening to a preacher that is straight as a stick and after coming off of three second flashes on television. Even when they watch a newscast, they've got all of the war and planes and everything going on in the background on video.

Clark
Exactly. That's exactly right.

Wright
Well, what can a children's minister do, or even a parent, to see when they look past the shell of a kid or a teenager?

Clark
Having been a youth pastor and children's pastor, I would say the most important thing you have to remember is that all they want is to be loved. Over the years, I have seen all kinds of kids. And while there is a different person in the shell, or skin, many times it is the same story. You have to realize that most things kids will do will be for attention. Understand that really all that kid wants is the same thing that we all want; we want to be loved. We want people to care about us. We want people to tell us when we have done a good job. Many kids do not get that today. I cannot tell you how many kids I have watched let there walls down when I helped them realize that they were safe and that they were loved. It's huge, David!

Wright

Most of the people that I know and see, even the church people, are hurting. I can just imagine when you augment that by being young, your hormones are raging, your body is changing and your mind is changing, it's so easy to look at all of the children that are hurt today. How do you walk in forgiveness when you've been really hurt?

Clark

You know, that is a very good question. It is one that is still tough with me personally. People usually think more in terms of revenge than forgiveness, and that is natural. Remember, forgiveness came along after Adam and Eve were created. I remember a line from a musical I saw several years ago, "It's a good thing I'm not God, when the lady gets in the express line with 13 items, ... it's a good thing I'm not God, when the guy shines his high beams late at night..." It was great! David, everyone is going to be hurt in life, but we must forgive those who hurt us. You do not have to continue in the relationship, but you must forgive. If God can forgive me, knowing the things I have gone through, and done, then I must forgive others. That is what Jesus is all about, forgiveness.

Wright

What do you see as the single most important aspect in the life of a child?

Clark

I think children need stability, especially at home. I am a firm believer in loving your kids. This is so important to me. It amazes me, even in adults, what someone will do, or is capable of doing, when they know they are loved. David, most men would jump off of high buildings if their wives said to them, "I believe in you, and I love you." I know I would! Kids must hear those words from mom and dad as well. Hearing those words will breed in them a confidence, and a security that will give them opportunities that they wouldn't ordinarily have had. How does it do that? Well, we know that what is on the inside of a person is what carries them through, not what is on the outside. When a kid has a sense of security, they will attempt things that other kids will not. When kids are raised in a loving home, they will have a strength, and a character that will help them push through difficulties, and achieve greatness.

Wright

After being in the ministry as long as you have, what are some of the awards of ministry?

Clark

That's always funny. It is always funny being around ministers, we're all so "holy," you know and "well, brother you know our reward is in heaven," you know. Maybe I'm just not cut from the same cloth or something, but I believe that there are huge rewards for people right now. Just last night I was in a kid's service; I was leading praise and worship with the kids. I saw a little girl. She was on the front row, left hand side of the room. I can see her right now if I close my eyes. I can see her worshiping God. David, that is the reward of ministry to me. There is just nothing like that. I am addicted to watching kids worship God. I mean, it's just amazing. You know, only one time in Gods word did He describe heaven with a group of people. He said it was like children. A lot of the times, we overlook kids in different areas of life, but when you get a kid that really knows what it means to worship God and you watch that kid worship, then you're seeing heaven. That, to me, is the reward. There's a lot of other things I think that could be considered rewards, but that's huge for me.

Wright

When you were explaining your work with churches, you said that instead of going in and locking horns and knocking out everything they've been doing and changing them, you actually lock arms with them and lift them up and add to their ministry. Why is teamwork so important to you?

Clark

When I was getting started in ministry, I thought I could do everything myself, boy was I wrong. I had no concept of teamwork, and at least for the first several years, I was working myself closer and closer to an early grave than towards a successful ministry. I finally wised up about six and a half years ago and decided that I wanted to learn more about teamwork. I began to pray that God would open my eyes and He did. He sent me a couple that worked with me in both children's and youth ministry. This couple was amazing! It was through working with them that God showed me many of the basics of teamwork. That team grew and other players were added to the team, but I was always incredibly thankful for that first couple. When people really understand their roles inside the team environment, then is when the team will see success. It is having the right players, in the right positions, at the right time, that makes teamwork so fun. A mentor of mine used to always say, "many hands make light work." Well David, God only gave me two hands. I must need some help.

Wright

As you go about teaching people, training people, helping people and uplifting people, you would be viewed by others, I'm sure, as a leader. What is the hardest part of leadership for you?

Clark

The hardest part of leadership for me is having to realize that you're going to come across people from time to time that just don't want to go on the journey with you. And you see, I'm the type of person that when God gives me an idea I just want to grab everybody in the room and say, "Come on, let's go! Let's do it! Let's go after it! This is your job and this is you job, and I'm going to be doing this. We're just going to tackle the world." And win the entire world for God. Because of that, the hardest part of leadership for me is to realize that every now and then you will come across a person that says, "You know what? I like where I am. I don't want to go any farther." That is always sad to me because I can already see what they are going to miss out on. But, that's where they are in life and if that's where they are, then the best thing you can do for the rest of the team is to let that person be what they want to be, even if they aren't going to come along.

Wright

A management consultant told me many years ago, "David, you cannot reach down into the muck of life and pull up people who do not want to come. There are so many people that you need to be spending your time with that actually do want to go with you." I felt exactly the way you did and because of my Christian upbringing, I didn't hear these words very well.

Clark

Right, that is so true.

Wright

It was a tough lesson and that thing about shaking the dust off your sandals and walking away has never set very well with me.

Clark

It's the toughest thing for me, that's for sure.

Wright

So, what are your plans for the future? Do you have any immediate goals or any long-term goals that you want to accomplish in your ministry.

Clark

At the forefront of all my dreams and goals, is the growth of the children's department at The Dacusville Church. When I say the word growth, I mean in every aspect. Spiritually, numerically, in relevance, in effectiveness, in every area. I even want to play better games than we ever have! I love to see growth. I want to see churches begin to once again become some of the major influences in the lives of kids. We also want to start to do some more citywide events as well. Instead of just doing single churches, we'd like to do some citywide events that would allow churches to come out of their shell. Churches so many times seem to be afraid of each other, and that's not God's best. God's best is for us to work together to promote his kingdom and to promote the love of God. So, that's another area we want to work into. I believe fantastic things will happen for God when cities come together. That's a couple of dreams that we have right now and I believe we will see those happen.

Wright

It sounds exciting!

Clark

It'll be awesome. We're looking forward to it.

Wright

Well, Travis, I really appreciate the time you have spent with me today in *Conversations on Faith*. I wish you the very best as you minister to the children. They are so important to us all and I'm sure that you know that better than I do. We have been talking today to Travis Clark. He is the children's pastor at The Dacusville Church, in South

Carolina. He also travels evangelistically, speaking at camps, and doing kid's rallies in local churches and as we have found today, committed to the call of ministry to children. Thank you so much, Travis.

Clark

Thank you, David, I appreciate it.

About The Author

Travis Clark is the children's pastor at The Dacusville Church, in Upstate South Carolina. He has been "rocking" children and youth for Jesus for nearly nine years. He says there is no reason why the church, if relevant to today's culture, can't be the biggest influence on the life of a child.

Travis Clark
Phone: 864.360.7356
Email: Travis.Clark@TheElementGroup.Net

Chapter 6

DR. LAWANA S. GLADNEY

THE INTERVIEW

David E. Wright (Wright)

Today we are talking to Dr. Lawana Gladney, the motivational specialist and president and C.E.O., of Gladney Associates. As a speaker, author, and trainer, she has energized audiences nationally by providing them with the tools to keep themselves motivated to achieve their goal. As an energizer, Dr. Gladney has operated her own business, obtained her doctorate degree, ran an organization, all while raising her four children. In 1992, God revealed his purpose for her life. After suffering tragedy and loss, she began her heart felt journey of healing and wholeness. Through her journey, she came to understand that God wanted her to speak into the lives of others to encourage, motivate, and help build vessels for the edification of the body of Christ. For more than a decade, Dr. Gladney has given speeches and training sessions in the education, corporate arena, and churches. She spent several years researching the field of motivation and understanding human behavior. Her education background combined with her life experiences have placed her in a unique category to be used by God. Dr. Gladney's energetic presentation style coupled with her ability to connect with the audience is an explosive combination that leaves the audience inspired and desiring to learn more. God has inspired her to start a non-profit organization for women called the Six Million Dollar Woman's Club. Her audiences are comprised of corporate entities, women's organizations, and educational institutions and churches. Dr. Gladney, welcome *to Conversations on Faith.*

Dr. Lawana Gladney (Gladney)

Well, thank you. I'm glad to be here.

Wright

When did you first come to know Christ?

Gladney

I came to know Christ as a child at the tender age of eight. I can remember feeling the tug at my heart to want to let Christ live within, although I didn't fully grasp the concept. My earliest memories include church. We would attend services four to five times a week, three times on Sunday, once on Wednesday and once on Friday. If there was a revival or a camp meeting going on, we would attend up to three services in one day for the entire week. So, it was not unusual to feel the pumping of your heart at a very age. I believe giving my heart to Christ at an early age, spared me from a lot of negative experiences that other people share growing up as teenagers and young adults.

Wright

That's good. Tell me about your spiritual upbringing.

Gladney

As I stated previously, I was literally raised in church. The church I grew up in could be classified as somewhat legalistic and tradition led. So, many different traditions determined your spiritual walk with Christ. There were many aged traditions that governed the places you went and the clothes you wore. For instance, we didn't have a television or go to the movies. There was a great deal of emphasis placed on your clothing, inasmuch as wearing a pair of pants was tied to your salvation. As a young person, I went through a difficult period because I wanted to go to the movies and attend sporting events. Many times I felt confined and restrained. But, I lived by the rules because I didn't want to interfere with my relationship with Christ.

Wright

Were you like me and thought you were going straight to hell or get killed by a lightening bolt on the first movie you ever saw on Sunday?

Gladney

I can relate to that, only my experience happened at a basketball game. The first basketball game I attended, I remember standing there and my heart was beating so fast, and I just thought, "Oh my goodness, something bad is going to happen to me." And I just thought God was going to do something terrible to me because I had attended that basketball game. Of course, that was not the case.

Wright

How long have you been married?

Gladney

I have been married over 17 years.

Wright

You are in a marriage enrichment ministry right now, aren't you?

Gladney

Yes. I am not only in the marriage enrichment ministry, but my husband and I are the marriage enrichment ministry leaders. And as veterans of 17 plus years it puts us in the minority, and particularly married to the same person. There are many couples who are in their second marriages that have years under their belt, but few that have been married to the same person for several years. And my husband and I are still young which means that we have spent over half our lives with each other. It's really challenging and very exciting to think that we have been together so long. We've made it through with God's grace.

Wright

You know it's strange. We were talking about it before, but I was surprised when I read the statistics. The divorce rate is the same with Christians and non-Christians. I also learned that behavior was not viewed by the citizenry as being different, if you are a Christian or non-Christian. That's kind of scary, don't you think?

Gladney

Definitely. There are some very gray lines here. As marriage ministry leaders, that's one issue that's very troubling to us, that there are no distinctions between the Christian marriages and the secular marriages. You think that there would be, because as Christians, you should be able to get together and say, "Hey, let's pray about this particular situation and we'll work through this." As Christians we do have God's Word that we can fall on to carry us that non-believers don't have. However, that's not the case, and what we're finding is that there are only a small percentage of couples that even pray together. Prayer is not integrated into their lives; daily, weekly, and sometimes not at all. Couples don't have a place where they can go and actually spiritually nourish each other outside of the church.

There are a lot of couples who have serious issues that are unaddressed and they start to deteriorate the marriage. They don't go and ask for help from the church or anyone else, because they don't want others to think they have issues. It amazes me how we look on the outside of someone's marriage and conclude that they are happy because they "look" happy. We all are devastated when a couple splits up who appeared not to have any problems. In the Christian arena, I actually think that we become masters at faking happiness and wearing mask. We are inclined to act one way at church, and a different way when we're at home. There is a tendency to hide your problems without seeking help until you've reached the point of helplessness.

Wright

Besides marriage enrichment, what other ministries are you involved in presently?

Gladney

Presently, I sing in the choir and help to direct the choir part time. I'm on the praise team, and I also help out with the parent group for children's choir when necessary, and then I lead praise and worship during Vacation Bible School.

Wright

How many children do you have?

Gladney

We have four children, three girls and one boy. My son is the oldest. At times he gets overwhelmed with girls, particularly when they invite friends over. Our house is always full of life, never a dull moment.

Wright

I made sure mine was. I've got a 41 year old daughter, a 40 year old son, and a 14 year old.

Gladney

Whoops!

Wright

That's what I said, "Whoops!"

Gladney

Oh my! So you guys decided to start over again?

Wright

Absolutely!

Gladney

Oh, wow! But I'm sure that is just a thrill. That is a joy for both of you.

Wright

Oh, yes, it's a blessing.

Gladney

Yes! Children are definitely a blessing.

Wright

Having or being marriage ministry leaders, what do you think are the greatest challenges to Christian couples as they face life?

Gladney

I think one of the greatest challenges is the whole surprise of living with another human being and thinking that your love is going to pull you through. Many times people think "God put us together" and so everything is going to work out fine. But, reality sets in and you find that you can't relate to this person. Communication or the lack thereof becomes a major issue. Couples really have a hard time talking to each other. The problem can turn into an issue when one person will not share what is bothering them. We can't discount that fact that there are many differences in the way in which men and women communicate. A failure to understand the differences results in additional problems.

Couples are challenged with sharing with each other their true feelings. In our experience, women typically feel as if they have shared with their mate just how they feel, but when the behavior doesn't change, there is a tendency to feel annoyed and rejected. On the other hand, the husband says, "She didn't come out and clearly say what she wanted, she thought I should know." It just becomes a vicious cycle. What we see is that couples get caught up in a cycle and it's hard for somebody to *step out* to break the cycle. As humans we have an incredible need to be right. You would rather be right than at peace.

For many couples, counseling is the best solution. Let's face it; counseling is not at the top of the list of desired activities. Unfortunately, there appears to be a stigma that goes along with seeking counseling. It really boils down to the communications and the expectations that couples have for each other. The couples don't clearly articulate their expectations going into the marriage. When these unknown expectations are not met, it leads to disappointment, which leads to anger and resentment, which inhibits communication. This leads to another vicious cycle.

Wright

Having been on a church staff for 40 years, I have noticed down through the years that there's kind of a glitch in the system. When you do go to counseling, it's expensive; if you go to church counseling, you run the risk of the entire congregation knowing you're meeting with the minister.

Gladney

Exactly.

Wright

And it's one of those things that the church is going to have to take a look at and get away from, because people just don't like for their friends to know that they're having troubles.

Gladney

Right, that's exactly it. The stigma related to counseling and the fact that someone knows I have problems. One of our challenges as ministry leaders is being transparent. When someone comes to me and says, "Oh, you guys are such a great couple. You seem to have the perfect marriage." I am a real person, and will quickly inform them that no marriage is perfect and as a matter of fact, just this morning, I got on his nerves and he got on mine. I want to state loud and clear that everyone has problems and marriage is work. Even with the length of years that we have been married (17 plus years) we still have concerns and issues that come up that we have to address.

Wright

You mean when you become a Christian, all of your problems don't—I thought they stopped for the rest of your life.

Gladney

I wish we could let everyone know that is a myth. Everyone has problems, believers and non-believers. The blessed benefit as a believer is that you have someone to handle your problems for you. One of the fallacies is people believe with Christianity once they are a believer, their problems will cease. No, your problems and life will continue, but now you can take your burdens to Jesus and leave them there.

Wright

What has been your greatest challenge as a couple?

Gladney

I think our greatest challenge as a couple was when we suffered the loss of two of our children.

Wright

Oh, my!

Gladney

Our firstborn children were twins, and they were born premature. My son Charles, III, he lived for a day, and our daughter, Chelsie, lived for three and a half months. She spent her short life in a hospital and never was able to see the flowers nor the trees. Prior to this tragedy, I read that over 70% of the couples that lose a child, their marriage will end in divorce. I remember thinking, "How in the world do you break up during tragedy?" That seems like a time when your relationship will bond together.

In reality, when you suffer tragedy, such as the loss of a child, it is devastating because you don't ever expect that your children will die before you do. You anticipate as you get older that some day your parents will leave this earth before you, but you never expect that a child to die. So, to be thrown in a situation as young people, we were still in our twenties, which we had to face the fact that our kids are not here; it put us in a totally different frame of mind. Coming to understand that men and women grieve differently was also an eye opener. It was very, very challenging because my husband was moving toward healing faster than I was and I thought that he didn't care as much as I did.

Wright

Right.

Gladney

I begin to feel as if they were "my" children. I had the children, so of course, he couldn't feel the same effects, and really what we learned was that a man's first concern is his wife and then the children. For a woman, it's her children, then herself. You know, I'd die for my kids, and men, it's a different hierarchy. In essence, they may feel like, "I'll give my life for my children, but I really want to keep my wife." Woman are the nurturer's and tend to feel like we don't care if we survive, let my children live. So, it was very, very challenging just because there was so much that took place during that time.

I had many spiritual challenges to battle. Growing up I was taught that faith was believing in Gods divine healing power without the help of a doctor. My faith was challenged since I knew that my daughter was breathing because of the life support. During my daughter's short life, we found out that my son's death was caused by the doctors. I was in shock. My daughter fought for three months and passed away. I basically hit the bottom.

The experience changed us in such a devastating way and we began to change as people. I knew that I was not the same person he married and he was not the same person I married. It was God's grace that got us through that journey, and of course, they say what doesn't kill you makes you stronger, and that's so true. Our marriage survived only because of the prayers that other people prayed for us, and His grace that He bestowed upon us.

Wright

What has been your greatest challenge as a Christian?

Gladney

That for me is probably one and the same. The greatest challenge as a couple and the greatest challenge as a Christian was that whole experience, and trying to understand how it happened, why did it happen. I was just trying to decide who God was for me, and trying to understand what this was all about. All my life I was trying to do what I thought was the right thing to do and to live a holy life before God. I couldn't understand how he could "punish me" in this manner. As a Christian, I was surprised to find out that my life and the way I lived didn't have anything to do with the cause of my children dying. It was just a really *big paradigm shift* for me.

As a result of the experience, I left the church that I was raised in. As you can imagine, that was totally a different type of journey to go through. That decision affected a lot of people who were a part of my life. At the time, I felt like I needed to step away from everything. I would say that my greatest challenge as a Christian was trying to redefine who God was to me and to find my way through the wilderness that I found myself in.

Wright

Well, the fact that you're still a Christian is a testament to your faith under girding everything that you went through. Do you have a definition of faith, a personal definition of faith?

Gladney

Yes, I do. I have come to believe that this is one of the most confusing areas for Christians. There are many Christians that talk about faith on a frequent basis. We use clichés such as, "You just didn't have enough faith," or "Your faith needs be the size of a mustard seed," everyone seems to be able to quote a scripture regarding faith. But, when it really comes to a test or trial, do we really know what faith is?

I had a difficult time with the concept of faith in dealing with Chelsie and her physical condition. She was born with a heart defect. I was convinced that God would give her a new heart. I knew that he could give her a new heart because he has the power. My thought was *I'm just going to believe that and pray in the name of Jesus.* I'm just going to kneel down and I'm going to pray and fast, and do all of the things that the scripture says that I should do. I believed when the scripture said where there are two or three are gathered together, you can ask what you will and it shall be done unto you. Our entire church family chose a day to fast and pray for her healing. In addition to our church family, there were several other friends that we asked to fast with us. I believed with my heart that she was going to get well and pull through this disease.

When she died, it was very devastating to me to say, I had to look back and say I didn't have enough faith. I guess it was me. I internalized that something was wrong with me, which led me down a negative path. It brought about a series of issues that I had to overcome and deal with. What I found out is that faith is the substance of things hoped for and evidence of things *not* seen. But, faith really means an absolute trust in God and His decisions. It's knowing that whatever He decides to do, I will believe and trust in his decision. Faith is not just looking on the outside of a situation for God, to raise your child, or heal your body, or if you give me a job. Those are all evidence of things seen.

We are looking for things that we can **see** and say, "You can tell I have the faith because my prayer was answered." Faith is just the complete and absolute trust that you have in the decision that God makes for your life. If I would have known that prior to going through this experience, then it would have been a completely different experience for me.

I really thought that faith meant if you believed hard enough in something, it would happen. And if you didn't believe hard enough, that it wouldn't happen. That's not what faith is. I have seen so many other people devastated in their lives because they felt like "God you did this to me even though I prayed and believed." So many people get hung up on this particular area. I think it would help Christians understand faith if they don't look around at the things that you can tangibly touch and see and claim that is faith in God.

Wright

In view of your life experiences, is there some message that you would like to share with others?

Gladney

Oh, yes. There are several messages that I would like to get across to other people. One big message is about faith, with the definition of faith in God. Another message is to get to know God for yourself. Find out who He is for yourself, establish your own relationship with God. The scripture says to work our own salvation with fear and trembling. Recalling my upbringing, I found out that so much of what I was doing was about other people. It was because somebody said that this was how God was and this was what He would do to you, for you, with you, through you, whatever else. But, so much of it was centered on people. What somebody else said, thought, or a word that they felt like they received from God.

I know in the Old Testament there were a lot of prophets and they would be sent out to prophesize to the people. I'm not saying there are not prophets today, but what I am saying is that you have to establish your own relationship with Christ and not depend upon others. I had to get to the point where I said, "You know what, I have my own relationship with God. I know Him personally for myself."

I don't just go to church and depend upon what the minister is saying or the word that he is giving on that Sunday. I read and study the word myself. It's not about what somebody else said. The ministers are helping to impart the word for your life, but you will not be able to live a flourishing Christian fulfilled life in Christ if you are just depending on what somebody feeds you for thirty or forty-five minutes on a Sunday morning. It is daily food that we have to be given, and it's through establishing that relationship with God for ourselves. That was just such a life defining moment for me. Finding out who God is and not concerning myself with what others thought because he speaks directly to me.

Wright

How do you know when God is speaking to you?

Gladney

I know when God is speaking to me because I hear his voice through my spirit. He speaks in a voice that if you were in the room you could not hear it. But, it is because of having a relationship with Him, that I can hear it. He speaks into my spirit in an audible voice. When God revealed his purpose for my life, He spoke very clearly to me in showing me what He wanted me to do. He told me that I would be a speaker, sharing my testimony and changing people's lives through the experiences he brought us through. I really rejected the idea at first because I couldn't imagine myself being at place where I wasn't hurting. But God is patient. Through the process, I started speaking on other topics in many arenas until I was ready. I was pruned in the process so that I can be prepared to minister to others.

He speaks so clearly into my spirit. He reveals things in different ways. Sometimes he speaks directly to me, and other times he sends a messenger with confirmation. Sometimes, we will have conversations like you and I are having. I'll ask questions and he just pours the answer right back into my spirit. It's just the most amazing and unbelievable thing, and it's nothing that I can invoke.

The last time He spoke to me so clearly, I was driving down the street and I asked Him, "God what do you want me to do about a speech I have written entitled *Six Million Dollar Woman?*" He spoke the words into my heart to start the Six Million Dollar Woman's club. He explained that it is an organization for women to enrich and develop them to live meaning and purposeful lives. He began to reveal to me His will, and what He wanted me to do. It is just an amazing thing.

If I could, I will reiterate the point that it is essential to have a relationship with Christ, and then you won't be in doubt when God is talking to you, or what he's saying because you're so close to Him. To use a real life example, think of how you are close to a friend, a sibling or spouse. When you have a relationship with someone you can communicate words to them through a look. That person knows exactly what it means because of your intimate relationship. It's the same with Christ. That's the type of relationship I that I strive for with Christ. It's just marvelous. That's all I can say. It's really great to be God's child.

Wright

What a great conversation on faith. I really appreciate the time you have taken with me today to enlighten me, and I'm sure our readers will be enlightened by your story and by your testimony and the depth of your faith. I really do appreciate this time.

Gladney

You're welcome.

Wright

Today we've been talking to Dr. Lawana S. Gladney. She is a motivational specialist. She's president and CEO of her own company, Gladney and Associates. She, as a speaker, author, and trainer, has energized audiences nationally. She provides them with the tools to keep themselves motivated to achieve their goals as we have found out here today. Thank you so much for being with us on *Conversations on Faith.*

Gladney

Thank you, I enjoyed it.

About The Author

Dr. Lawana S. Gladney has spoken to audiences throughout North America. She dedicated to helping women become emotionally empowered. As a columnist for Today's Virtuous Woman magazine and Family Cents, Publication, she shares with thousands of readers her knowledge and experiences to help individuals develop personally, professionally, and to learn how to live purposefully. She is the founder and president of a non-profit organization called **The Six Million Dollar Woman's Club, Inc.** which focuses on developing and enriching the lives of women to live the most fulfilling life possible.

Dr. Lawana S. Gladney
PO Box 833605
Richardson, Texas 75083
Phone: 972.889.9656
www.DrGladney.com

Chapter 7

REV. DR. ED TAYLOR, D.D., TH.D.

THE INTERVIEW

David E. Wright (Wright)

Rev. Taylor has been a church-ordained minister since 1958. He was educated at East Tennessee State University, Tennessee Temple University, Southwestern Theological Seminary, Fort Worth, Texas, and received his doctorate from Emmanuel University in North Carolina. Rev. Taylor is senior minister of Gatlinburg Ministries; a Christian organization established 25 years ago with a reputation for upholding traditional family values by conducting Christian ceremonies based on the Biblical principle that marriage is a divine institution. From a small marriage chapel 25 years ago, Rev. Taylor oversees Gatlinburg Marriage and Enrichment Center, which includes three chapels, a proposed Biblical museum, and a 500-seat Christian concert hall. Rev. Taylor, welcome to *Conversations on Faith*.

Rev. Dr. Ed Taylor (Taylor)

Thank-you, David. I'm delighted to be able to share some of the experiences I've had over the last 25 years. We're celebrating our 25th anniversary this year.

Wright

That must be nice. Twenty-five years is a long time, especially when so many businesses in this economy fail.

Taylor

Well, you have got a point. We just want to keep on, keeping on in what we consider a life's work, a ministry from which there is no retirement. I could retire, of course, in just a few months I'll be 73 years old, but I still get around very well. My energy comes from running 2 ½ miles each day—six days a week and eating nutritionally. I feel as energetic now or perhaps more than I did 25 years ago. Yes, I am excited about my life's work.

Wright

Rev. Taylor, you are affectionately referred to as "Rev. Ed" by the thousands of people you have performed ceremonies for, can you tell our readers what led you into the marriage ministry?

Taylor

David, it began 25 years ago. I was in the Gatlinburg, Tennessee area looking for a meaningful ministry. Then, while jogging in the park one day, I had this strange sense from within, of a Scripture I had not considered for many years, "Behold I set before thee an open door and no man will be able to close it." I said, "Well, Lord, do you have a ministry here?" At that time, I didn't know what God had in store for me. Anyway, we started a ministry to tourists, we had by-laws, and a list of things we wanted to accomplish in the future. So, we began a tourist ministry as a motel "chaplain on call." Later, I started reading Dr. Norman Vincent Peale's book, *The Power of Positive Thinking*, written many years ago, and he wrote, "We need to find the need and fill it; find the hurt and heal it; find the problem and solve it." So, we looked and saw the need. People came here from all over the country asking about getting married, and the local clergy didn't want to marry them since they didn't want to get involved marrying transit folk. In fact, I don't think they marry people even today, unless they marry their own people. So, I saw the need to give dignity, sanctity, and credibility to couples marriage ceremonies. I had heard horrible stories about how people had gotten married by the Justice of the Peace at the local feed and seed store, or by the JP at the service station behind the grease rack, or at the little country store where the JP stood with tobacco juice dripping off his chin.

These were referred to as civil ceremonies. We felt that they were not Christian ceremonies in any respect. So, when I heard these stories I saw a need to give the dignity to marriage that it deserved. Marriage was being denied, the spiritual marriage, to people coming into our county. It was then that I realized that God had a purpose for my life, and I started the ministry which has become an industry, the third largest in our County. We established a church at that particular point, a non-profit organization, and not a wedding chapel. We started a marriage and enrichment center and we're still here for the need; not the greed. We operate as a non-profit organization with church worship services on Sunday and we will continue to do so, just as any church in the area.

Wright
You said you were celebrating your 25th anniversary. Have you seen any changes in the attitudes of the couples you have seen over the years?

Taylor
Over the last 25 years, we have married over 85,000 couples. Many of the people who come to us are referred to us because we are a church and have church-ordained pastors who are certified marriage and family counselors, and we have encouraged many thousands to build their marriages according to our guidance and to build their marriage within the church. We know that the Bible says we are not to forsake the assembling of ourselves together in the church, and that's why Christ came into the world. It says in Ephesians that Christ died for the church. We encourage (the couples) very explicitly to get involved in church. We've had a tremendous influence in getting thousands of people into church in these many years. To answer your question, attitudes of the couples have not changed. Most believe that marriage is a sacred bond approved by God.

Wright
You know you referred to the marriage industry as the third largest in Gatlinburg, Tennessee. For our readers, Gatlinburg is a small resort city with over 12 million visitors each year. With wedding chapels sprouting up all over, what makes yours different from the others?

Taylor

First of all, we are a church. We're here with church values and with the purpose of God. We were the first marriage chapel in the area. We don't particularly like the name "wedding chapel." We are a marriage and enrichment center. And we don't claim to be affiliated with the wedding chapel industry. We are the only church marriage facility in the Smoky Mountains. The whole organization is owned by God, a non-profit, ministry organization. We feel we are here for the need and not the greed, and all other chapels are owned for profit or for business. We give all of our couples marital counseling. Our services are called in-marital counseling, and last for 15 to 20 minutes, where most of the walk-in, walk-out wedding chapels last about 3 minutes. We do post-marital counseling as well, and we stay in touch with the people. We give them books; we give them a Bible and literature on how to be successful in marriage. We tell every one of them, including the guests, that they are now members of "their church away from home" and down through the years, thousands have come back to visit us when they vacation here. We have a new congregation every week.

Wright

When you consider the statistics, that 50 percent of all marriages end in divorce, do you do anything in your ministry to try to lower the statistics, and if so, what? For example, you said you give them a Bible.

Taylor

Tennessee is the second largest divorce state in the country. We've been very successful in lowering the statistics through the presentation of the Bible, and we offer every couple a written guarantee of success if they follow the marriage manual, which is the Bible, the concepts and precepts which are in the Word of God. The statistics, which have gone from 30 percent over the last 25 years to over 50 percent now, are cause for alarm. As a minister of the Gospel, I am alarmed at the breakdown of morality in America. There are all these new developments in the moral standards in our nation: road rage, violence in schools, destruction of the twin towers in New York, anthrax in the Post Offices. We as Christians must do all that we can to change society for the better, and that starts within the home. As goes the home, so goes the nation. We try to build some solid homes and marriages as we stand before these couples, counsel them, and strengthen them in the faith.

Wright

Dr. Taylor, this is a book about faith. Down through the years, has your faith kept you on track, or did you ever question whether God was with you as you continued your work?

Taylor

Well, there have been times in the 25 years that if I wanted to, I could have thrown in the towel. But every time I throw in the towel, the Lord throws it back. And then I remember my faith and I remember the call from God that occurred to me some 25 years ago, to keep on keeping on. The Bible says the calling of God is irrevocable. And it also says we shall reap if we faint not. We keep on keeping on, because the Bible says we live by faith and not by sight. Again, the writer of Hebrews says that "without faith, it is impossible to please God." Yes, our faith is increased day by day by day. We look upon Him for guidance every day of our lives.

Wright

In a recent interview, a great pastor and religious teacher told me that today's preachers need to have more courage and preach the truth from the pulpit. Too many preachers, he said, want to keep people in the pews and are afraid of offending anyone because they might stop giving their tithes and offerings to the church. What do you think?

Taylor

I think he's very much on key. The Bible says the truth shall make you free. It will liberate you. Knowing the truth will establish us in the faith. I have said many times that we are misjudged, misunderstood by the community, misquoted by the media, misused by some local so-called ordained ministers, but yet we're still here. We're called by God as ministers. Did you know, you can go online and in three minutes you can print out your own ordination certificate. The Tennessee Senate and House have set some laws and voted 94-0 that this ought not to be allowed to happen. They haven't put any teeth in the law as yet. Certainly they aren't real ministers since one of the attributes of a minister is to preach the Gospel, to tell the truth, regardless of the impact on the tourism dollar. We know where we're coming from because we know what works with people in marriage.

Wright

What part can the marriage chapel play in the continued life of the couple in the church?

Taylor

We strongly assert that the couple should get involved in a church when the couple gets back home. Find a church where they can put into practice the principles of the marriage union. That within the church they build their network of Christian friends that will help them build their marriage. God's plan includes worshipping together; reading the Scriptures together, praying together, and these precepts will result in their staying together.

Wright

Is there a specific Scripture that propels your work, that under girds your belief that marriage is ordained by God?

Taylor

Since the beginning of time, in Genesis, it says that a man should leave his father and mother and cleave only to his wife, and the two shall become one flesh. Jesus performed his first miracle at the marriage of Cana in Galilee. As Paul said in Ephesians that we should love each other, as husband and wife, as Christ loved the church. These scriptures are very specific about the sanctity of marriage. He elevates the position of marriage to its highest pinnacle when he compares the marriage of husband and wife to that of Christ and the Church. Yes, marriage is a spiritual union.

Wright

In a Christian ceremony, if you take seriously the command to love each other as Christ loved the church, and you realize that Christ died for the church, it puts it in perspective, doesn't it?

Taylor

That's the reason the church was formed, so that homes and families and marriages could exist and be strong. One thing that makes America what she is today is our churches. Without them, marriage cannot be built upon the principles that God gave for it. He said we are not to forsake the assembling of ourselves together in the house of God and that includes the marriage ceremony.

Wright

What is your mission and vision for your personal and professional life in the future?

Taylor

This ministry is like a marriage. I'm married to the ministry and in one respect married to God. I will continue this ministry until "death do us part." We have a wide variety of things we are accomplishing and looking at: our museum, where we've been able to collect a lot of biblical artifacts down through the years from Israel and Egypt and different parts of the Bible world. We're working now as part of the Bible Heritage Museum of London, England. We've been able to get many artifacts and Biblical pages from there, that go back to the 12th and 13th centuries. We have many of those on display presently and we have many more things that are being held for us for our museum. By his time next year, we hope to have everything in place for a world-class Bible history museum. We're also looking for things to come along to have the 500 seat Christian Music Hall that will also be here. We display the Christian flag and the American flag outside of our marriage complex. We have the Ten Commandments on display for everyone to see. And it's been engraved in granite, the most lasting material we could find. We want to do all these things to promote the ministry of marriage, because that's what it's built upon.

Wright

I remember visiting in church and was fascinated with the artifacts, especially the lamps like those carried by "the young virgins." Also, I enjoyed looking at some of the coins. It was like going back thousands of years. Where did you get all of those?

Taylor

Most of those came from the Bible History Museum and the Bible Heritage Museum in London. Just recently we were able to acquire a full Geneva Bible, printed in 1560. That's the time the Bible was first put into verses and is the Bible our Pilgrim forefathers brought with them on the Mayflower. It was 50 to 60 years after that, that they would even accept the King James Version of the Bible, printed in 1611. In addition, we have several pages of the original King James

Version Bible here. It's ironic that some people don't know that every page was once worn by some person. What I mean is that every page was made from rag paper. Rag collectors in carts would go up and down the streets of London and collect rags and pieces of clothing and make paper from it. It's amazing how God allowed that to be preserved. Some of these pages look like they are only a few years old, even though they date back to the 12th and 13th centuries. We also have an original page of the Aiken Bible, the first bible printed in America in 1782. It is very rare. It's the Bible that the U.S. Congress approved as a pious work; it was called the "Bible of the Revolution." We also have a document from the United States Congress that goes with it that says, "This Bible was recommended to the inhabitants of the United States for reading in homes and schools and wherever." We have come a long way since that time.

Wright

Dr. Taylor, do you think that faith in God works for everybody?

Taylor

I think faith in God is always rewarded. The Bible says that faith comes by hearing, and hearing by the Word of God. It is our calling to share the Word because the Bible says, concerning faith, that by grace you have been saved through faith. God is talking to everyone in that scripture. It says you have been saved by grace through faith, and that not of yourselves, it is the gift of God, not of works, lest any man should boast. We're sanctified by faith and saved through Jesus Christ, the Bible says in the Book of Acts. And without faith it is impossible to please God, says the writer of Hebrews 11. So yes, without faith we are total failures. It is a necessity. It's through faith that our eternal salvation is based. It's based on faith in what Christ did on the Cross, over 2,000 years ago.

Wright

Now that you have been in the Christian vocation for over 45 years, what are the challenges of operating your business and your life in faith?

Taylor

We're going to continue to do what we are called to do here. We will build these dreams that we feel that God has given to us. We'll be traveling more into the Holy Land areas and collecting more artifacts.

We're looking to have a local radio station here, and build that into a television ministry as well. We have great challenges ahead of us and we're excited about them every day.

Wright

Lastly, if I were a young man, and was entertaining thoughts of getting married and spending the rest of my life with one female, what would you say to me? In other words, if you were talking to a couple contemplating marriage, what would you say to them to ensure that their marriage didn't become one of those statistics that we heard so much about?

Taylor

First, I would talk to them about their personal spiritual experiences through life. Regardless of their denomination, if they have had a personal relationship with God through Jesus Christ, that is half the battle. Then, as they build their marriage upon the framework of the church, I tell each couple that if they will read the bible that I am going to give them and make it part of their life, and let the past go, not holding each other at fault or failure, and forgive as Christ forgave, they will succeed in marriage. Last week, we performed a marriage for a couple. The groom called back and said, "Rev. Ed, I must tell you something. At our ceremony you performed, there were two couples there who were ready to throw in the towel. They were contemplating divorce. But, because of what you said, they went back home and began to talk to one another about forgetting the past and about loving each other and getting into church and now their lives are better than before." And so we reached not only the couple, but we also, over the years, have been able to touch thousands of people who were guests at the ceremonies.

Wright

What an interesting conversation. I appreciate the time you have taken with me today to ensure that this chapter in our book on faith, having to do with marriages and weddings, is put forth in a Christian way. I want to thank you for being here today on *Conversations on Faith*.

Taylor

Thank-you, brother. It's our intention to stay in the battle until the Lord comes again.

About The Author

Reverend Ed Taylor has provided thousands of couples with beautiful memories that they will cherish for a lifetime. To them, he is affectionately called "the marrying man of the mountains." For twenty-five years, Reverend Taylor, an ordained minister, has been performing beautiful, meaningful, Christian ceremonies at his church wedding village in the Great Smoky Mountains in Tennessee.

Rev. Dr. Ed Taylor, D.D., Th.D

209 Reagan Drive

Gatlinburg, Tennessee 37738

Phone: 800.346.2779

www.gatlinburgchapels.com

Chapter 8

JENNIFER O'NEILL

THE INTERVIEW

David E. Wright (Wright)

Internationally acclaimed actress, film and television star, successful spokeswoman, composer, author, artist, proud mother of three, and grandmother of four, Jennifer O'Neill has accomplished enough for a lifetime. Jennifer began her international modeling career at the age of fifteen, after her family moved to New York from her native home of Rio de Janeiro, Brazil. Her career in the entertainment industry boasts twenty-eight feature films including the classic, *Summer of '42*, numerous television movies and three series to her credit. In addition, Jennifer held a thirty-year position as spokeswoman for Cover Girl Cosmetics. Following the success of her biography, *Surviving Myself*, Jennifer adds her latest book, *From Fallen to Forgiven* to her list of accomplishments. She continues to carry a full load of upcoming projects and speaking engagements in addition to the late spring 2002 release of the feature film, *Time Changer*, as well as the *E True Hollywood Story* on her life that is currently running. She serves on the board of Media Fellowship International as well as the advisory board for "All-Stars", is the spokesperson for Woman's Well Being Corp., and will be filming her women's conference *All You Can Be* in January 2002. January will also mark the release of, *All You Can Be*—an original album written and performed by Jennifer herself. Mrs. O'Neill, welcome to *Conversations on Success.*

Jennifer O'Neill (O'Neill)
Thank you, thank you.

Wright
In your first book *Surviving Myself*, you write about the addiction that would afflict you most of your life, not alcohol, drugs, or sex, but an insatiable need to be loved. Why did you think you were not loved?

O'Neill
As I have come to my faith, I have learned that the opposite of love is not hate, but rather indifference. As a child, although I adore and respect my parents and I make that clear in my books, in fact, they live with me to this day and have given me many wonderful things; they were completely involved with each other. I believe that the core or the beginning of that feeling invisible, unloved, not good enough, and not wanted was just a sense of indifference towards me as an individual. Everyone handles those feelings differently; some become extremely withdrawn, others become over achievers or perfectionists. So, at an early age I believed and took on the notion that I could earn love. If I got straight A's in school, if I was a good girl, then I would get my parents attention. Let me say here that dinner was always on the table. Mike—my brother—and I were well taken care of, but as I say, I believe that Mike and I were pitted against each other for my parents attention. They just were not parents that were kids' people and involved with their kids. For young children, even if they are fed and they have clothes and all of that, at least for some of us, the core kind of that "I'm not good enough" negative tape that starts in our minds. I believe confirmation and affirmation are what children need.

Wright
How much did your early life and family shape the Jennifer O'Neill we know today?

O'Neill
I believe that family and early life really forms who we are. I was very inspired by my parents. My dad was a war hero and my parents have an on-going and great love story to this day. They just had their

58th anniversary and they still *Boso Nova* at lunch. They gave me a great model for marriage, but not for parenting. I believe that we are pretty much who we are at a very early age in terms of personality traits, security, a sense of being loved and all those places that need to be solid for a child to grow and go into the world with a sense of confidence and balance. Children that are brought up in un-churched atmospheres and aren't going to Bible study don't have a sense of a higher love, which is from Jesus Christ. They really are reliant on those who mirror, at least in their own little minds, who they are. So if they feel invisible, unlovable or empty in this place, God fills up that empty void, not people. I found that out when I came to my faith in Christ at 38 years old. But, with the lack of that, the parental surroundings and family surroundings are extremely important.

Wright

I've got a 41 year old daughter, a 40 year old son, and I also have a 14 year old.

O'Neill

Oh, wow. I've got a 36 year old, a 22 year old, and a 16 year old. I've almost done what you have.

Wright

I have found that it's very different parenting between the generations.

O'Neill

Absolutely. What we have learned is also very different. I believe that I was pretty much the same parent to my daughter that my mother was to me because that's what you're used to.

Wright

Correct.

O'Neill

For example, I was chatting with my parents about this the other day. They weren't close to my brother or me when we were kids and they aren't close to their grandchildren or their great grandchildren. I said, "It's interesting Dad, I have never gone and had a pizza with you and you've never thrown a ball to your son, your grandson or your great grandson." And he said, "We take care of you, but I'm not a *kids* person." That would then beg for the question, "Why did you have kids then?" It was the thing to do in their generation. In my mom's case, she came from a large family. My mother is English and from a very closely knit family where her mother was very, very involved with the children, but did not have a good relationship with their father. Therefore, my mother—growing up one of seven children—had experienced a great closeness with her siblings and her mother, but saw this great divide between her parents. She was determined not to have that in her marriage. Therefore, sometimes the pendulum swings the other way before it rights itself. I think that with my parents, their marriage came first. I think that is actually biblically correct. But, kids don't want to feel invisible. That's where a lot of the insecurities come from.

When I wrote *Surviving Myself* and even *Fallen to Forgiven*, not only did I concur with my parents, I asked their permission to write. I only deal with the early beginnings of some of these feelings that became very negative in my life, because they have to have an origin. If you don't understand from whence something comes, it is not the worldly view of dwelling on your past. It is not a finger pointing mission. I do not blame my parents. They did not do anything maliciously. Regardless, that damage was done. You have to call a spade a spade and recognize it so that you do not dwell or blame them. Recognize it, understand it, believe it, and heal it. That never came for me until I found Christ. You can psychologically understand it and you can go to therapy, which I am not against, but I've never seen it work without Christ in the center of it. Forgiveness is the core of all healing. I don't want to sound like sour grapes. I always say if you throw dirt you lose ground. My books are not a finger pointing mission, nor is this discussion.

Wright

Someone asked me recently why all my life I've always gone to church. It's just a part of who I am. It's a part of who all three of my children seems to be. They said, "Do you go to church to stay out of hell?" And I said, "Well, I don't know about that, but when I die and I go through the pearly gates, I'm not so much worried about anybody other than my mother. When I meet her, I don't want to have to answer the question, "Why didn't you go to church, son?"

O'Neill

That's funny. Well, it's interesting because there are so many church people that aren't born again and are going to miss the boat even though they're sitting in a pew. This is disturbing unto itself.

Wright

It's really strange when you read articles in some of the books that are coming out about faith. The actions of the people in the church are no different than those who are outside the church. This has always amazed me.

O'Neill

Well, those are the ones that are just keeping the bench warm instead of having a relationship. It's a relationship with Jesus Christ, that God is looking for and through free will. When you receive the Holy Spirit, then your life changes. So, there are misconceptions about what God put so clearly in His word that so many people aren't hearing.

Wright

It seems that you've always loved horses. What is it about horses that captivates you and gives you such joy?

O'Neill

I've always had a love of horses. I've always had a huge love for animals. I think that was born from my desire to have a relationship. Animals are fantastic. They love you unconditionally. They wag their tail if you have a bad hair day. It doesn't matter, they are always there for you. That need that I felt innately, my relationship with animals filled. I was pretty happy. But, this was another thing that my parents missed in me. My mom grew up in London and just didn't relate to animals. She didn't necessarily want to be in Connecticut where we were. Although I was in the perfect place to have animals, it was years before I was allowed to have a cat and then a dog. I used to take care of other people's horses. I lived in an area where the kids grew up with pony club; they had been there all their lives and there was a lot of horse activity. I was in seventh heaven in that respect, but it was something my parents didn't recognize. They didn't go to the pony club shows and all that support system.

Wright

As a young girl in the spring of 1962, you actually attempted suicide. What did you learn from that ordeal?

O'Neill

Well, my animals were my world. My parents decided to send my brother away to boarding school at 14, I was 13. I was to go into Manhattan to attend Dalton which was an all girl's school. What that meant to me was that I had to give up the horse I was taking care of. I just wanted to be able to take my dog. That was just unacceptable to my parents. She wasn't allowed in the house. For me, that was my whole world. You know how teenagers are. Teen's don't know this too shall change and they will overcome. In their barometer with their hormones raging and everything, losing a boyfriend or losing what they perceive to be the center or core of their world can throw them into a great depression. In my case, my parents took my dog to the pound. I didn't want to die, I just wanted to be heard. So, I took my mom's sleeping pills. I think a lot of teens who are trying to kill themselves are angry or want to be heard. They want to express how much they hurt. Not all of them want to actually die. I deem this as one of the first times God held his arms out to me and I didn't succeed in that mission. I was in a coma for two weeks. When I came out of it, my parents referred to the event as a stunt; the dog went to the pound and I went to Manhattan. What happened in my life then was that even a stupid, potentially lethal, dramatic expression of trying to be heard was unheard. I was never understood, recognized or healed. It just added on to my negative tape. That negative tape was that I was not worthy or loved; I was invisible and I didn't count. I was kind of a dichotomy because I had this very tenacious side to me. I think that's why I named my book *Surviving Myself*; the side that kept me going was equally as strong as the side that was hurt, depressed or in pain. When I went into Manhattan, just to round out the horse show and the animal deal, I was 15. I started to model. I felt very skinny, gawky and ugly. Yet, Ilene Ford felt that I could model. I had an Aunt Ellie that took me in there. My thought was that I would be able to buy my own horse. The independence had started. If I wasn't going to get my parents attention, get their love or get them to hear me, then I was off on a mission to do it myself.

Wright

I wonder how many worldwide models could say they went into modeling to buy a horse.

O'Neill

I don't know, but that was all that mattered to me. What was interesting is that when I got my horse and modeled for a couple of years, there still was this empty hole in my heart, David. That's what's so interesting about the biggest lessons I learned as I came around to my faith in Christ. Only God can fill that hole. If you perceive that someone else or something else is going to fill you up, you're going to be on a search that ends at an empty line. I became the billboard for that on a mission.

In my teens—in the brilliance of a teenage mind—I concluded that I should get married, because if I got married I would be adored like my dad adores my mother. So, that was the logic and my next mission. I married at 17 and had my daughter when I was just 19. Yet, none of the issues of my earlier life had been dealt with by myself or my parents. I always got straight A's in school and behaved myself, but there was this seething unhappiness and emptiness that I kept trying to fill up with. This is more common than you can believe. I speak to tens of thousands of women and men that feel that emptiness—the purpose of telling my story is certainly not to listen to myself talk. It's amazing how much in common we all have even though we have differences in details of our lives. The needs that drive us as human beings from the heart with the absence of Christ is a tale that is usually riddled with unhappiness, ups and downs and needs that are met in anger and depression as you are not heard. When we're babies and we come into the world, you can see right off the bat that they are completely self centered. As beautiful, gooey, wonderful and fabulous as they are, I had occasion to understand sin nature when I finally did come to my faith. I said, "God, that's an ugly thing to be carting around." And He gave me a wonderful illustration. I went to visit a nursery and there were these toddlers playing and parents standing around just cooing over them. Then, I noticed the babies' behavior. A big toddler would go over and knock the little one down and grab the toy from it and pull his hair, and I just went whoa! What occurred to me at that point is that as the parents came over to those toddlers and said, "Say please. Say thank you. No don't, now share," was that we can learn manners in our life, but we cannot be transformed without the grace and the power and the love of Jesus Christ.

Wright

Interesting.

O'Neill

I was just a grown up toddler emotionally. Looking for love in all the wrong places, I married a guy six years older than I and the marriage lasted six years. That was during a period of time when I did suffer from depression. I did not want to be suicidal at all; I put myself in the hospital. I had shock therapy because none of the issues that had been seething in this cauldron of negative—I call it negative tape—had ever been dealt with, understood, grieved or healed. I got a lot of therapy then and I could understand what was going on mentally, but I could never connect it to my heart and heal until l found Christ.

Wright

In all of the therapy that you had did any of the therapists add God to the mix?

O'Neill

No.

Wright

That's unfortunate.

O'Neill

Oh, it's lethal. It's absolutely lethal. It's a psychological, Freudian approach and what it does is it creates a well. We buy the therapists their homes and send their grandchildren to college, because it's a never ending cycle. When there is a void of forgiveness, you don't change. You just control. We can learn better manners, but we're never healed in our hearts.

Wright

Most therapists that I have ever met are into non-directed therapy and it seems that God is awfully directive.

O'Neill

Exactly.

Wright

Therein lies at least one of the rubs.

O'Neill

One of the rubs definitely. You just keep going around. Everything that we need to know on every aspect of life is in the word of God, everything from even where to put yourself in a theater of seats. The truth does set you free. Talking about life without God as opposed to with God is just a good platform. You can take one life and you can see what God can do and the difference he can make in anyone's life.

Wright

Let's talk about your latest book From Fallen to Forgiven, A Spiritual Journey into Wholeness and Healing, how did this powerful book come to be?

O'Neill

Well, that was really interesting. When I wrote *Surviving Myself*, which as you can imagine extremely lethargic, I was determined to write an honest account and it was so scary. God is so faithful and I thought at first why would I write about my life? Number one, who would care? Number two, whose business is it anyway? But, I wanted to write about a life—mine—that on the outside looked so good—it was in many ways with all the travel, the fame, fortune, and the opportunities—but on the inside was so empty and damaged. I almost died three times, had nine miscarriages along the way of having my children and many failed marriages—I am embarrassed to say. I sent it to Elizabeth Taylor and we had a good hoot. She said, "Well, we didn't date men we married them, and we're both hard to kill." It was a life that was really a dichotomy again. I wanted to write the book because I wanted to tell the truth. God can take any life, at any age, no matter where you've been or what you've done and His arms are wide open to each and everyone of us. When we accept Christ as Lord of our lives and are saved, He transforms you. It is never too late. A lot of people need to know that, especially when I speak to kids in high school or even un-churched kids and they think that they've messed up because they've had a relationship with a boy or a girl. God can make you white as snow. When I married my husband, I was

48 years old and we've almost been married seven years now. At that time, I had three grandchildren and was a mother of three. I had gone through all the failed marriages and relationships and when I met my husband we did it God's way. We waited. When I walked down the aisle on my dad's arm, at age 48, I felt white as snow, and I was. That was so exciting to tell teens and it's so exciting to tell adults that have had failed relationships.

Wright

That's a reoccurring theme now. Connie Selleca advocated that did she not?

O'Neill

Yes. Yes, absolutely, and that's what He promises through the Blood of Jesus. There is nothing that is unforgivable if you repent and accept His grace. This takes me to *From Fallen to Forgiven*, both books deal with top issues, the teen suicide, abortion (God has put me on a path with the Silent No More Campaign), my new book that will be written this summer, the work books about the abortion healing process for those millions and millions of walking wounded that were told that it was nothing and their lives are destroyed. Of course, the baby is the cornerstone of our concern. But, once an abortion has taken place, the ripple effect of damage is just phenomenal. I wrote *Surviving Myself* that also dealt with sexual abuse, as requested by my daughter. My daughter was sexually abused for four years and no one knew it. The experiences in my life are pretty extreme. I can't sit in a room full of women and not know that 43% of women who reach the age of 45 have had an abortion. This means we all know someone who's had an abortion and this is coming out now. We've got a president that's going to deal with partial birth abortion and *Silent No More*.

The enemy loves to keep us locked in lies; the same goes with sexual abuse. Generational sin can stop and God tells you in His word exactly how to do it. That's what *Fallen to Forgiven* is about. W Publishing came to me and asked me about the last 17 years of my life, since I came to the Lord. I thought that I had really visited all my demons when I wrote *Surviving Myself*. But not so, there were deep crevices that we all push away, things that we don't want to deal with, that the enemy uses to bind us and lock us to our past. We can be eternally saved, David, as you know, but daily we can be tortured by things through shame, guilt, anger and awe. If you don't get to the core and let God through the power of the Holy Spirit clean house, then you are going to be bound to your past even though you may have eternal life. God wants us unencumbered from our past. He says, "Give it all to me." Accept Jesus, make Him Lord of your life. He says, "Leave the retribution of your pain to Me. Let me heal you, but you have to come through." Our un-forgiveness is the block. We walk through life holding on to un-forgiveness to others and to ourselves that rob our lives. God says what My Son did on the cross, the blood of Jesus covers all of your sins. This means that forgiveness is there for abortions and for sexual abuse. If you keep holding on to those places, my children need to give me those places and He tells us exactly how to do it. *Fallen to Forgiven* is a biblically based step through in dealing with our un-forgiveness. God says, even in the end of the Lord's Prayer he reiterates, that if we hold anyone in un-forgiveness to deal with that so He could forgive us and heal us. It's not a request, it's a commandment; he empowers us to do it. Jesus did not one a thing on the face of the earth without the power of the Holy Spirit. It's really the key.

Surviving Myself is a terrific book for teens as well in terms of what not to do, and what God can do in your life. But *Fallen to Forgiven* is for believers who are ready to engage the power of the Holy Spirit in their lives, to improve their lives. God's biblical way through their un-forgiveness to reach a point where they get to clean house and get all their ducks in a row. Because you can't give what you don't have, once you allow God in, once you feel less abandoned, the more you are bonded to God. Once you thwart the enemy's evil plans by just covering it in prayer and doing it God's way, all of a sudden you are released to be a billboard. You become a better mom, a better dad, a better friend, a better citizen, and that's what God wants for his people now. That's why it's such an important book.

Wright

You have written that whenever you are in a room full of women religious or not, you know in your heart that you are surrounded by many with unresolved, un-forgiven, unhealed issues.

O'Neill

Yes.

Wright

Are these people's battle scars, as well as your own, the reason you believe in the healing power of God?

O'Neill

It all starts with my own, but I believe in the healing power of God because I see the transformation once you invite Him in and let Him deal with your un-forgiveness and your hurt and your pain. Whether you've victimized or you've been the victim, He can take care of the retribution. Forgiveness doesn't mean you have to do business with the people that hurt you. They don't have to be any part of the process. That's a misconception that the enemy keeps over our heads saying, "Well, you know, that means it's okay." No! It just means that you are released from it and you are healed from it, then you can go and move on in your life. God does not want us stuck in our past, like our names on a bunch of cemetery blocks.

Wright

You stated that when God closes a door in our lives and hasn't yet opened a new one, it can be extremely uncomfortable. You go on to write about waiting on God. What do you mean?

O'Neill

First of all, God's never late. We set an agenda and if we keep bumping into closed doors or find ourselves in that transition, uncomfortable transition period, it just reminds us that change doesn't come from pain. If we're complacent in where we are, sometimes we don't grow as much as God would intend if we were in His will. God wants us, first of all, reliant on Him, period. I spent years negotiating with God when I first came to my faith. It is hysterical when I look back. I'd say, "Ah, I've got to take care of this, but God I'll give you this one." God says give me everything, especially the tough ones. As soon as I got to the end of myself and I realized that through my own might, I was continuing to live a limited life.

As soon as I gave it to God and rested in Him in those areas where the door had been closed and I didn't know what He was going to open next, and I got that peace beyond understanding, then the doors opened and they opened faster and faster. I really believed His words when He says, *"In Christ all things are possible."* I really knew that it wasn't by my might that something was going to happen, but by His. God speaks very highly of horses in Revelations and there's a wonderful analogy, that's why I love horses. Unlike most animals, he holds them in high esteem, and he in fact is going to come back on a white horse. Horses are very elegant and noble, particularly for little girls. It's a wonderful sport because they are so tender in a way and so powerful. As a little girl, you can groom them and love them, and care for them. It's not like the bicycle you have to throw in the corner. They have personality. They can snuggle. They have great breath. But, when you get on that pony or that horse, you feel the power and you feel the partnership, and you can fly through the air with the greatest of ease. In the beginning of, *Surviving Myself,* I wrote a really strong description of how I feel about horses, and also in *From Fallen to Forgiven* there's a poem called *My Horse,* and that answers it.

Wright

You have said that some people whom you had loved respect your faith, but do not share your beliefs. You go on to talk about being empowered by the Spirit. How do you deal with unbelievers and still respect the fact that God loves them?

O'Neill

Well, I know God loves them. It also, the whole adage if you walk into a town and you plant the seed, it's the Holy Spirit's job to convict these people. If they don't respond you dust your feet off and go on. I've had a lot of dear friends that I've witnessed to for years. It kills you because you love everybody and want everybody to know this joy. But, if you personally love the people, you can't imagine how they cannot see it. This is just so incredible. This is eternal. It's the truth. How do I deal with it? I cry a lot at night, but I keep praying. That's the most important thing. I was 38 years old when I came to the Lord and I found out afterwards, David, that there were people that prayed for me for 20 years that didn't even know who I was. When we have kids that we just don't know what to do with anymore, give them to God and cover them with prayer because He will protect them. What I do with that is still love them. I don't know if I'm answering the question like you wanted, but I love them and I pray for them. If they are respectful to my beliefs, then I can continue to have a relationship. We have to have a level of discernment. If you're listening to the pursuing of the Holy Spirit, you'll know that some relationships, once you've set the seed in front of them and told them the truth and they don't respond or its negative in any way, you need to move away from

115

it. But, if it's still loving and it just hasn't registered yet, stay on and keep praying. Even if you move away, you can always pray. That's the point.

Wright

It's really nice to know that people are praying for you. I remember a few years ago my wife almost died of cancer. It was very serious and people all over were praying for her. I thought it was just around my neck of the woods. They put her on prayer lists. I found out that tens of thousands and perhaps hundreds of thousands in every country in the world were praying for her.

O'Neill

And it worked, as you know.

Wright

It absolutely worked.

O'Neill

I had an aunt and when I just did the *Women of Faith* a couple of weeks ago, it was the first time I ever spoke about her and I was just led to by the Holy Spirit; I could barely speak. I loved her so much and she spent a little bit of time with me. She played cards with me. I used to go into her apartment in New York and play on the piano. She left me her piano and I carried it around for 30 years. When she was dying of cancer, and would come out of a coma—I had just had Amy and I was just 19—she would come out of all this pain and just say, "Tell me about the baby." She was my godmother. She had a huge faith and even though she didn't talk to me about it, I know she prayed for me. She actually walked the walk. She was the most godly person I knew. I didn't know what it was about her that I loved so much until I came to my faith. And then I went "Whoa! There it is."

Wright

In your case, aren't you glad that you will get the opportunity to see her again?

O'Neill

Yes, I can't wait. I really can't wait.

Wright

Today we have been talking to internationally acclaimed actress, film and television star, successful spokeswoman, composer, artist, author, proud mother of three, grandmother of four, Jennifer O'Neill. It's certainly been a pleasure. I really appreciate you being with us on *Conversations on Faith*.

O'Neill

Oh, thank you.

Jennifer O'Neill is by far one of the world's most Beautiful Hollywood Film God-desses of all time. She started her international modeling career at the age of 14. She then became a film star in some of Hollywood's most bankable films like *Rio Lobo* (with John Wayne) and the award winning classic film *The Summer of '42'* (this movie made Jennifer a household name). She is best known as the #1 Cover-Girl spokes-model in the world. Her face & glamour made Cover-Girl make-up the best selling make-up for 30 years. Jennifer is also an animal activist, she races, trains, & breeds show horses, and is an advocate for charitable causes like the American Cancer Society & other women's issues. Jennifer's career has been a dream come true, but her life was a nightmare of broken marriages, near death experiences, emptiness, abuse, and even her daughter being sexually abused by one of O'Neill's husbands. She turned her life around by becoming a born-again Christian & now ministers to hurting people world-wide through seminars and her two books that she wrote herself called, *Surviving Myself* and *From Fallen to Forgiven*. The books have won critical acclaim & her seminars are packed-in by the millions (all of them long to find hope to life's toughest problems). Jennifer is an amazing lady, a mother of 3 children, a grandmother, she's a survivor, & has become a role model to all who hear her story.

Jennifer O'Neill
Email: jennifer@jenniferoneill.com

Chapter 9

CAROLYN BROOKS

Dedicated in loving memory of
my dear mother, Irene (Reese)
Slaymaker Phelps

THE INTERVIEW
All Scriptures Taken From King James Version, except where otherwise noted.

David E. Wright (Wright)
Carolyn Brooks is a dynamic motivational speaker, inspiring author and successful business professional with a career that included
four promotions and spanned more than 28 years. She is a member of
The Professional Woman Speaker's Bureau and speaker with Christian and Professional Women's Clubs. Carolyn is a former model and
nominee for the "Women of Excellence" Award in 1997 and 1998 for
exemplary career with SBC Communications Corporation and community involvement. Carolyn appeared on the nationwide television
broadcast "Life Today" and is co-author of book, *What I Learned From
God While Cooking*, by Barbour Books, to be released in the fall of
2004, is a contributor to book, *But Lord, I Was Happy Shallow*, by
Kregel Publishers to be released in 2004, and she is the author of a

booklet *Biblical Work Ethics*. Carolyn, welcome to *Conversations on Faith*.

Carolyn Brooks (Brooks)
Thank You. I am happy to be here.

Wright
Carolyn, what does faith mean to you?

Brooks
With betrayal and deception at every turn in today's society, faith is difficult to understand and realize. Faith, however, touches the heart of God to move on our behalf. It can be defined as complete trust or confidence, a firm belief not requiring logical proof. Here are a few scriptures that help us understand faith.

Now faith is the substance of things hoped for, the evidence of things not seen (Hebrews 11:1). Let us hold fast the profession of our faith, without wavering, for he is faithful that promised (Hebrews 10:23).

Faith is the foundation in the life of a Christian. It is confidence in God. In the midst of pain and suffering, faith can provide a song in our hearts. We can't see the answer or good news, but by faith, we know it is coming! *We don't have to enjoy suffering, or to seek it out, or to stoically endure it in order to be considered faithful. We just have to go through it knowing, the wilderness never has the last word (Virgil M. Fry). Often, the only way out is through.* Faith provides our lives with strength and determination. When presented with a challenge, I know there is absolutely nothing that God and I can't handle. With God's help, I will go over, go around, or through the storm. Giving up is never an option. Faith is the catalyst changing the impossible into possibilities. God makes a way when there is no way. Some of our victories, however, are still in the making. God's "no" today often means a better "yes" tomorrow. Faith opens the door to our greatest potential. God holds nothing back to those of faith. Maturity and personal growth are by-products of faith. Growth means to increase in value, to cause to be strong, to have the power of resistance, not easily overcome or disturbed, well supported, and irrefutable. *Growing old is mandatory; growing up is optional (Margolyn Woods and Maureen MacLellan).*

The storms in life are growing exercises dispersed by a loving God to shape our character and deepen our faith. Problems call forth our courage and wisdom; indeed they create our courage and faith. They cause us to grow mentally and spiritually. *Life poses an endless series of problems. It is the process of meeting and solving problems.* Faith gives us the courage to stand in the midst of great conflict, difficulty and pain. We know God will work things out. Have you ever been in rush hour traffic, trapped behind a large truck with traffic on all sides? Your vision is limited, and all you can see is the rear of the large truck ahead. Then the traffic clears, and you have a way out. Suddenly, you can see clearly down the road. In life, our vision is obscure and limited to the problem at hand. Faith allows us to trust God, who sees down the road of our lives. He is capable of handling all the curves, the delays and "traffic jams" in our lives. *We are not born with roadmaps for our lives, but God's word reveals the way.* Faith brings us through seasons of waiting. This is the hardest thing for me, because I don't like to wait. However, time and waiting are God's best tools in our lives. *Knowing this, that the trying of your faith worketh patience. But let patience have her perfect work, that you may be perfect, and entire, wanting nothing (James 1:3-4).* Patience is perseverance, ability to endure, tenacity or fortitude. Faith also contributes to our destiny. Faithfulness in the small things brings larger opportunities into focus. *He that is faithful in that which is least, is faithful also in much (Luke 16:10). One does not discover new lands without consenting to lose sight of the shore for a very long time (Andre Gide). Faith leaves footprints in our hearts, and in the hearts of others.*

Wright
Where does faith begin?

Brooks
Faith is born when one comes to know God personally. My journey in faith began in August, 1982. As a small child, I remember attending church and vacation bible school. I heard my father and many others preach in my home town Buna, Texas. I was baptized at the age of nine. My mother sang in the choir and performed many solos in church. She owned and operated Irene's Beauty Salon for thirty-three years, and she always showered us with love and affection. Mother made sure piano recitals, country club dinners, and celebrity charity horse shows in Beaumont, Texas were a part of our lives. Her brother, Jordan Reese Jr., made it possible for our exposure to these events. Mother did not work in the salon on Wednesdays, and she

always went into town to go shopping. My sister and I would get off the school bus, hurry inside to see the portrayal of beautiful clothes that she had bought for us. This was so exciting! After high school, I attended modeling school in Houston. I married early my first year in college and later began my career with SBC Communications. My life, by all outward appearances, seemed to be successful, but something was terribly missing. I lacked purpose, meaning and a reason for living. Peggy Lee wrote a popular song called "Is that all there is?" I felt this had become my life's theme song. I sought help through doctors and psychiatrists, but despite my search, I still felt empty and unfulfilled.

One day in August, 1982, I returned home from work as usual. This day, however, was no ordinary day. I stood by the window watching it rain, reflecting on the many times I heard sermons on eternal life and something called "born again." In that moment, my heart cried out "Oh, God, please help me." A miracle took place in my life. My mind began to clear, and over the next weeks and months, the void in my life was replaced with real joy, peace, and purpose in my life. I had finally experienced what I had heard about all my life. The mystery has been solved. Within the human heart, there is a God shaped void. Only God can satisfy the longing in our hearts, and provide meaning and purpose to our lives.

And ye shall seek me and find me when you search for me with all your heart (Jeremiah 29:13). . . .Marvel not that I say unto thee, ye must be born again (John 3:7). For by grace are ye saved through faith; and that not of yourselves; it is the gift of God: Not of works, lest any man should boast (Ephesians 2:8-9). For God so loved the world, that he gave his only begotten Son, that whosoever believeth in him, should not perish, but have everlasting life (John 3:16). Philosophers can debate the meaning of life, but we need a God who declares the meaning of life.

Wright

What contributes to the growth of one's faith?

Brooks

I am convinced that faith grows every time we give something of ourselves away. Faith enables us to give to others what has been given to us. I have a couple of stories to share with you.

The Twenty Dollar Story:

Growing up in a small town presents many challenges. One challenge, is the required travel to nearby towns for shopping. Silsbee was a small town nearby, and whenever I drove my car from my home in Buna to Silsbee, Texas, I always took a shortcut that led me by rows of small wooden framed homes. These homes reflected the struggles of the people who lived there: peeling paint, overgrown yards, and small children dressed only in dirty diapers. In larger cities, one might call these homes the projects. As I drove by, my heart always broke with compassion for the people living there, and I always prayed, "God, please help them."

On one occasion, I stopped to cash a check for twenty dollars before traveling to Silsbee. As I approached the shortcut leading by the homes, I decided not to take the shortcut. Driving away, I felt strongly the need to turn around. I was puzzled by this, but continued to drive away. The urging persisted, so I turned around and proceeded down the familiar path. As I approached the first home, I felt I needed to stop. I felt confused and struggled to understand, but said out loud, "God, if you want me to stop by one of these homes, you are going to have to show me which one."

I pulled up in front of the first home, waited a moment, got out of my car and walked to the front door. A small child, about three years of age, opened the door. I asked "Is your mother home?" A voice from inside answered "come in." A middle-aged woman dressed in a worn cotton robe was sitting at the kitchen table. Another lady was standing behind her rolling her hair for a home permanent. I hesitated a moment, then said, "My name is Carolyn . . . and I was sent here." The lady seemed puzzled by my words, and then asked "By who?" I said nervously, "By God. . . and He wants to give you twenty dollars." I reached into my purse for the twenty dollars, and extended the money towards her. She burst into tears. Sobbing, she came running up to me, grabbed me and hugged me, and she would not let go. She said, "God bless you." Then we both cried. *It's different once you've been there.*

Be willing to enter the pain of fellow travelers, in the name of the one who shares our grief (Duke–employee at MD Anderson Cancer Hospital).

I will instruct thee and teach thee in the way which thou shalt go; I will guide thee with mine eye (Psalm 32:8).

Lena Ketner – Room 13B:

One Sunday afternoon, I decided to stop by a local nursing home in Euless, Texas. I asked the receptionist if there were residents who did not have family or friends. She thought a moment, took a small piece of paper, and wrote something down. I opened the piece of paper and read the words, "Lena Ketner, Room 13B." I thanked her and then left. I drove to a local Eckerd's and bought bath power and lotion. After wrapping the small gifts, I returned to the nursing home. I saw many frail elderly men and women with longing eyes that seemed to cry out for attention. I asked for directions to Lena's room, and walked down a long hallway and came to room 13B. I knocked on the door and a voice from inside replied "come in." Inside was a very young looking lady, about fifty-five years old with short straight gray hair. I introduced myself and spent about an hour getting to know Lena. She told me about the automobile accident that left her with minor brain damage and the inability to speak clearly. Lena said she did not have family to help care for her.

Over the next six months I visited Lena many times, bringing Thanksgiving dinner, pecan pies, socks, and other things she liked. One afternoon, we talked about God, and I told Lena how much He loved her. I shared my simple story of how God had changed my life. Lena listened, and tears began to stream down her face. I felt that this was a divine moment, so I took her hands in mine and asked Lena if she knew God personally. More tears fell. We prayed a simple prayer, and right there she invited Christ into her life. *Teach me to listen Lord, when you speak in whispers (Lois T. Henderson).*

Preach the gospel at all times, using words only when necessary. Sometimes, our lives speak louder than our words.

Giving is one of the best rewards. It is the prerequisite for experiencing the fullness of living. It is taking what we have and offering it to another so that they may gain. It has untold worth that ripples through the lives of those touched by it. Giving has immense power when it is done in the dark. Giving blesses the giver before it even gets to the receiver. For the greatest gift is being For-Given (Duke–employee at M D Anderson Cancer Hospital).

Wright

What other factors contribute to the growth of one's faith?

Brooks

I am a firm believer in having mentors both professionally and spiritually. I was a member of Southwestern Bell's Professional Women's Mentoring Program. This program afforded me with the opportunity to regularly meet with high ranking executives within our company, e.g., Vice President—Market Area, to learn from their strengths and successes. I also conducted benchmarking meetings with executives from other companies to learn and share ideas. I liked one idea called "One Stop Shopping" in the area of staffing. I submitted a proposal and recommendation to the President of South-western Bell requesting our company implement a similar process. The proposal was approved and initially implemented in five states. This new process resulted in an annual savings of more than two mil-lion dollars for our company. The process was then implemented throughout SBC's thirteen state region, including Pacific Bell and Ameritech. *"He that walketh with wise men shall be wise" (Proverbs 13.20)*. Also people are placed in our lives to encourage and develop our faith. My greatest mentor was my former pastor, Dr. James T. Draper. For twelve years he was my pastor, friend, and mentor. He is now president of Lifeway Christian Resources. He used to always say "Nothing can touch our life that has not first gone through the hand of God, through the hand of Jesus, allowed to touch our lives, and it will be always be for our good." In addition, I have found attending church and studying God's word often to be significant in developing our faith. *So then faith cometh by hearing, and hearing by the word of God (Romans 10:17). Looking to Jesus the author and finisher of our faith (Hebrews 12:2).*

Faith is much like a flower. It starts with a small seed. The right soil, plenty of water and sunshine produces a beautiful flower. *If you have faith and doubt not, ye shall not only do this which is done to the fig tree, but also if ye shall say unto this mountain, be thou removed and be thou cast into the sea, it shall be done. And all things, whatso-ever, ye shall ask in prayer, believing, ye shall receive (Matthew 21: 21-22).*

Wright

Does faith please God?

Brooks

Faith, I believe, causes God to smile. It touches and moves his heart. Parents love it when their children have complete faith and trust in them and simply obey their instructions. The parent loves it when their child obeys simply because Mom or Dad says so. Love and gratitude for the child embraces the heart of the parent. So it is with our Heavenly Father. *But without faith, it is impossible to please him;*

for he that cometh to God must believe that he is, and that he is a re-warder of them that diligently seek him (Hebrews 11:6).

Wright

Does Faith Affect One's Work Ethic?

Brooks

Absolutely, yes! My career with SBC Communications included four promotions and spanned more than twenty-eight years. The Bible is our greatest inspiration and tool for professional success. I am convinced that we should work the hardest and give above and beyond expectations. During my career, I wrote a booklet, *Biblical Work Ethics.* This booklet was purchased by Family Christian Stores and distributed to all their employees throughout the United States. Several executives of SBC contacted me for copies of the booklet. I am currently re-writing a modern version to be entitled, *What Does God Have To Do With It, Faith in the Workplace.* I am of the opinion that success follows those who work hard and apply themselves. Some of the topics include employee responsibilities to management, management responsibilities to employees, the importance of authority, and basic keys to success. Those in management positions should develop great "people skills." I believe a successful manager learns to interact and communicate with others the same way God interacts with us. *People may not remember exactly what you did, or what you said, but they will remember how you made them feel (Margolyn Woods and Maureen MacLellan).*

Wright

What is Faith Vision?

Brooks

Faith vision is seeing beyond the moment of crisis to the anticipated end and promises that God has in store. Faith is ever hopeful, seldom doubting. We refuse to accept anything less than God's promises. Faith vision affects our thoughts, actions, and vocabulary. People of faith are the greatest optimists. Difficult circumstances seldom cause them to be negative for long. They are back on their feet, anticipating what lies ahead.

Wright

Does Faith provide one with God's favor?

Brooks

Yes, it certainly does! Throughout my career, I sensed God's favor. I had the difficult task of submitting recommendations for employee terminations, encountered union grievances, and faced betrayal. Each event was very difficult, but management support was always there for me. Reorganization occurs often in corporations. When SBC merged with Pacific Bell, reorganization was to result in my return to a department where I had previously encountered hostility and betrayal. One week before the reorganization, I received a telephone call from a department wanting to schedule an interview for a position that would result in a promotion. The day after the interview, I was offered the position. God provided the way out through a promotion. In the story of Joseph, which is discussed later, God gave Joseph favor with the King of Egypt which led to his appointment as governor. *A good man obtaineth favor of the Lord (Proverbs 12:2). So shalt thou find favor and good understanding in the sight of God and man (Proverbs 3: 4). When a man's ways please the Lord, he maketh even his enemies to be at peace with him (Proverbs 16:7). For thou Lord, will bless the righteous; with favor wilt thou compass him as with a shield (Psalm 5:12).*

Wright

Is it possible to have faith during difficult and trying circumstances?

Brooks

I have a few more stories to share.

When we don't get the first promotion:

Soon after I began my career, I wanted to be promoted to the position of District Secretary. This was an entry level management position. I applied for the position and waited. Another candidate was selected, and I was crushed. About three months later, I heard of another opening for a prestigious position in staffing. This was a higher level management position. My supervisor recommended that I be considered for the position. I was interviewed, and promoted one week later! God's "no" today often means a better "yes" tomorrow. Sometimes we have to wait for the best to come our way. Sometimes our greatest blessings are unanswered prayers. *An individual can succeed at almost anything for which he has unlimited faith. Faith is often the first chapter in the book of excellence. Cheerfulness, it would appear, is a matter which depends fully as much on the state of things within, as on the state of things without.* Faith grows more in the highways of adversity than in the rose gardens of life. Disappointments often mean God's appointment. Faith has been my strength to emerge through many difficulties. I share some of my experiences when I speak for Christian and Professional Women's Clubs in my talk "Overcoming for Successful Living."

God is God of the mountains, the valleys, and the places in-between. Our difficulties are God's proving ground; his personal handiwork to mold and shape our lives. *For when our faith is tested, your endurance has a chance to grow. So let it grow, for when your endurance is fully developed, you will be strong in character and ready for anything (James 1:3-4).[1] And we know that God causes everything to work together for the good of those who love God and are called according to his purpose for them (Romans 8:28).[2]*

God has not promised skies always of blue, but grace sufficient to see us through.

From the Pit to the Palace:

In Genesis 37, we find of the story of Joseph. Joseph was loved by his father Jacob more than his other children, because he was the son of his old age. Jacob made Joseph a coat of many colors. Joseph's brothers were moved with envy and hatred when they saw their father loved Joseph more. Joseph had a dream, and told his brothers in his dream he reigned over them. This caused his brothers to hate him even more. They conspired to kill him, place him in a pit, and claim a wild animal killed him. His brothers decided instead to sell him into slavery in Egypt for twenty pieces of silver. The story continues, and we learn while Joseph was in slavery and in prison God was with Joseph, and He made all that he did to prosper. *And the patriarch moved with envy and sold Joseph into Egypt, but God was with him. And delivered him out of all afflictions and gave him favour and wisdom in the sight of Pharaoh King of Egypt, and he made him governor over Egypt and all his house (Acts 7:9-10).*

Can you imagine what Joseph must have felt while he was in the pit and in prison? I am sure he felt confused, afraid, and betrayed by those closest to him. However, he would not have been appointed gov-

---

[1] Scripture taken from New Living Translation.
[2] Scripture taken from New Living Translation.

ernor of Egypt without these experiences. We must always remember when we are in the "pit of circumstances" God has something great in store for us. He is always working towards a greater end. *The process from where we are to where God moves us is often along the road of hardships. Trust me in your times of trouble, and I will rescue you, and you will give me glory (Psalm 50:15).*[3] *Sometimes I get the feeling the world is against me, but deep down I know that's not true. Some of the smaller countries are neutral (Robert Orben). Have you ever heard of the term "growing pains?" Focus on the "growing part." Mother Teresa was once asked if she wished she had done more, to which she replied, "God called me to be faithful, not successful."*

Irene (Reese) Slaymaker Phelps, Room G-1253, MD Anderson Cancer Hospital:

July 28, 2002 began my sweet Mother's courageous battle with cancer. Mother has been my greatest inspiration on how to live life, and she is now my greatest inspiration on how to face eternity. Often, we would sit side by side holding hands, and gaze out the hospital window. Sometimes there were words, sometimes not. We spoke of Heaven, the angels, and how our finite minds could not grasp eternity or the wonderful things God had in store for us.

Mother sang many of her favorite hymns. She once sang a solo for a volunteer in the music therapy department, and she sang it just like she did over thirty years ago! She also quoted Scriptures, "Eye hath not seen nor ear heard, neither have entered into the heart of man, the things which God hath prepared for them that love him" (1 Corinthians 2:9). "Oh what a beautiful place God has prepared for me," and "Yea, thought I walk through the valley of the shadow of death, I will fear no evil; for thy rod and thy staff they comfort me" (Psalms 23:4). We talked of going to Heaven much like going to a place far more beautiful than Paris or any place here on earth. It would be similar to our old Reese family reunions with great celebrations. Those of faith will receive a personal invitation, but each invitation will have a different postmark. We will attend one-by-one.

The best kind of friend is the kind you can sit on the porch and swing with, never say a word, and then walk away feeling like it was the best conversation you've ever had.

Mother often talked to other patients saying, "Oh honey, God is going to help you. I will be praying for you." She seemed to be more con-

---

[3] Scripture taken from New Living Translation.

cerned for the other patients and for the nurses providing her care. Mother often said, "There is nothing going to happen to me today that God and I can't handle, and we live by faith, not by sight." She is facing eternity with ultimate hope, peace, and joy, and her life and grace have touched so many at MD Anderson. One doctor said, "Mrs. Phelps, you have a grace about you that is evident to everyone here." A nurse told Mother, "You have no idea of the lives you have touched here."

Throughout her life, Mother provided love and generosity to all her family, and now her family is giving back to her. I am sure the balance can not be made equal. Illness results in many financial needs, but God has provided all of mother's financial needs. The outpouring of love and support has been tremendous. *Faith escorts us into the presence of God.*

God moves beyond the walls of a church building and meets us directly in the middle of our sorrows and our joys. The place of crisis and tears is not the end of the story. God's Word reminds me that He is in control. This year with Mother has truly been God's gift to me. The conversations have been priceless . . . the memories great. The way has been difficult, but I could not have received a greater blessing.

He knows not his own strength who has not met adversity (Ben Johnson).

Faith during difficult times:

- Allows us to have a heart for others.
- Enables us to give to others what has been given to us.
- Equips us to be a light in someone's life.
- Sustains during difficult times.
- Provides peace in the midst of storms.
- Opens doors to unlimited possibilities.
- Develops our greatest potential.

Faith is like angels who lift us to our feet when our wings have trouble remembering how to fly.

Friends can hold our hand at the deathbed of our loved ones, but we need a God who has defeated the grave.

August 10, 2003

Mother went home to Heaven.

Wright

Well, Carolyn, I have certainly enjoyed this time with you today. I appreciate you taking the time to share with us your view on faith.

Brooks

Thank you, David.

About The Author

Carolyn Brooks is a dynamic inspirational speaker, inspiring author and con-sultant. She is a member of The Professional Woman Speaker's Bureau and speaker with Christian and Professional Women's Clubs. Carolyn is a former model and nominee for the "Women of Excellence" Award in 1997 and 1998 for exemplary career with SBC Communications Corporations and community involvement. Carolyn appeared on the nationwide television broadcast, "Life Today," and is the co-author of the book, *What I Learned From God While Cooking* by Barbour Books to be released in the fall of 2004, is a contributor to book, *But Lord, I Was Happy Shallow* by Kregel Publishers, also to be re-leased in 2004, and is the author of booklet, *Biblical Work Ethics.*

Carolyn Brooks
Simply Divine Communications
Houston, Texas
Phone: 832.978.3242
Email: carolyn.brooks@sbcglobal.net
Website: www.carolynbrooks.com
Website: www.protrain.net
Website: www.womenspeakers.net
Website: www.BookASpeaker.com

Chapter 10

DARRYL C. WALLS, CSP

THE INTERVIEW

David E. Wright (Wright)
Today we're talking to Darryl C. Walls. An accomplished leadership developer, and keynote speaker, Mr. Walls always makes a profound impact on his audience. A former Fortune Five Hundred team leader, Mr. Walls has an insight into what people want and thrive on from their leaders. He has dedicated his time to coaching and empowering students, faculty, employees, supervisors, managers, executive staff, and faith based institutions while observing what's effective and what isn't. Under his leadership his teams have been recognized with consecutive National Leaders in Excellence honors, and Exceptional Contribution Awards. Early on, Darryl was encouraged to hone his gift for speaking. This eventually led to countless appearances and promos at prestigious religious institutions, spoken word competitions, national conferences, and leadership workshops. He was awarded the Mayoral Citation from the city of New York, and has received national awards, certificates, trophies, and honors for his talents. His leadership, team building, goal setting, and communication techniques won him the honor of being awarded the Driving Force Award for exhibiting exemplary leadership skills. Darryl, welcome to *Conversations on Faith*.

Darryl C. Walls (Walls)
Thank you Dave.

Wright
What would you like people to know about you?

Walls
I would like people to know that I love my family that God has blessed me with, and I praise Him for allowing me to share in this joy of foundation (of marriage). I want people to know that by no means am I perfect. I don't sit on a pedestal, nor do I wish to. Although, I may send a message with my body language, or tacit communication, maybe even possessions I have worked hard to acquire over the years, I have faults, challenges, skeletons, and pet peeves just like everyone else on these mundane shores. I'd like to challenge people to look beyond their perceptions and ascertain the rich substance of my character.

Wright
What church are you a member of?

Walls
I'm a member of Cornerstone Baptist Church in Brooklyn, New York. Our Pastor Harry S. Wright just turned over the spiritual leadership baton to a young dynamic "preateacher" Reverend Lawrence E. Aker III. By the way, that's spelled P-R-E-A-T-E-A-C-H-E-R, because just like his predecessor, Rev. Aker is a preacher *and* teacher, which are much needed today.

Wright
What intrigues you about your church, or church in general?

Walls
I think watching God provide unwavering leadership and needed change consistently. I've had the good fortune of experiencing the changing of God's soldiers, if you will, on more than one occasion at my church. I've seen the infamous Rev. Dr. Sandy F. Ray as our leader during his thirty-five year tenure, and after he passed, I watched our very own Rev. Henry G. Scott effectively maintain a well-lit torch to be passed on to the Rev. Dr. Harry S. Wright. Dr. Wright, who carried the torch for about twenty-one years, took Cor-

nerstone to new heights, introduced different levels of leadership, teachings, membership, and change. Now, we again have been blessed with what appears to be a *"dual powered distance sprinter."* He appears to have the flexibility to sprint when needed and go the distance through this transitional period. God's churches are guided by His leadership assessment process and <u>no one</u> can interfere with the end result.

Wright

What pivotal points in your life strengthened your faith in God?

Walls

Wow! That question could fill a book all by itself. But, let me try to give a synopsis on a few points. God had blessed me with a job as a correctional officer years and years ago. I was making thousands and thousands of dollars, could spend thousands on clothes and entertainment, and I could go from my apartment in Brooklyn and retreat to a home in Jersey and things were wonderful. I even purchased a studio in the Metro Tech area of Brooklyn as a profitable investment. Then God began what I call the cleansing process of Job in my life: incarceration, my father's death, the loss of my job, and legal separation from my wife. Each of these brought a taste of different, unpalatable and indescribable levels of pain that ultimately created in me an increased sense of faith in God.

For instance...Incarceration: A few years before I was married, I made an extremely poor decision that haunts me still this very day and I was incarcerated for it. I made a left turn when I should've turned right, I looked down when I should've looked up from whence cometh my help. I disgraced my family by going astray. It didn't matter whether I was helping someone I loved who claimed they were dying from leukemia or getting money back that was owed me from another friend. They both *appeared* to be in need. Regardless, it was the wrong way to go about it. Fortunately for me, my mother and father never left me; they stood by me and stood up for me and **NEVER** stopped loving me! If I could equate God's providential care and degree of love to someone, my parents would certainly take the blue ribbon! I am truly blessed!!

During this period there were people I considered friends who stopped coming to my home. Other people who used this against me. There were people who had too many political concerns to help me significantly because they felt their "reputation" would be at stake.

And then, there were the rumormongers. I was bitter, paranoid, scared, terrified and petrified of the events I would soon have to face. I lost over 20 lbs rapidly and my health began deteriorating. The questions started, *"You don't look well D, are you okay? You've lost a lot of weight, what's going on?"*

So, I experienced and continue to experience what might be categorized as a "disability" as a result of making that tremendously wrong decision many years ago. And unfortunately, society exacerbates it by labeling incarcerated adults as a type of plague. But, this strengthened my faith because it opened my eyes to the people who truly had my best interest at heart and those that were fair weather friends. God was cleansing my spiritual atmosphere. People like Dr. Fred Lucas sat and talked at length with my parents (he was the only minister to do so) and prayed with them during the time leading up to my sentencing. God will send His angelic soldiers to protect His children.

Then there's my father's death. Always remember: Pray to God before the battle...even though no visible sign of victory...but, don't forget to PRAISE GOD after the victory (I Chronicles 16). My father left me that scripture several months before his passing and it hangs in my bathroom. I just made time to read the entire passage this summer; and WOW! I had a lengthy talk with my sister Gail and she told me to make sure I never let his memory or legacy die. She said to always keep that flame burning brightly! She couldn't have hit the bull's-eye any better and I'm looking forward to hopefully completing a project with my mother by 2005 to help support his memory & legacy. The magnitude of the man continues to unfold. My father had a particular love that was tangible, fresh, real, warm, affectionate, endearing and unconditional. He had the capacity to touch my most inner feelings just by sharing a laugh with me. You didn't have a choice *but* to love him back; if you failed to show love for him it was only because you were forcing yourself not to. I've learned so many things from my father and had no idea that these things would come back to mind in a flurry of waves after his home going. I cannot get by one day without doing something that he would have done, exactly the way he would have done it. His laugh is my laugh. His definitive looks with his eyes and eyebrows are the same as mine. His chess playing style is mine. His out of the box thinking is mine. His love for his children is mine. His love for his wife is mine. His analytical way is mine. His enjoyment of watching his culture dominate sports, music and entertainment is mine. His playful tendencies with all who knew him...we share. Tossing me in the air in our backyard and catching me without fail...I share with my children. *His futile attempts at cooking, well...they are not mine by a long shot!* When people talk to me on the phone, they get chills because we sound identical. They even have mistakenly me for him. I am proud to be able to call him my father. He lived vicariously through me many times when I would have team meetings at my Fortune 500 job. I am proud in knowing that he provided a positive example for me to emulate. I start my presentations off with *"If I were 1/5th the man my father was, I would be 5 men."* You can see everyone trying to do the math. No matter how much time I put into our relationship, no matter how much I knew he knew I loved him...by show and tell, it could never be enough to completely fill the void I carry because I miss him.

You see, my father died in my arms. Although I was able to identify that he needed a lifeline, although I was CPR trained, although I was sleeping right next to him, although emergency medical service was a call away, although I administered that very CPR technique, had all my faculties working properly, God had other plans and they were being executed exactly as His will so said. I helplessly watched my "twin" be absorbed in the providential care of God's unchanging hands. These are things that made his departure so difficult for my family and me. There's a song title that best describes my heartache..."Sweetest Pain." It's a wonderful feeling to know you can love and miss someone so much! We were two of a kind and despite his physical presence being absent; he is very much with me...daily! In his death came faith refinement, knowing that the enemy could not negatively impact my memory nor could he touch my father's spirit. Death, where is your sting? Through his death, I identified a higher level of faith that I had NEVER seen before. A strength in God's sovereign power, grace and mercy by way of my mother's behavior. I watched her hold our family together through prayer...**never** ceasing! She comforted me when I thought I would be comforting her because I was her "sun" (that's what my parents call me)! She held me in her arms because I was crying uncontrollably. She spiritually transferred her strength to me that I would be able to perform a song for my father. I was supposed to shine for her at this time! I was supposed to "lead by example" and be strong for her and my family...but I could not. I needed her. And through an extension of her faith, I was able to see my way clear of this tragedy-coated triumph. Through her faith and prayer, I could continue once again. Through her faith, I could breath. Through her faith, I learned how good God can be and how He cares for **ALL** His children. It is readily apparent to me that she has a special relationship with Him and can effectively use His hands to provide "baskets of somehows" for our family. Many people can attest to the special love we share as mother and "sun" and they know that I am so thankful for all she has done and continues to do **WITHOUT** the thought of getting something in return. Her commitment to her church far exceeds anyone else's I know! She puts God first in her life and challenges me to do the same. She is not the person who looks to talk the talk; she is definitively the woman who **walks the talk** and I praise God for allowing me to spend time with one of His "borrowed arch angels". My church will never realize how important she is until she is gone. But I am laser clear on her importance to me and my family, her love for me, and her faith in God. She doesn't give of herself sporadically or with ulterior motives, she simply gives...consistently! I love you Mother and I thank you for your unconditional love!

Then the loss of my job: This was a significant happening because like my old boss Al would say about corporate America, "**Well, Nobody Cares.**" **WNBC** ideology. This was their (corporate America) line of thinking. *Your* family or *your* well-being didn't matter! Whether you are doing nothing at your job or you are churning away consistent record breaking unprecedented results, the bottom line ultimately rings with a resounding "needs of the business" bell! You could have nominations (I had that), awards (I had that), rewards (I had that), recognition for outstanding achievement (I had that), have cleaned their worst division in the company (I did that)...**Well, Nobody Cares—you were still expendable!**

I had a good paying position managing a highly energized team. One day, I came to work and tried to use my email, but the system wouldn't allow me access. I went to the technical support team and they had no answer. A well orchestrated dismissal! Or as they say...separation! I received a call to report to an office and upon my arrival, I was informed that I had 3 choices: either take a bulk sum of money that includes my salary and time on the job pay and say goodbye, receive a bulk sum for time on the job and have payments made to me for one month in the same amount to "give an appearance that you're still employed for another month," or take **no** package (what I call *keep quiet money*) and my salary and seek legal advice. I chose the latter and what a battle it has been.

Your family is counting on you, the bills always arrive on time, you're in the process of growing a business, you're applying for job after job after job after job and no one hires you—I'm talking about over 50 jobs—and you're watching your children so your wife can go back to school and get her degree. You feel like there's a hole in your *faith ship* because things aren't moving the way you want them to move.

Then God began to send me speaking engagements. Not just any kind of keynote speeches, but keynotes where the topic was about Him or trying to be more like Him. Keynotes where He would provide me with ***"divine intervention patches"*** to help seal up the holes in my faith ship. This too has strengthened my faith by teaching me to wait on the Lord.

Finally, my marital separation: (This combines all the levels because there's a connectivity between each of them—what I mean by that is by going through each of the other trials, He was preparing me for this particular one). My separation has made all of the other pivotal points of my life feel like a summer breeze on the shores of Tahiti. Even with all the leadership training, faith based teaching I've received, and motivational speaking I've done, I've allowed divorce to take me through a daily mental and emotional shredder. I know He has something great in store for me and this is just a means of getting me there. He is molding the characteristics He needs me to have when I get there. It's just been extremely difficult to comprehend. The separation process tears at the very thread that holds the fabric of my heart together and to intertwine that with watching my children deal with such a monumental emotional transition is crippling! I will always love my wife and am confident that God will watch over her and our children. I have to take full accountability for any part I've played in this end result and pray that none of the negatives of this separation process bleeds onto or remain embedded in our children. My faith continues to grow through His plan and it has further taught me how to ***"let go and let God."*** These are definitely the pivotal points I've been dealing with.

Wright

You mentioned the negative societal impact of your incarceration. What exactly do you mean and is there an example you would like to share with the readers?

Walls

Society—and believe me, I was one of them—labels you based on their perceptions and says, "We have to put this one in this pile."

When I was first released, I can remember finally getting a shot at an interview for a huge company and fortunately for me, they were in dire need of people and were willing to disregard my record at the time. I recall the interviewer telling me "We really need people right now, so I can get you in regardless." I just wanted a job, so it didn't matter what she said. I would call that Divine intervention where God gave me what I **wanted** and **needed at that time.** We all need to understand that He's not always going to do that.

For instance, when my entire unit was terminated as a result of "downsizing" as I mentioned before, I was back on the jobless terrain again. I received a call from my buddy Bill, who told me there were positions available at an installation company and I should look into it. Upon my arrival, I completed the application, which includes an account of your criminal record. The general manager interviewed me for almost 2 hours reviewing the initiatives, processes, and personality assessment tools I put in place with my former employer and told me it would be great to have me on their team, but I was overqualified for the position I applied for. However, he said there's a supervisor position available that you could fill. If you were a fly on the wall, you could probably see how excited with anticipation I was! He then turns to the page that has the criminal record breakdown and excused himself to go speak to one of the managers outside the office. Upon his return he said, "You know Darryl, you are light years ahead of this company and it would probably be best not to place you in a position that may not suit your challenge level." End of interview! Well, welcome to the real world! Funny, just a minute ago, I was going to be a great addition to the team. I would call that Divine intervention too, but this time God was molding me for what he wanted me to do <u>NOT</u> what I wanted to be done. These tribulations are snapshots inside a chapter of my life story. I don't normally go outside my family circle with these pieces of me, but I believe this may very well be the right time.

Wright
What do you mean the right time Darryl?

Walls
The right time because God expects us to share ourselves as a means of testimony, healing, and teaching by example. The right time because he's providing me with so many signs that can't be ignored or set aside. The right time because there is probably never a right time

for how we want things to happen. The right time because I believe I need to not only learn the process of cultivating faith, but begin to fully implement and monitor an element that on many occasions is part of the faith process—forgiveness. I am suggesting that as you go through, or after you have gone through challenges, it's likely that the next step may be to forgive someone or even yourself. In each of the incidences that I mentioned prior I had to do one or both. You know, I listened to Dr. R. T. Kendal on *WMCA* here talk about finding true forgiveness and it continues to assist me with my healing process and has tempted my faith to believe it will work. It literally raises the forgiveness bar. You see Dave, we are all diamonds in the raw and God is going to place people, things, events, accidents, incidents, challenges, storms, trials, tribulation, strife's and strains, detours and derailments just to stir us and shake us up, because He loves us and wants us to be the kind of people He intended us to be. It's His molding process. Therefore, we must learn to exhibit the same forgiveness practices He has demonstrated to work towards walking in His footsteps.

Wright

You said *"monitor it"* regarding forgiveness. Are you suggesting that there's some good to be derived from forgiving?

Walls

Absolutely! In fact, theoretically, the greater the level of circumstance for forgiveness the more God recognizes and rewards us for forgiving. In other words, if I have to forgive you for stealing my favorite ball point writing pen verses forgiving you for hitting a child while drunk driving, my blessing for forgiving you for the drunk driving incident far exceeds that of the pen, and God's reward will be predicated on your level of forgiveness.

Wright

What keeps your faith strong?

Walls

Well, God has provided me with a mother and father who have been deeply rooted in His word and he has taught me as my mother's favorite Philippians verse says, *"I can do all things through Christ who strengthens me."* Key members of my family and close friends have helped to keep me on the right path and given me scriptures, pamphlets, and emails to peruse that help to keep me rooted. Their prayers and unwavering support are the very fabric of my spiritual motivation. It's people like my Aunt Cookie who introduced me to Psalms 91 that says, *"He is my refuge, and my fortress, my God in whom I trust."* Then, there are other angels that God sends your way with keynote messages that you know only God could have sent. You have to have your theological sunglasses and what I call celestial hearing aids on to make sure you see what he wants you to see, and hear what he wants you to hear. In fact, I remember speaking at an affair at Cornerstone and a wonderful person Mrs. Joiner took me aside and told me "God is molding you right now Darryl, and He is preparing you for something great." I couldn't stop myself from crying that day because there was no way that this woman, who I rarely speak with, would know that I was dealing with a heavy burden in my life unless she was connected directly to my Heavenly Father. Just thinking about it fills me up with a high level of joy. Then, there are other angels like Mrs. Majette, and Mrs. Jeffries. Mrs. Majette sends me mail periodically and it arrives at key times that I need to read His word. My Aunt Chequita has been and continues to be part of my *"faith ensemble"* as she demonstrates her faith lasting (not shallow), faith leading (not just following), faith living (not just surviving) power in Christ! These things keep my faith strong, David.

Wright

What are you doing with your life right now?

Walls

Well, I'm focusing on putting the big rocks back in first.

Wright

Big rocks? Now, what's that?

Walls

Well, there's a story that talks about an Ivy League Professor I'd like to share with you. He was an Ivy League Professor of Physics and he arrived at his lecture class with several items: a large fish tank, four big rocks, gravel, sand, and water. He proceeds to advise his students to observe the demonstration. He puts the four big rocks in first, and asks the class if the tank is full. One scholarly gentleman with a 4.0 GPA stands up and says, "Well, anyone can see it is full now, sir." But, the professor says, "No, it is not." He continues the experiment and pours the gravel over the big rocks and repeats his question "Is the tank full now?" Another bold student raises her hand and says, "I would think it so professor." "No," he replied. Frustrated the students began talking amongst each other trying to determine where the professor is going with his experiment. He then pours the sand in the tank and shakes it up so the entire area is covered top to bottom and asks the students again, "Is it full now?" And a resounding "Obviously" from the entire class rings out. He calmly says "No." He takes the water out and pours the water over the sand and into the tank waiting for it to rise to the surface and then asks for the last time "What do you think now?" And with skepticism circulating the students say together softly "Yes." The professor replies back with a smile "You are correct!" He asks them "What does this teach us?" And one of them stands up and says "Well, that liquid is an element that..." and he says "No, no, no, it teaches us that if we don't put our big rocks in first we will never get them in at all."

Wright

What are the big rocks in your life?

Walls

Well, my big rocks are receiving God's approval in all of my endeavors, and getting to the point of total submission. The health, interest, mind, skills, friendships, work, dreams, and ministries of my darling little angels in the *"whole wide world,"* Darryl Christopher Walls II, Amara Aurelia Walls, my relationship with my beautiful wife Francisca, my relationship with my mother and her well-being, rebuilding my relationship with my brother Joe, the continuous strengthening of the relationship with his wife and my sister Gail, insuring my numerous Godchildren and niece Jasmyne have a relationship with me and our children, and the rest will come in His time. I've got a friend Mike who introduced me to a book a little more than a year ago and I shared it with my brother. You may know the author David, Bruce Wilkinson. The book is entitled, *The Prayer of Jabez Devotional,* the first chapter is called: The favor of the Father. It starts off with a bible scripture for each chapter. The scripture he starts with is I Corinthians 2:9, which says: *"Eye has not seen, nor ear heard, nor have entered into the heart of man the things, which God has prepared for those who love Him."* In other words even if we use our imagination's imagination we still can't fathom the rewards God has reserved for us if we just follow Him. He moves forward to share with his readers how his 23-year-old son creates dead silence during family talk time by asking his father to bless him. This reminds me of my son, because he's so sensitive and loving, much like Bruce's son. Bruce told his son David, "You know I do bless you." David responded saying "No, Dad, I want you to _really_ bless me." And he says "Do you know what flooded through my heart at that moment? I felt a tremendous desire to bestow on him every possible good thing. Here was my own child waiting at my feet telling me by word and action that he wanted most, was what only I as his father could give him." And he says he put his hand on his shoulders and started to pray. He prayed for his mind, health, interest, skills, for friendships, his work, his ministry, his dreams for the future, and for every part of his life in Jesus' name he poured blessings and blessings upon him. He didn't stop until he was certain that he not only _was_ blessed, but that he also _felt_ blessed. That's a powerful statement Dave. This has been my prayer for my family and my children since their birth. I've asked God to touch their ears so that they would hear what He wanted them to hear, and touch their mouths and tongues that they would say the things that He would have them say, to touch their eyes so that they would see the things He would have them see, and touch their minds that they would soak up His gospel and excel academically and so on. Prayers for our children to recite from their Godmother Carol have supported our vision for our children and have been handed down 2 generations. David, hands down these are my big rocks!

Wright

What projects are you looking to initiate or complete in the next year or so?

Walls

Well, depending on how successful God allows this project to be, I would like to see a follow-up leadership development book in the works that focuses on the elements of fear and how to prevent them from negatively impacting our decisions and ultimately our lives. I also envision a biography in the works in two or three years. In addition, I would like to achieve complete understanding of my new recording studio, see a leadership CD package produced and distributed, and possibly obtain a record deal or have my songs published. Speaking of projects and relating them to faith, I asked God to provide me with additional exposure for my motivational speaking business before the year was out and a director at Berkley College, Richard McCulluch offered an opportunity for me to be a writer for a full-page column in their quarterly newsletter focused on leadership development. Now, this should help me in creating material for my leadership book and strengthen my personal leadership development by serving the community. I thank God for sending people like Richard my way to help support my endeavors. These are just some of the projects I'm looking to complete.

Wright

What morsel or tidbit of faith can you provide our readers with that might help them along the way?

Walls

I would say to open their Bibles to Malachi 3:3 where it says, *"He will sit as a refiner and purifier of silver."* It comes to mind because I spoke with my Aunt Flo a while ago and she shared this story with me that goes along with this scripture that her daughter Lorri sent her by email. The author's unknown, but it says that a woman wanted to fully understand what the scripture meant, so she made an appointment to visit a silversmith to watch him at work, and never mentioned anything about the reason why. As she watched the silversmith, he held a piece of silver over the fire and let it heat up. He explained that in refining silver, one needed to hold the silver in the middle of the fire where the flames were hottest as to burn away all of the impurities. The woman thought about God holding us in such a *hot spot*. Then she thought again about the verse that says H*e sits as a refiner and purifier of silver*. She asked the silversmith if it was true that he had to sit there in front of the fire the whole time the silver was being refined. The man answered, "yes," he not only had to sit there holding the silver, but he had to keep his eyes on the silver the entire time it was in the fire. If the silver was left a moment too long in the flames, it would be destroyed. The woman was silent for a moment and then she asked the silversmith "Well, how do you know when the silver is fully refined?" And he smiled at her and answered, "Oh that's easy. When I see my image in it." So, if today you are feeling the heat of the fire remember that God has His eye on you, and will keep watching you until He sees His image in you.

Wright

How deep is your faith?

Walls

First, let me say that I don't know how much faith I have, nor can I say how deep my faith is. For me, only God knows. Let me try to paint a couple of pictures on *my canvas of faith* to offer up some type of faith measurement tool. There I am...completely alone...climbing Mount Everest for well over 5 days. Just before I reach the top I slip and begin to fall! Suddenly, I'm able to grab onto a branch protruding from the side of the mountain and there's nothing beneath me to jump on to, no buffer, nothing to cushion my fall; the branch stays intact and I hear a voice say, *"Be not dismayed my child, let go and I will take care of you."* I don't know that I could let go of that branch. Then suddenly the branch begins to give way and it's only a matter of time before it won't matter either way and AGAIN I hear that same voice calling unto me *"Be not dismayed my child, let go and I will take care of you."* It would be at this point that I could see letting go as an option.

If I use Job as a comparison to the tests I've had, I would say that not only am I not in the ballpark of Job's trials, but I'm not even on the bus to get to the parking lot *at* the ballpark. Job had an abyss of faith! This makes me even more thankful because notwithstanding my level of faith, God still loves me and trusts me to handle His *"pre-approved"* exams of faith. If there's one thing I've begun to get a firm grip on, it's that *if He brings you to it, He'll get you through it.* So, I must rejoice in the opportunities He provides me with to display and increase my level of faith and I only pray that when all is said and done, I have pleased the Lord with my "faith" results.

If we go back and examine the "hanging on the side of the mountain" scenario from a leadership and behavioral perspective, we would look at the dynamics of the ever small in size, but huge in impact...Amygdala. There's a saying I've extracted from a book my cousin Jon leant me entitled, *What Color is Your Parachute,* by Richard Nelson Boles that says something to the effect that it is often the mosquito **NOT** the dragon that can slay you.

You see, the amygdala is the mosquito of your brain. As part of the limbic system, it plays an important role in **motivation** and **emotional behavior.** Therefore, it has the potential to STING and/or suck out the motivation and emotional behavior you need when it's time to use it effectively! The **amygdala** is the creative portion of the brain. The **Core** of the brain surrounds it. The **neocortex** is what overlays the Core of the brain as your brain develops. So, the more that happens in your life, the more layers you achieve. When we are faced with fear/stress/conflict, we pass through the f³ process. Either we FIGHT, FLIGHT, or FREEZE. Initially, the brain can't tell the difference between a saber tooth tiger and a surprise party! If we **fight**, we might physically, emotionally or mentally *"put up our dukes,"* if we **flight** we run or avoid the issue at hand, if we **freeze** we choose to do absolutely nothing and in doing so, we have made a choice to leave our destiny in something or someone else's hands. At the point of fear/conflict/stress the amygdala actually gets "hijacked" and it is then that we need to have faith in His sovereign power.

I am suggesting that we envision Jesus at the helm of our neurological control center and tell Him to take complete control because the storm/fear is difficult to see through. He remains in constant communication with God so your message gets delivered instantaneously! Then stand back and get out of your own way and watch Him do work! In other words, don't pull out the devil's Renoir de la **De**saster, pull out God's Renoir de la **Thee** Master and let Him take care of the paint on your life's canvas! This has helped to create a deeper sense of faith for me.

Wright

Darryl, I read your bio and noticed that you are also an accomplished musician and songwriter. Are there any songs you've written that apply to our faith theme?

Walls

There are two that come to mind Dave. The first is, *In the Spirit of Christ*, that my mother sings, which tells us that "through all the pain and strife, stay in the spirit of Christ." Then you hear a sweet saxophone melody in the background played by my *"other brother"* Leo. The other song is entitled, *He Didn't Bring Me This Far to Leave Me*, which is pretty self-explanatory.

Wright

What was the determining factor that made you know you have faith?

Walls

Well Dave, we all go through levels of gethsemane (an instance or a place of great suffering) and we either realize that we were not alone and didn't accomplish getting out of the storm by ourselves, or we decide to believe that we handled the situation without divine intervention. There have been many instances that made me aware that I had Someone watching over me. That's a capital S Dave. But, the determining factor on a large scale would have to be the process leading to my incarceration and the aftermath thereof. I can remember asking God to keep me out of harms way and do what is best for me. I prayed for the people involved. I didn't receive what I thought was best for me, but I did get what He knew was best for me. I spent more quiet time with Him, and for that He began blessing me with a fresher focus on my family, my music, and my speaking that I thought I already had. He allowed me to create numerous songs in both secular and non-secular categories. He moved me to write songs praising Him. He allowed me to achieve accolades even while incarcerated. He nurtured and strengthened my relationships with my immediate and extended family. He had me touch the hearts of others through songs. All because I let my faith in Him guide me, and He still isn't finished!

Wright

Do you witness to others?

Walls

Absolutely! I don't have a choice but to witness to others, because He's been so good to me. I've been witnessing throughout this entire interview. I have friends and family going through or heading towards the same devastating wall I've hit, and I believe He has put us in each other's lives to meet at this crossroad to share so we can salvage our families. He's been so good to me to the point where I question whether I'm worthy. I mean why should He take care of me when I have not traveled in the footsteps of His son...consistently. I can only surmise that He knows my heart, and just like a father, as I mentioned earlier with regards to the Jabez book, He desires to give us all we need and then some. That's a powerful proclamation; and subsequently blessings are bestowed upon us even when we fall short, because we serve a most gracious and merciful Lord. I have told many a person that if God were only about justice, if we were getting what we deserved, neither they nor I would be standing amidst each other, because we have not come close to what He wants us to be. Fortunately, He is a forgiving God.

Wright

What areas of faith do you feel you're weakest and strongest at, Darryl?

Walls

I am a very logical and analytical person. When you examine the dimensions of behavior known as the DISC model, you can place me in the "Dominance" quadrant. This means my personality tendencies include: getting immediate results; causing action; accepting challenges; making quick decisions; questioning the status quo; taking authority; managing trouble; and solving problems. So, when God places me in a position that I cannot rely on my dominant style tendencies and I have to rely on Him, it temporarily destabilizes me. It is at this point that I am weakest and begin to reach out to God for a better understanding. I will also seek out my spiritual support system within my family and friends circle like my mother & father (with me in spirit), Aunt Cookie & Uncle Greg, Aunt Flo, Aunt Sara, Joe & Gail, Yvonne, Jon & Joy, Uncle Al, Alan, Leo & Karen, Lauren & Brian, Angie & Demetrius, Albert & Toni, Jai, Eddie, Joe, Gary, Greg T., Lawrence W., Mo, and others so I can exchange thoughts and see if I may have missed something. During this strengthening process, I include the dynamics of the Situational Leadership model I discuss in my academic, corporate and faith based presentations. Designed by Dr. Paul Hershey, this model identifies the follower's readiness and how a person or team moves through the four phases of "readiness" or what I call "followership." For example, if I place God as the leader, and myself as the follower, I can see of how He moves from *telling, to selling,* to *participating with me,* to finally *delegating* tasks **to** me that will demonstrate and strengthen my faith. Every time I used to get introduced to a new challenge, I would revert back to the 1st quadrant of being *"directed"* for a certain period of time (destabilization). As my faith grows, I can see it takes **_less_** time to make the transition from quadrant 1 (being *directed* by Him) to quadrant 4 (where He is just *observing*) and I can effectively measure the time it takes me to ramp back up to the 4th quadrant.

Insofar as my strongest is concerned, I feel that would be when the challenge parallels the dimensions or traits of my dominant style behavior or when I am lifting the spirits of another. I've been blessed with opportunities to share my thoughts at Bishop M.D. Williams' church and at the 43rd Sandy F. Ray Institute's Christian Education

Week where I will facilitate a one-week Leadership Development
Workshop for the youth and community.

Wright

Have you ever lost or questioned your faith?

Walls

I can't say I've ever lost faith. I can only attest to the fact that my
faith continues to be challenged, and refined, and that God has carried me many times when I thought I was walking along side Him.

Wright

What value does faith have in your life?

Walls

Everything and everyone revolves around faith. It's the very core
of the mental, spiritual, and emotional dimensions we call life. Without faith, I'm merely surviving. Faith gives me the opportunity to live
and feel the connectivity between my confident expectancy and what I
like to call His limitless deific deliverance.

Wright

How do you know that *you* know what faith is?

Walls

I know because there are other people who did not have faith in
God, and have dealt with the same, similar, or greater drowning circumstances and never made it above life's waters of trials. Some have
even committed suicide. I remember my Uncle Greg telling me a story
about a friend of his who went through a devastating divorce and he
was never himself again. He spent countless hours just staring out
the windows as if his family was going to return home or the answer
to all of his problems was going to suddenly appear. I understand
that feeling, I relate and I empathize with the feeling. I know because
God has provided a myriad of examples of faith dating back before
and after His son's death. I know because there was a woman who,
because of her faith level, stopped Jesus in his tracks and when she
touch the hem of His garment it made her whole. You know about
that, Dave. I know because of the men in the book of Matthew that
were once blind, but Jesus told them that if they had faith in Him, if
they believed that He could restore their sight, they would be able to

see, and they did! I know because in the same book of Matthew He renders yet another example of having *little* faith when His disciples woke him up while crossing the lake to calm the storms. God has given us faith measurement tools so we can effectively gauge ourselves and make modifications in our behavior accordingly. God meets us at our level of faith; the greater the faith, the more powerful the encounter, the richer the blessing. What an incentive! I know, I know what faith is!

Wright

Is there a message that you would like to leave with our readers?

Walls

You know, it's often said that faith is believing on the unseen. That's almost a norm. That's what everyone relates to. That believing on the unseen is faith. If we take a closer look at that statement, if we pull out what I call our Renoir de la Thee Master instead of our Renoir de la Desaster this is what we will find: Lets say a child wanted to be a neurosurgeon when he grew up. We would have to prepare him and ourselves in and effort to try to get him there. Remember, I said *try*. We would have to make sure we fed him right, clothed him right, so he would be comfortable as they learned, send him to the right schools, have the money to pay for the schools, contact others in the field to get recommendations on steps we might have to take, establish how much time it might take, ensure the child studies daily, instill the right ethical and moral values to support his endeavor, provide exemplary levels of encouragement, create a nest egg for potential specialized academic tutors targeted specifically at mind proliferation, and the list goes on. We have to do all this just to give our child a fighting chance. All of this is based on the anticipated and hopeful results. In essence, it's the unseen. Unseen, because we can't tell the future, there's no guarantees. The future, is the unseen. It's just like the wind. I mean, it's passed you by. You knew it blew by you, but it remains unseen. Yet we are banking on the results and might even be disappointed if it is not achieved. But, all God asks us to do is read, study, follow, and spread His word. In short, the acronym that's used in behavioral training is EX-DEM-PRA-FO; explain, demonstrate, practice, and follow-up, and He will prepare a place for us in His kingdom. It's that simple. A place where attendance is taken everyday, and sickness, pain, strife, stress, cancer, leukemia, sickle cell, aids, common cold, surgery, asthma, heart attacks, blindness, old age, death, drugs, alcohol, divorce, 9/11, fighting, fornication, adultery, stealing, distrust, lying, pedophiles, rapist, arson, cults, and all that's negative on these mundane shores, nonproductive, and evil would not answer when they are called. Most importantly, God guarantees it, but it is predicated on your level of faith. That's your key to the entrance to the gates. So trust God! There will be times when God doesn't lift the darkness from you, but you should trust Him anyway. Have a pre-established conviction that He will come through for you and will do what's in your best interest. Not what *you* may think is in your best interest, but what He knows to be in your best interest. You know, as I heard Reverend Ireland who pastors Christ Church here in Montclair say, "Know that if He is testing you, He has already approved you and you must thank Him for having the faith in you to handle the challenges He sends you." I agree one hundred and fifty percent. You have to... Dave, you have to know. And you can hear I'm excited about this. You have to know that when you come through those rolling sea billows, His process will strengthen you and give you a better understanding of His way not yours! Eventually, you will sing with an emphatic conviction, "*It Is Well With My Soul.*"

Wright

Today we have been talking to Darryl C. Walls who is an accomplished leadership developer, keynote speaker, trainer and teacher. He empowers people and as we have found out today, is a man of faith. Thank you so much Darryl for being with us today on *Conversations on Faith.*

Walls

Thank you very much Dave, and I'm looking forward to future interactions.

About The Author

As the founder of **MINDS**, Darryl C. Walls specializes in leadership development and keynote speaking, possessing 25 years of combined experience. Coaching one-on-one or speaking to crowds in excess of 2000, he resonates a spirituality that flows as a conduit throughout his presentations. Awarded numerous accolades and honors for his leadership and teambuilding skills, his timeless message of practical goal setting, and his road map for optimizing professional potential is a testament to the mantra **M**ental **I**ntensity **N**aturally **D**etermines **S**uccess.

Darryl C. Walls

MINDS

Mental **I**ntensity **N**aturally **D**etermines **S**uccess

Phone: 973.675.3467

Fax: 973.414.9245

Email: dcwminds@verizon.net

www.darrylwalls.com

Chapter 11

BOB LENZ

THE INTERVIEW

David E. Wright (Wright)

Today we are talking to Bob Lenz. Bob Lenz doesn't want to see young people cheated out of life. The most devastating thing he has ever seen is that 60% of all youth at some point consider death to be more appealing than life. Bob wants to help youth embrace life, not give up on it. Through his speaking opportunities, he easily connects with youth by sharing valuable biblical principles intertwined with stories and personal experiences that help them deal with real life. He explores sober issues facing youth while using his unique gift of humor and his message of hope, worth, courage, and respect to help ignite their faith and capture purpose in their lives. Bob Lenz speaks to over 100 thousand teens and parents across North America each year through school assembly programs, community outreaches, professional conferences, and state or national church events. His range of topics vary greatly, but he is especially effective in the areas of making positive choices, leadership, self image, suicide prevention, as well as preventing drug and alcohol abuse. In addition to speaking, Bob is president of Life Promotions, a non-profit youth ministry located in Appleton, Wisconsin, with a mission to build bridges to youth through authentic, relevant, and relationally based programs and events. Bob has spoken in 49 states over the past 20 years as well as internationally, and is a member of the National Speakers Association. Bob Lenz, welcome to *Conversations on Faith*!

Bob Lenz (Lenz)
Thank you, David.

Wright
Bob, you work in the public school system. What do you see as one of the biggest concerns of teens today?

Lenz
Well to me, David, I think one of the biggest needs is to convince youth they are valuable, and that they can choose to live life to the fullest. I see so many kids today not knowing their value, not knowing their worth. Look at what happened on September 11th. We lost over 3,000 lives on that day—3,000 *valuable* lives. It's obvious from our reaction to that event that we view life as valuable and important. Just look what we are doing for the fight against terrorism so that another 9/11 doesn't happen again. Over 100 billion dollars is being spent on the fight against terror.

Yet, every year in America alone, we lose 30,000 lives to suicide. So my question is, "What are we doing to fight this domestic terrorist, the internal terrorism that's going on called 'suicide'?" Every two hours another teenager commits suicide. That's twelve teenagers every 24 hours! Every two hours a young person makes the ultimate and desperate statement, saying, "I'm not valuable. I have no purpose. I have no meaning for my life, and the pain is so great that I just want to check out... forever." I don't know about you, but I see that as a problem, and I want to challenge people by asking "What are we doing to convince these youths that their life has purpose?" We're putting billions into the fight on terrorism that took those 3,000 lives, but what are we doing for the 30,000 lives in America every year that are taken from our society through self-inflicted suicide? These young people are convinced they're not worth anything, and I want to do everything I can to convince them of the truth—that they do have value and purpose.

Wright
What are the issues in a youth's life that would be driving this reality?

Lenz

You know, David, before I even answer that, I want to confess that sometimes our answers, as Christians, may sound simple. Maybe that's because the gospel really is simple. But, when we over simplify the gospel in areas of application, we insult the educated. We expose our own ignorance, and I think we blaspheme the God who is all-knowing. We still need to address the realities of depression and things that are treatable through professional help and medication. But, with that said, I believe if you look at it, the answer to what is driving the difficult issues facing youth today is community, or the breakdown of it.

When somebody is suicidal they talk about giving things away, and that happens in 31% of the cases. Many talk about writing a goodbye letter. That happens in about 33% of the cases. But, youth who make a statement indicating their lack of value or feelings of despair happens 78 to 81% of the times—statements of helplessness, statements of hopelessness, and statements of worthlessness. They are saying, "No one can help the situation I'm in. There is no way out. It's hopeless. There's no light at the end of the tunnel, and it's not going to get better." Without hope, there's no purpose and there's no future. Youth contemplating suicide feel worthless. They believe that no one could possibly understand or know where they're coming from. They can't imagine anyone understanding their pain. Once they're convinced they're alone *in* society, they're convinced they have no value *to* society. They think, "What worth could I possibly have?"

So, I believe that the ultimate issue, or breakdown in the lives of many youth, is found in the absence of community. More specifically, the breakdown is revealed in an absence of community found in a personal relationship with God through Christ Jesus. There is a vacuum in our lives, an emptiness, a God-shaped void. I believe that it is best filled only through Christ and His community, a community of family, a neighborhood, a youth group, a team. Yes, I'll be even so bold as to say a community of believers called the church. I believe that the breakdown of the community called the church is the main reason driving this reality for young people today. You see, Christ, God himself in the Trinity, exists for community and relationship. The Father, Son, and Spirit are the perfection of love. That's why Hebrews 10:25 tells us not to forsake the assembling of believers. Hey, keep getting together. Here's what we're told to do: Stimulate one another to love and do good deeds. First is love. That's relationship. That's meaning—relationship with God and relationship with one another. Then, it tells us to do good deeds, meaning what? Significance. That's purpose. There's a reason you are here. There's a purpose you are here. It's to live in relationship with others and to make a difference.

Wright

You seem to be pessimistic about the state of youth. Shouldn't we look at the positive?

Lenz

You know, I'm in high schools almost every day of the week during the school year, and one of the biggest problems I see youth, especially the non-churched youth, having with the church or Christians today is the same problem that Jesus had with the religious people 2000 years ago. We like to think that our society is so advanced, but the state of human nature hasn't changed. You can hear youth saying, "You know, you look good on the outside. You look and sound so optimistic, and you're being really positive, but something's not right." What's not right? Youth are smart enough to know when people put on a front showing that everything is great on the outside, that those people are most likely dying on the inside. "They're full of dead man's bones," is what Jesus said. You know what Jesus is really saying? You're fake! You're living a pretense. I think Jesus would say that kind of faith is a phony, pretentious, religious front that can't handle the real issues of the world. I think a lot of Christians today, because of that, hide out in church, and we preach a positive self-image instead of preaching the Cross of Christ. And we preach a phoniness of 'just smile, God loves you' instead of the cross that really will produce character. One of the biggest things I've seen a longing for among youth today is authenticity. They want people who are real, and youth have an innate sense to know when something isn't. Religion is not true Christianity when it just wears a mask to avoid the pains of life.

Wright

To hide out in church is a scary thought.

Lenz

Exactly. If Jesus' plans and the historical reality of his empty tomb are true, then He can handle the realities of my life. That's not pessimism. It's realism. We can have a God who steps into our pain instead of using religion, or church, as a way to avoid and cover up the pain.

Wright

So, if there is a God, then why is there so much suffering today?

Lenz

You know, a lot of people use the realities of suffering as their argument against a loving God. I know that there is suffering, and we live in a broken world. We live in a world that was designed to be in relationship with God and in relationship with one another. We were designed to choose love as the major reason and force in our lives, to know God and to love others. But, I think what has happened is we chose power and possession instead of love and relationship. I think it's clear that the word of God says in John 10 that the enemy comes to kill, steal, and destroy. Why does God come? So that you might have life. I'll just be honest and say that I don't understand it all, but I know that the words of Elizabeth Elliot have really helped me, "If God was small enough for me to understand, he wouldn't be big enough for me to worship." Even when you can't understand why, the one thing we need to know is that God is still good, and he still is sovereign. I personally don't believe that means God causes the pain. I believe what sovereign means is that he's bigger than it. Somehow we have a God that can work the worst things in this world out for the good. I've seen it so many times. We have a God who understands. He took pain, he took suffering and he entered the real world. We don't have a God that just sees us as "out there." We have a God who understands and "is there" for us.

Wright

A young person may say, "Bob, it's easy for you to talk about suffering, but you don't know what it's like to live in my pain." How do you respond to that?

Lenz

I think one of the first things that we as a church need to stop saying is, "We understand. I have been there." Because, you know what, even it if looks like we're going through the same thing, we can't understand the uniqueness of that individual. What we can do is listen, share our own pain and empathize with theirs. We have a God who understands, but as people we can only say, "Hey, this is what I've been through." For myself, I think the biggest thing I could do to answer that question is tell them my story.

I was raised in a family with two handicapped kids. My sister, Lois, has mental retardation, and my brother, Tim, who I learned so many lessons from, had cerebral palsy, along with mental retardation, scoliosis and curvature of the spine. Half of his body grew and half of it stopped. He had epilepsy with grand mal seizures and eventually died from his physical problems when he was 19. I remember so many times when I was mocked. In the first grade I found out I had a speech impediment and was put in another class that was specialized—you know, "Special Ed." Other kids would say, "There goes Bob. He's retarded just like his brother." Everybody laughed, except me. It hurt so bad. Eventually, I had to ask the question and say to myself, "What am I going to do with all this pain? Do I have value? Does my family have value? Then why all this suffering?" While my situation was unique, my pain was real. That is one thing that each person has in common. Every person has pain. We have a God who doesn't just say, "Hey, make believe it's not real." But, he'll enter it and through his cross will show us that even in pain, there is meaning. Even in pain, there are lessons. God can turn something that looks bad to the world into something wonderful. That's true of my brother, Tim, and my sister, Lois, who have been one of the biggest blessings in my whole life.

Wright

How can you personally believe in a God who loves you when you've had so many hard things happen in your life?

Lenz

I don't know where else to turn. Just look at the world and see the things it keeps turning to in an effort to deal with the hard times in life. It's not working. It's just like Peter said, "To whom would we go? You alone have the words that give eternal life." When I look at the atrocities of life and the philosophies throughout history they don't hold up and they don't offer lasting answers. But, when I look at the ultimate example of Jesus who won the fight against evil, who cared about the injustices in the world, who communicated that every person needs to know there is a reason for them and needs to have a reason to live, I am convinced that he truly is the way, the truth and the life. I've been told by some people that I'm just using God as a crutch. I'd say, "You know what? You're right!" The cripple are walking again. The blind can see. The dead, people who have been dead inside, including me, are alive. We have found real life. So, the real question is: Do you want to be bitter or do you want to be better? I've seen that God isn't someone who just disassociates himself from suffering, but is right there in the midst of my suffering with me to help me through.

Wright

There's a lot of theology or teaching that says, "If you just have enough faith, nothing bad will happen to you." How do you view this?

Lenz

Let me just say loud and clear that I think it's wrong. I don't believe that. When I was in fifth grade, I asked my religion teacher why my brother, Tim, was handicapped and why I was 'normal'. And out of her ignorance, she said, "I guess God loved you more than he loved your brother, Tim."

Wright

Wow!

Lenz

I was filled with such rage at her answer that I got up to kill her. I didn't know how I was going to do it—maybe with lead poisoning from a #2 pencil. But, a bunch of others stopped me and one of my teachers, Mr. Romenesko, who was a coach of mine, grabbed me and said, "Bob, she's wrong." I was swinging, and thrashing, and crying. I knew she was wrong, but deep down inside there was a part of me that was afraid she was right.

Years later I realized that I needed to see this from the perspective of God's word itself. It says in Matthew 5:45 that the sun comes up on the righteous and the unrighteous. It rains on the good and the bad alike. It doesn't say that if we just have more faith then nothing bad can happen to us. God is not out to hurt us. In Matthew 7:25 it says there were two builders. One builds on the solid rock. One builds on sand. On both of them, the winds come. The rains come. The storms of life will come. So, it doesn't say that if you just love God there won't be any storms. Jesus himself said, "In this world you will have tribulations. But, be in good cheer. I have overcome the world. I am bigger than that." There's a theology being taught in many circles today that tries to convince us that, "if we just have a little more faith, then…"

It's what's called a theology of glory, not the theology of the cross. You've got to see a God who is not just going to ride in triumph one day, but a God who humbled himself and became Man and took on the cross and suffered. He's personally familiar with our suffering because he became like us.

Wright

If God is in control of all things, in other words if he is sovereign, then why doesn't he stop some things like rape? Where is he when bad things like that happen?

Lenz

That's a tough one. I've talked to people who have been raped and I can see the shame and the stripping away of dignity that happens. I've found it hard to find the right words to say to them, because there's nothing that can take away their pain. What I do have to say is from what I know of God and what I know of the man Jesus—God who became Man. It's what I know from his word and from my relationship with him.

When I've talked to girls and guys who have been sexually abused, I've said, "Think back to the day this person hurt you. From what you know of the bible, if it would have been Christ there instead of that person, do you believe you would have been violated and abused? Would he have done it? Would it have happened?" And they all have said, "No, of course not." Then, I ask, "If the person who did this to you was truly surrendered to the lordship of Christ in their life, would they have done it?" And they say, "Well, no! But still, why didn't Jesus stop it?" That's so hard to answer, but you know the fear, degradation and lack of dignity you felt when you were being forced to do something against your will? Well, would you expect Jesus to force himself on you or anyone else to make you do what he wanted? Wouldn't it result in the same feelings? Jesus would never force himself on us like somebody who rapes and does evil things to someone else. God is love and love does not force. Love does not instill fear. It casts it out. God wouldn't force us or the person who did this to you to respond to his will and desire for us. It's our choice to receive or reject him. Isaiah 54:15 tells how if you're fiercely assailed, if you're attacked or if you're hurt by somebody, that it is not of the Lord. But, in his bigness, he can turn it around into something good. That doesn't mean it's from the Lord. The Lord doesn't want evil for us. He knows the plans. In Jeremiah it says that God wants to prosper us, not to

harm us. But, there will be a day when all wrongs will be made right
and justice will be served.

Wright

If God doesn't promise that nothing bad will happen if I believe
then, what good is faith?

Lenz

Without faith, there's no way to please God. There is no hope.
What faith does is bring hope in the midst of the pain. It brings reason. Look at some of the people that are really making a difference in
this world today. It's because they are people of faith. They are people
who can have faith in the midst of the storm. There's a guy named
Joseph in the Bible, you know, the one with the coat of many colors.
His jealous brothers beat him, threw him in a hole to die, and then
said, "Ah ha! Let's sell him. Let's get some money off him." But, when
you fast forward through the story you'll find that the very thing that
seemed a tragedy ended up working out for the good of an entire nation because of the faith of Joseph, even for the good of those who intended to kill him. What man intended for evil, God turned into good.
Look at Christ in the midst of when he himself came to the point in
his suffering where he cried out to God and said, "My God, my God,
why have you forsaken me?" Even in the midst of his own pain and
suffering he was an example for us. At that turning point in history
our only hope said, "Into your hands I commit my spirit." When you
have the kind of faith that's displayed through obedience and surren-
dering your life to God despite your suffering, it's the very thing that
can turn the world around.

Wright

Do you believe that God still does miracles or was it reserved just
for Bible times?

Lenz

I believe that God is the same yesterday, today, and forever. I believe in the God of the Bible. Those aren't just stories. I believe the
Bible to be true. I believe what it says, even the parts that are hard
for me to understand or explain. I believe that God still does miracles.
But, the biggest thing that I know God wants is to advance his kingdom, to show people that he is who he said he is, and it results in big
miracles. I believe the biggest miracle of all is still a changed life. Je-

sus himself said that he was sent to heal the brokenhearted, to proclaim liberty to the captives and recovery of sight to the blind, to set at liberty those who are oppressed. The biggest miracle is still "I was lost, but now I am found." The biggest miracle is, "I was a detriment to society, and now I am being a blessing. I was part of the problem, now I'm part of the answer. I caused pain for many, and now I'm trying to bring comfort and hope and healing." That's still the biggest miracle.

Wright

So, you're implying that people should spend most of their spirituality searching for wholeness?

Lenz

I guess it depends on how you look at that. If I'm saying that we need to live the rest of our lives in just finding purpose and meaning for ourselves, boy, all that sounds like is selfish philosophy. I really believe that we can find wholeness, but it's not in getting. It is found in giving yourself away. Remember those 3,000 who died on 9/11 and the 30,000 who die every year in America alone to suicide? On top of that, let's include the 30,000 children who will die today, yes, just today, from starvation or complications that are preventable. If we only search for our own wholeness, where does that leave others who may be facing a similar demise? Can you imagine if everyone just spent their time searching for ways to fulfill their own personal wholeness? I can't even imagine what the world would look like. Jesus said that, "My meat, my food, my nourishment, my *wholeness* is to do the will of the Father who has sent me and to finish his business." I think we have work to be done, and I think that real wholeness is not just about getting more medicine for our own souls, in whatever form it may take. Ironically, the medicine for our own souls is found in the words of Jesus; "freely you received, now freely give." I want to cry out to a youth generation out there to say, "There are 30 thousand kids dying. Don't tell me you don't have a purpose. We need you! Be a part of the answer. Be a part of the message." We see one out of six kids in America alone living in poverty, and I say, "We need you!" We see our streets deteriorating and I say "We need you!" We see our school systems being invaded with drugs and alcohol and 1.8 million teenagers in 2001 alone that were victims of violent crimes, and I say, "We need you! We need teachers. We need nurses. We need coaches and people as pastors and moms and dads. We need you so." The biggest wholeness is not in finding yourself, but in giving yourself away! There's a call, and that's where purpose is found.

Wright

You know what confuses me more than anything else is when people ask me, "Does God still perform miracles?" You know, my question is not, "Does God perform miracles?" My question is, "Why in the world don't you see the miracles?"

Lenz

Exactly.

Wright

In my opinion, not only does he do it, he does it more often because there are more people.

Lenz

That's right.

Wright

And I would hope we'd be getting better at it too.

Lenz

Right. Well, he said, "You'll do greater things that I." Because when he walked the earth, even though he had miraculous powers, Jesus was limited to the humanity of one person. Now he's saying, "You are my church. You are my hands. You are my feet. Go out and do an act of kindness. Go out and love in my name, and bring that home. Bring it to the people who are suffering from anorexia. Bring it to the people who are suffering from depression and thoughts of suicide. Bring it to the people who have been abused physically and emotionally and sexually. Bring it to those who are part of a broken society. Go and bring them home."

Wright

What would you say in closing to convince someone that God still loves them even when things are going badly?

Lenz

You know, I think my mom taught me best. She said, "If you look at circumstances, you'll always question if God loves you. But, if you look at the cross there's no way to doubt his love." If the claim is true that Jesus was really God come to earth, Emanuel, God with us, and you really look at the verse that says, "For God so loved the world that he gave his only Son," you can't deny that his love is true. Look at the cross and see it for what it really is—the ultimate demonstration of love. The cross shouldn't just be lifted high in our cathedrals and churches on Sunday morning, but in our everyday walk of life, for there is hope. There is comfort. There is purpose. There is the reason for life itself. There is the thing that can fill the vacuum inside and cause us to go out and make a change in the world.

Wright

What a great conversation! I've learned a lot today. Some of the things I probably didn't want to know; the statistics about youth suicide are just really, really scary.

Lenz

It's still the third leading cause of death for people ages 15 to 24. The number one thing that kills young people is car accidents, and sadly, 90% of those fatal car accidents are caused by someone who is intoxicated. So, even in that statistic you can see how youth are searching for ways to find meaning and significance. We've got to give them hope and a purpose. The scarier fact is that while 12 teenagers are committing suicide every 24 hours, as many as 1200 to 1800 are attempting it every day! They are looking for hope. Many of them are saying that they want to live and they want to die in the same breath. What they're really saying is, "Help!" They're saying, "Is there hope?" If there is just one thing I can close with, David, I would cry out to every teenager on this planet starting with America and say, "You are valuable! You have worth! There is hope! There is help available and it's in God and his people."

Wright

Today we've been talking to Bob Lenz and we have also found out he is at least one person on this planet that doesn't want to see young people cheated out of life. Hopefully, our readers will join him in his quest. Bob, thank you so much for taking your time today to be with us on *Conversations on Faith*!

Lenz

Hey, thank you, David, and God bless you.

About The Author

Considered one of the nation's top youth speakers, Bob easily connects with his audiences by sharing valuable biblical principles intertwined with stories and personal experiences that help youth deal with real life while re-igniting their faith. He explores sober issues while using his unique gift of humor. His messages of hope, worth, courage and respect ignite an interest in young people that results in adults and youth alike being moved from laughter to tears, leaving with a message they won't soon forget.

Bob Lenz speaks to over 100,000 teens and parents across North America each year through school assembly programs, evangelistic rallies, professional conferences and state or national Church events. School assembly programs are often followed by an evening community outreach where Bob is able to share the Gospel message of grace and the unconditional love of God.

In addition to speaking, Bob is the President of Life Promotions - a non-profit youth oriented ministry located in Appleton, Wisconsin with a mission to build bridges to youth through authentic, relevant and relationally-based programs and events. Bob has spoken in 49 states over the past twenty years, and is a member of the National Speakers Association.

Bob Lenz

Life Promotions, Inc.

213 E. College Ave.

Appleton, Wisconsin 54911

Phone: 800.955.5433

Fax: 920.738.5587

E-mail: speaking@lifepromotions.com

www.lifepromotions.com

Chapter 12

GAIL RICHARDSON

THE INTERVIEW

David E. Wright (Wright)

Today we are talking to Gail Richardson. Gail is a Certified Public Speaker. She is the host of "Word Up" a gospel talk show on WGBB 1240AM in New York. She is also the President of the New York chapter of the National African-American Speakers Association. She is a certified consultant on women's issues, diversity, and youth and young adult issues. She is an excellent workshop presenter who is experienced in working with women and troubled adolescents. Gail is a Missionary who led a group to Nairobi, Kenya to explore the situation with AIDS Orphans in 1996. She is the author of *Prepared To Be Married*. She recently released a CD entitled, *Can We Talk—It's A Sista' Thing*, a series of inspirational sermonettes for women. She has appeared on Praise the Lord on TBN. Her latest project is a videotape entitled, *Sex Sells Your Soul to Hell*. Gail Richardson, welcome to *Conversations on Faith*!

Gail Richardson (Richardson)

Hi, I'm so glad to be here.

Wright

Tell me, in your opinion, what is a faith driven Christian to you?

Richardson

A faith driven Christian to me is one who walks not looking, not seeing, not knowing, just trusting. So many times we have to have an outcome or have knowledge of what the outcome of something is going to be before we will attempt it. So, to me a faith driven Christian is one who just doesn't know, but trusts.

Wright

How would that fit into goal setting. A lot of people in business today are goal setters. Are you saying that you just go and trust and not set personal goals?

Richardson

Oh, no!! I'm a very firm believer in goal setting and writing the vision down so that you may run when you see it. But, for instance, like with the African Ministry, I was very clear that God had told us to go to Africa and to help the AIDS orphans. At that particular time Daniel Arap Moi was the President, and he was not even acknowledging the fact that there was a problem with AIDS orphans. The Lord spoke to my heart all the way over here to go and to make people aware of what was going on. I knew what I had to do, I just didn't know how. I didn't know who He was going to use to help me to get it done, but I just had to start somewhere. So, that's what I did.

Wright

What other experiences have you had that identify you as a faith driven Christian?

Richardson

I would say even in everyday life. When I first got married, my husband and I had an apartment. The people who owned the apartment above us were from Haiti. They were getting ready to move some of their relatives in and told us that we would have to move. The Spirit said to me that we were going to get a house. I told my husband, "We have to buy a house." He's looking at the income and he's looking at the fact that we are a young married couple with no credit and no experience, not a whole lot of money, and he's saying, "It's utterly impossible to buy a house." And I said, "The Lord said buy a house." He said, "So, what are you going to do about that? That's what you're telling me, but the facts say different." I said, "I'm going to go to a realtor, tell him the facts, and tell him that we need a house." That's exactly what I did. I can be honest with you. He didn't go. I went by myself. What I can tell you is that we did end up getting a house. We didn't go to another apartment. What happened was we were able to rent the house with the option to buy. It was cheaper than if we had gotten an apartment.

Wright

What has been the largest challenge to your faith in God?

Richardson

The untimely death of my husband. He succumbed to colon cancer at the age of 33.

Wright

My goodness!

Richardson

Yes. That left me a widow at 34 with three children.

Wright

My wife is a colon cancer survivor.

Richardson

Praise God!

Wright

Some make it and some don't. I think the ratio of survivors is still pretty bad. It's 50%.

Richardson

It's very slim. Very slim.

Wright

So, during that time, was your family in an upheaval?

Richardson

Well, you know based on our faith, I can honestly say, "No." The one who felt the impact the hardest, I do believe, was my firstborn son. He was 11 and just going into adolescence when this happened. My other son was six and my daughter was two and a half. They were very young and they were looking to me and I knew it. I realized that whatever they saw in me was how they were going to react. So, I really had to rely on my faith in God and the belief that God doesn't make mistakes, that He doesn't do anything wrong and believe that my husband was in a better place. I was actually with him when he died. I knew that he was with the Lord, so I had that peace. I had to be able to convey it to the children in a way that they would really know mommy means what she's saying. I really had to let my faith kick in. I had to be able to do it with a firm belief that if we live the same way daddy lived, we'll all see each other again. The most important thing I can do is to live that way and help you to live that way too.

Wright

In my case, when our family went through that, I was overwhelmed by the help, the love and the consideration that the church community gave us.

Richardson

Yes!

Wright

Was that your experience?

Richardson

Yes, and it was two-fold with us because by the time he passed, my father was Pastor in our church and we had support from the church that we came out of. There were two church families, the Salem Missionary Baptist Church family and the Shiloh Baptist Church family that were there for us during that time. The outpouring of love and support that came from both church families was just amazing.

Wright

How has your faith affected your life to date?

Richardson

I believe sometimes it causes me to go through experiences that are sort of "Job" like, because living by faith, you're living the substance of things hoped for, the evidence of things not seen. I tend to live my life according to what God says and not what man thinks. A lot of times I would be the rebel without a cause to people who wouldn't understand what God is telling me to do. That affects my life from time to time.

Wright
What Bible person do you identify your level of faith with? You just mentioned Job. Is that the one you most identify?

Richardson
No.

Wright
Thank goodness! I was thinking of saying, "poor old Gail!"

Richardson
No, not Job. I would say Joseph.

Wright
Joseph? How so?

Richardson
Well, throughout my life, in different encounters, I've always had favor from God and I know it. On jobs and places that I've gone to, I didn't always know why. I understand now the relationship that I had with Him. I just knew that there was something different about me. When you are young, you can sometimes tend to be kind of cocky and other people aren't too pleased with you.

Wright
Right.

Richardson
I can understand how Joseph could bring on the ire of his brothers because of his favor. I know I brought it on in many situations in school and different things because of the confidence that that favor gives you, and people mistake it for arrogance or conceit.

Wright
I assume you stay away from bright colored coats.

Richardson

I love them.

Wright

You'd better watch it. Somebody will throw you in a hole.

Richardson

Oh, they've tried, believe me!

Wright

How would you describe your personal relationship with God?

Richardson

Intimate, I'm very much in a committed relationship with God.

Wright

How does one keep a relationship like that going when things are not going so well?

Richardson

Well, you know, some friends of mine are working on a book titled, *I love You, But I Don't Like You Very Much*. It's talking about how to work through difficult times in your marriage. What I've come to understand is that the joy of the Lord is my strength. I have to work at my relationship with Him just like I had to work at my relationship with my husband. There were days I didn't like him very much. There were days that things didn't go very well, but I always had to love him. That's the same method that I use to sustain my relationship with God. Even when things are bad certain times in my life I know I'm doing what God has told me to do. I will encounter different things, financial difficulty, and then I read things like He makes provision for the vision. I'm saying, "So, where is mine, because this is not my vision, this is yours?" Even being completely honest, when my husband first passed, my inner thought was "I'm doing everything just the way You told me to. I've been faithful all these years. I've turned my life around. I'm walking with the Lord. We're both in church. We're training the children the way they should go. And, now you are taking my husband and other people's husbands live." But, then I had to say, "your will and not mine," knowing that God knows what's best for me. Whatever it is, He doesn't make mistakes. Staying in the Word, having a regular prayer life and constant communication is what keeps me close to God.

Wright

I've been asked the question about prayer so many times in my life, it's strange when people ask me if I pray. And when I say, "Yes, I do," they say "Well, does God ever talk to you?" I say, "Yes, He does." They say, "Have you ever heard Him?" I say, "Well, to be honest with you, not audibly."

Richardson

No?

Wright

I guess the fact is, whether or not you believe that prayer works is a function of whether or not you believe someone is listening.

Richardson

Yeah, it would be. I know He listens because He has responded to me on more than one occasion audibly, and I know He's talking. I mean I've had that "The Master's World" experience with God where nobody is hearing anything but me.

Wright

That would be a little scary.

Richardson

The first time it was. It really was, but it doesn't happen a lot. When He wants to get my attention, if He doesn't come to me directly audibly, He will come through a *preached* word. He'll come through a prophetic word from somebody I have never seen in my life and they know nothing about me, and they come and tell me something that I've been discussing in my private time with God. That has happened to me on more than one occasion. But, the audible stuff is usually correction or chastisement when I've been given a directive by God and I do something different, or refuse to do what He tells me to do. That doesn't happen often, but every once in a while, if the truth be told.

Wright

After all the Christian upbringing and the Christian work that you've done, to whom do you minister today?

Richardson

Mostly to young people. God has given me what He's entitled a Marriage Preparation Ministry. I've found out that young people can relate, not just young people, most people can relate to the fact that what it takes to make a relationship with a man or a woman work is what it takes to make a relationship with God work. When I use that as an analogy, then people understand and they are able to grasp it. There's a group of young people that I'm working with, I've worked with numbers of young people that have come out of our church, but this particular group that I'm working with now, I call them "The Joshua Generation." I really see a breakthrough and they're coming through with an understanding of holy living. Not just what it is, but the application of it where a lot of young people at that particular age don't want to live holy. These are high school students. These are junior high school students. Young people in college. And they're in Bible study. They're in prayer meetings and they are going into the ministry. They are looking at careers in Christian entertainment. They are looking to see what they need to do for the Lord and discovering their purpose in the body of Christ. There's a group home across the street from me. I'm getting ready to start conducting Bible studies with the young ladies there at their request. Now, I just told them what the Lord placed on my heart and I said, "Do you want me to do this?" And they went, "Yes! Please!" I said, "Okay." So, they are going to start coming over and we're going to have Bible studies in the living room because they want a closer relationship, but they don't know how to get it. I host a radio talk show on WGBB 1240 AM in Long Island and that's another opportunity for me to teach life application of Biblical principles to anyone who listens. That's what I do because it's my passion that everyone know God the way I do.

Wright

I commend you working with youth. I say it's just unbelievable what they have to go through. I've got two children, a daughter that's 41 and a son that's 40, and then, I have a 14 year old as well. She just entered high school last week as a freshman. The first two, teaching them about God and having them try to live Christian lives was a lot easier in their time. It's unbelievable what all kinds of influences, non-God influences, come at my 14 year old through the internet and through the television set.

Richardson

Yes.

Wright

Television programming has just, I mean for Christians at least, has just gotten to be almost unbearable.

Richardson

It is awful.

Wright

It's really harder. A lot of people complain about the youth of to-day, but my heart goes out to them. I don't see how they get through it with all of those visual images through their mind daily.

Richardson

That's why it's up to us. We have a call to work with them on the transforming of their minds through the Word of God because we know that Greater is He that's in us than he that's in the world. It's up to us not only to create visual pictures for them, but to really be-come walking epistles, so that they can have Christian role models that they can really follow. People who say, "Okay, so and so is really doing this." You can tell them how you are doing it, not just that I do it, or do it because I do it, but why you should do it. It all goes back to one word—sex. That's what's tempting them. That's what they see on television. That's what drives advertising. That's what's on buses. That's everywhere you go, and they're adolescents. They are coming into the stage of their sexuality. They are entering it with all of this promiscuousness all around them, and being driven by it because what they see is saying, "That's where I'm supposed to be headed." We have to counteract it with something. The only thing we have is the Word of God. Then, we have to give it to them in a way, the same way that they get it on television.

Wright

Right.

Richardson

You can't sugarcoat it.

Wright

Where do you see your ministry going?

Richardson

Well, tomorrow I have an interview on *Praise the Lord* at TBN. I believe that God is opening a doorway to expand the ministry from radio to television. I actually see a worldwide ministry. And, not so much myself, but training other people in how to conduct a Marriage Preparation Ministry.

Wright

The Marriage Preparation, are you talking about premarital counseling or just what does that entail?

Richardson

Well, first of all, it starts with being prepared to be married to the bridegroom. So, when Jesus comes back you will be ready, because we don't know the day. We don't know the hour. But, it transcends from that also into marriage between a man and a woman. What I've come to find out is God never gives me something without giving me practical experience in it. Everything that I had been doing, the book I wrote, the CD that he had me put out, the book I'm working on now, and then, he wants me to do a video called *Sex Sells Your Soul To Hell* for young people; all of these things are part of this Marriage Preparation Ministry. What it boils down to is there are couples right now in church, and I'm not talking about outside of the body, who are having weddings, but they don't have a clue about what it means to be married. Therefore, they're entering into the institution of 'holy matrimony' with the concept of "if it doesn't work, I get out," as opposed to going in saying that we're making a covenant with God and this person that is not to be taken lightly. Going in with the means that you are going to go in and do everything you can to make it work, and when you can't, you will turn it over to God who is the head of the marriage." In terms of the wife, "I can't do anything with my husband, but you can God." Go interceding in prayer to my Father in heaven to take care of the matter with my husband and trust in God to fix it. If I chose God to fix it, I don't have to do anything. But, if I look upon my capabilities, Lord, I'm going to be in divorce court.

Wright

Do you plan to use the media to expand your audience?

Richardson

I believe that's what's going to happen, yes.

Wright

The very thing that causes a lot of these problems, you're going to use to solve it?

Richardson

Exactly. I'm already looking to go forward as a sheep among wolves. I already see that coming. That's why I stay as close to God as I can, because I need to be like Daniel. When I get into the den, shut the lion's mouth because they are going to try to eat a sister.

Wright

Oh my! What is your vision for your ministry say 20 years from now?

Richardson

Twenty years from now I would like to be conducting a school that just concentrates on holy living. It would start with the Marriage Preparation Ministry, because until you enter into that kind of relationship with Him, then you can't hear from God and you really don't know what His life plan is for you. I can't tell you what His life plan is for you, but I can tell you how to get in touch with Him so He can tell you. That's what I see happening all over the world. We won't be as hopeless about certain situations as we are now. We'll remember that God is in control of everything, the government, wars, rumors of wars, everything that's going on He's in control. Then we're able to operate and do what we are here to do. That's what I see.

Wright

Are you experiencing any successes in the young people, or any people for that matter, that you are introducing to *Prepared to Be Married* training at all? Have you been doing it long enough to enjoy any successes?

Richardson

Yes, there's a couple that I met, a young couple, and when I met them they were living together. I was drawn to the young man in the spirit. The more I talked to him, the more I found out that he was a former churchgoer. He was raised in the church and had left the church based on some hurt that he had experienced. The Lord told me to tell the young woman that he's going to marry you. I was like, "I don't know these people. Why are you telling me to tell her this?" He told me to tell her that he's going to marry her. On her birthday, God had me to give her a copy of my book, *Prepare to Be Married*, as a present. I gave it to her, forgetting all about the prophetic word that God had given me for her, and shortly thereafter he came to me and he said, "Mom, she read your book. She has totally changed and I'm going to marry her." I said, "My God," and I was able to be at the wedding and witness a powerful move of the Holy Spirit when this couple were joined together. I had never seen anything like it. I was so blessed! I would say that's one success story. I've had a number of young women who have turned away from fornication, because of the teachings of the Marriage Preparation Ministry, who are living an abstinent lifestyle, even a couple of young men, one of them being my son, who is now going into the ministry. At first, he didn't want to hear anything from mom. He went from not wanting to hear anything from me to constantly sitting at my feet wanting to talk about the Lord, walking with the Lord, living for the Lord and the challenges of it. My daughter did as well. Both of them are saved. I've got one more that I'm reeling in. I said, "God, go get him."

Wright

I think maturity must be kicking in. When I was about 16 or 17, my mother was so stupid! By the time I got 21, she sure got smart within a few years.

Richardson

Oh yeah! Maturity does kick in. It makes a big difference.

Wright

What a great conversation. I want to thank you for taking this time to be here today. I wish you all the successes in the world as you continue to talk to young people and people of all ages about marriage. I wish you great successes in your fight against AIDS. That must be a devastating task to go and see people who are dying so rapidly of such a terrible illness.

Richardson

Yes, I mean we've been kind of dormant for the past couple of years, but we're beginning to feel the urge to go forth. We've been doing a lot of research and gathering materials and stuff and putting together those support pieces that we need for a return trip, and it's about to happen. I will probably be in 2004. We'll be able to go back in a force and just bring the word of God and some relief. I do believe God is in the midst of getting ready to heal a lot of those AIDS orphans, because He's getting ready to do some miraculous stuff to let people know that He is still here, just like he was. Nothing has changed. We just are not using him like we are supposed too.

Wright

Well, today we have been talking to Gail Richardson who is a Certified Public Speaker, the host of Word Up gospel talk show, and as we have found out today, a dedicated Christian, who is living out her faith. Thank you so much, Gail, for being with us today.

Richardson

Oh, you're more than welcome. Thank you for having me.

About The Author

Gail Richardson is a mother of three, a Gospel Radio Talk Show Host, a Certified Public Speaker and a Missionary to name a few. She is an active member of Shiloh Baptist Church in Brooklyn, New York. There, she serves as the Minister of Music, Sunday School Teacher and Youth & Young Peoples Coordinator. Gail has recently completed a video presentation entitled, *Sex Sells Your Soul To Hell.* The purpose of this project is to encourage our Christian brothers and sisters to practice abstinence. Gail's website is: http://www.godswillproductions.com.

Gail Richardson
41 East 10th Street
Brooklyn, New York 11218
Phone: 718.703.0245
Email : WORDUPMINISTRY@aol.com
Email: prepare2bmarried@aol.com
www.godswillproductions.com

Chapter 14

DR. CHERI WESTMORELAND

THE INTERVIEW

David E. Wright (Wright)
Today we're talking to Dr. Cheri Westmoreland. She is an educator, motivational speaker and founder of CSW Consulting Group in Cincinnati, Ohio. Dr. Westmoreland is a visionary whose personal vision is to inspire and communicate God's purpose and plan for personal development, spiritual development and excellence in service. With over 20 years of professional experience in higher education and non-profit organizations, Dr. Westmoreland has dedicated her life to empowering people to make changes in their lives and reach their full potential in Christ. Dr. Westmoreland completed her doctoral research entitled, "Faith in Action: a Descriptive Case Study of a Comprehensive Juvenile Diversion Program Sponsored by the African-American Church." Through this comprehensive juvenile diversion program the community was touched and lives of youth and families were changed. True efforts and projects such as this are the beginning point to the healing and reconciliation process for families, communities and our society. From this work, she has provided service to non-profits in the training and development area dealing with leadership, conflict resolution and diversity issues. Cheri, welcome to *Conversations on Faith.*

Dr. Cheri Westmoreland (Westmoreland)
Thank you.

Wright

What is your mission and vision for your personal and professional life?

Westmoreland

As stated in the introduction, my mission is to dream, inspire and communicate God's purpose and plan for personal development, spiritual development and excellence in service. I envision my work helping people to dream and expand how they see themselves in the world. Experiential activities are the tools that I use to help individuals tap into what God's plan is for their lives and how to reach their full potential in Christ. The process begins with understanding your natural abilities, spiritual gifts, values and passions. Once an individual has explored these areas of his or her life and can recognize his or her strengths and abilities, the development of the mission and vision statement begins. These statements can be used for guidance and assistance in the decision-making process for next steps to future opportunities as individuals work to fulfill God's plan for their lives.

Wright

If they are non-Christian do you still work with them?

Westmoreland

The mission and vision statement is a process that any and everyone can use to gain control and find direction for their life. The process is a career exploration and development model with biblical perspectives. I use the model in both Christian and secular environments.

Wright

Since you approach it from the Biblical perspective, is there a scripture that propels you to do the work you do?

Westmoreland

The foundational scripture used is Romans 8:28, "And we know that in all things God works for the good of those who love him, who have been called according to his purpose." The significance of this verse for me is the promise of God's divine protection. I diligently pursue my personal and professional work with the belief that, whatever I do, it will work for my good and for the good of others.

Wright

How can you use what most excites you to affect or change what most angers you?

Westmoreland

What most excites me is working with youth and their families and helping them to realize their full potential. As I work with youth and families, I use this time as an opportunity to break down the myths and deceptions that many families have been told about their current conditions. The goal is to have them know that God has fearfully and wonderfully made them and that he has empowered and endowed them with gifts that will help them to have prosperous lives. I have turned my personal dislike for this kind of deception and lies around and it helps me to work and fight to break all of those curses and deceptions that have kept the youth and their families in bondage. In the end, my work becomes my blessing to youth and their families.

Wright

As you speak, train and do seminars for all kinds of people—whether it's a training seminar or a keynote speech—are there key elements that you want people to come away with after hearing you speak?

Westmoreland

Four key elements have evolved from my work over the years. The first key element is my sense of compassion and my desire to have people feel that I genuinely want them to reach their full potential and to be successful. Success is in the eye of the beholder. The seminars and workshops are designed to help the audience connect with each other and experience a connection with me. The second key element is the ability to communicate God's plan and purpose to everyone regardless of their level of understanding. My desire is for everyone to walk away with some knowledge or insight that will change his or her life forever. Thirdly, my objective is to help people better understand the gifts and abilities that God has given them. Lastly, I motivate and energize people to take the information that they have heard and apply it to their lives.

Wright

Down through my life, I've heard all kinds of definitions of faith. What is faith to you?

Westmoreland

From the Biblical perspective, "Faith is being sure of what we hope for and certain for what we do not see." Faith and belief are used interchangeably in many cases, but I have heard and agree with the following: To have faith is to trust God and to believe is to rest in Christ. Faith is the work required to move towards a paradigm shift in our thinking towards trusting and continually leaning on the Lord. Believing is an action step that physically moves and positions us to begin the process of operating in faith.

Wright

I like to see faith in action. I have two very close friends whose 30-year-old son had a massive heart attack and died yesterday. Even through this period of grief and sadness, I can still see that faith shining through that in the finality, things will come out the way God has planned. How does an individual increase their faith?

Westmoreland

In Romans, Paul tells us faith comes by hearing the message, and the message is heard through the word of Christ. Exposure to biblical truths, teachings, and biblical studies will increase your level of faith. Without faith, it is impossible to please God. Our experiences in life along with our knowledge of God through study will help us to do what God has purposed for our lives and will also help us to extend our territory and accomplish more things than we could ever imagine. In addition, there will come a time that our faith will be tested. When we are tested or challenged to take a stand for what we believe, we not only grow in faith, but in character.

Wright

I think you advocate faith teams, don't you? I'm not sure what that is.

Westmoreland

A faith team is a group of individuals working together to fulfill a God-given mission or ministry. I had an opportunity to be a part of a faith team that developed an outreach program for youth and their families. The team operated in three very key concepts: courage, conviction and commitment. The faith team began with a single vision to help youth and their families become whole. The work was accomplished through counseling, group sessions, mentoring, job training and placement and parent training and education. Team members were charged to work in a particular area that complimented their expertise. The ministry evolved through prayer and faith and over 50 families were provided services in a year with volunteer assistance. The ministry had very little resources and God provided as the need was spoken. The facility needed furniture and we prayed for furniture and a call came into the office from a church member about furniture from her company to be donated to the project. Several situations occurred like that from each team member speaking a need and God providing.

Wright

It's interesting that you should mention prayer and praying for each other. Sometimes, I think if I had been a disciple I would have been walking around the earth with one of the greatest orators and one of the greatest speakers and motivators and brilliance and all the enthusiasm, but rather than ask Christ to do anything for them or teach them anything, the only thing the disciples ever asked Jesus for was to teach them how to pray. So, it must have been very, very important. How important do you think it is?

Westmoreland

I know that prayer is the key to operating in faith. Prayer is the tool for communication with God. When we are not praying or in communication with God, we are operating in our own understanding. That's the time when we find ourselves getting into trouble. We have to keep the lines of communication open with God. The Word of God tells us to pray without ceasing. God desires constant communication with us because he wants to lead and direct our lives. As we function in this world, it is not about what we know, but it is about relying on God to navigate our course in life.

Wright

What does faith in action look like?

Westmoreland

Faith in action is the work that faith-based organizations are doing. It's moving from Sunday services to really having an impact in our community. It is exciting to see churches moving towards urban, rural, and foreign missions and outreach. This is taking what we have learned in all the Sunday sermons and Wednesday night Bible studies and applying it in the vineyard. The Word of God says that faith without works or deeds is dead. So, you can believe in God and you can trust Him, but unless you are out there in the community or have stepped out of your personal comfort zone to work; it doesn't mean anything. Faith in action is—seeing the church get out there and touching lives in meaningful ways.

Wright

How does a business or Christian outreach program operate in faith?

Westmoreland

Businesses and Christian outreach programs can operate in faith by utilizing courage, conviction and commitment. With courage, a business and Christian outreach program will have a single vision that will align with the Word of God. The convictions of the businesses and Christian outreach program will make them stand firm, unmoved, always doing the work of the Lord, because they will know that their labor in the Lord is not in vain (I Corinthians 15:58). Lastly, the commitment and charge will enable them to say as Timothy, "I have fought the good fight, I have finished the race, I have kept the faith." In the end, each group will be granted the words, "Well done, my good and faithful servant."

Wright

How do you see your work with diversity issues relating to faith?

Westmoreland

I've been doing diversity work for about 15 years. My work with diversity consists of workshops dealing with the awareness and appreciation of other cultures, ethnicities, and social conditions. There are two principles that help me to do diversity work, and they are courage and compassion. Courage is facing danger without fear. Courage is fighting when the odds are against you. Courage is not giving up. It takes courage, to stand firm and confront individuals and institutions that treat people unfairly and unjustly. Second, is compassion to accept people as they are. Not everyone may understand or have the awareness, sensitivity or even the exposure that they need to handle the many situations that arise around the issue of diversity. Compassion begins by seeking first to understand people and their differing views and beliefs. The work continues with assisting and encouraging individuals to take the time to appreciate the contributions that diversity in thoughts and values can offer in all situations and environments.

Wright

Does faith work for everybody?

Westmoreland

I believe that faith is most powerful to those who believe in Jesus as their Lord and Savior. We are all given a measure of faith and as we operate in that measure of faith, we are empowered to do what God has called us to do. Faith is a belief system and everyone believes in something. If you believe and receive Jesus Christ, faith will work for you. The ultimate and most powerful belief system is in Jesus Christ. Faith is belief and trust that God will work things out in your situation. Believing in God and operating in faith is a choice.

Wright

What are the challenges of operating in faith?

Westmoreland

The challenge of operating in faith is being able to stand and believe when there is no physical evidence to support what you are doing. The family that was mentioned earlier is operating in faith even though they are grieving and mourning now. There is no physical evidence for them to have the faith that they have, but they are standing anyway. It is difficult to operate in faith when your loved ones do not support your faith walk nor can they understand why you have taken your stance or position. In both of these situations, you realize that it is only you and God. God is going to be there to support you. The blessing is when you go through the situation and you see it to the end, FAITH ALWAYS WINS.

Wright

There was a Methodist minister back in the 60s who told me that faith without knowledge is superstition. This offended me until he finished his thought. Then, he said that faith was walking as far as you could into the light and then taking one more step into the darkness. Light for him was knowledge and darkness was not. So, that's basically what you are saying, isn't it?

Westmoreland

Yes it is. You need a foundation for your belief system. The strongest foundation or source of knowledge is Jesus Christ. In order to have faith you have to understand and know who is the most High God. I believe that the Bible is our manual for walking the Christian journey. I advocate for studying the Bible, because we need to know how to operate in this world and be prosperous.

Wright

You mean when I mess up I can go to the owner's manual?

Westmoreland

Yes.

Wright

Not bad advice. See, now all of that education is paying off. What an interesting conversation on faith. I really appreciate you taking the time to talk to me, Dr. Westmoreland. It has been very enlightening and I just wish you the best in all you're trying to do for people.

Westmoreland

Thank you, David.

Wright

Today we've been talking to Dr. Cheri Westmoreland. She is an educator, motivational speaker and founder of CSW Consulting Group in Cincinnati, Ohio. As we have found out today, she is also a committed and dedicated Christian. Thank you so much, Dr. Westmoreland.

Westmoreland

Thank you.

About The Author

Dr. Cheri Westmoreland is an educator, motivational and inspirational speaker who specializes in professional and organizational excellence. Currently, founder of CSW Consulting Group, a company designed to assist individuals and organizations with leadership development, cultural diversity and spiritual fulfillment.

Cheri Westmoreland, Ed.D.

CSW Consulting Group

Hebron, Kentucky 41048

Phone: 859.689.4529

Email: cwestmore_99@fuse.net

www.protrain.net

Chapter 14

CAPTAIN GERALD COFFEE, US NAVY (RET.)

THE INTERVIEW

David E. Wright (Wright)

Today we're talking to Gerald Coffee. Gerald has served our country as a naval officer for 28 years; much of that service was as one of the longest held prisoners of war in the communist prisons of Vietnam. His military decorations include the Silver Star, the distinguished Flying Cross, two Bronze Stars, the Air Metal, two Purple Hearts and the Vietnam Service Metal with 13 stars. He has received numerous civilian awards as well and holds a Masters Degree in political science from the University of California at Berkeley. Drawing from his own unique life experiences, he shares a message of going beyond survival. Through a national survey of corporate and association meeting planners, he was selected as one of America's top 10 speakers. He is considered by many as the most memorable speaker ever. His book, *Beyond Survival*, was featured in the condensed version in *Reader's Digest* and *Guidepost Magazine* and it was produced in audiocassette version by Nightingale Conant. Gerald Coffee, welcome to *Conversations on Faith*.

Gerald Coffee (Coffee)

Thank you. It is a pleasure to be with you, David.

Wright

You were a P.O.W. in North Vietnam for more than seven years. How did your ordeal begin? How did you arrive in such a predicament?

Coffee

I was a Naval Officer and pilot for many years before I was deployed to Vietnam. I was in a squadron aboard U.S.S. Kitty Hawk, which is now the oldest warship in the Navy—which makes me feel that much older, of course. We were flying a reconnaissance airplane called *The Vigilante*. We were on our last mission for that day. We were hit by anti-aircraft fire over the Southern part of North Vietnam. It disabled our hydraulic system, our control system, and ultimately caused us to have to eject from the airplane, as it turned out, at a very high speed—680 mph, as a matter of fact. Totally out of control. The ejection was pretty horrendous. As I explain to people sometimes, imagine bombing down the nearest Interstate Highway in your convertible with the top down at 680 mph and standing up in the front seat. That gives you some small idea of the impact. In any case, I was knocked unconscious, badly injured, broken forearm, shattered elbow, dislocated shoulder and many cuts, burns and bruises. I regained consciousness floating in the water sometime later. We were picked up almost immediately by Vietnamese communists who had come out in small boats. Then there was a fierce battle for our capture with airplanes overhead striking the boats and the Vietnamese fighting back. Ultimately, my crewman was killed and I was captured. I was taken over a 12-night period to the capital city of Hanoi and incarcerated there in the old French-built prison called Hoa Lo, which in Vietnamese means "fiery forge." That was the beginning of my seven-year ordeal. Thank God I didn't know at the beginning it was going to be that long. I don't know how I would have handled that.

Wright

What was it about your life before that experience that helped most in surviving it?

Coffee

I think there was a level of self-esteem I had developed over the years. I come from a very functional family, even though my father did have some alcohol problems. My family was very, very supportive of all of my athletic endeavors and school activities and so on. I had achieved some success in high school and college in academics and athletics. By the time I joined the Navy, I was a pretty happy, normal, stable all-American guy, I guess. As far as my spiritual development, when I was a kid I went to whatever Sunday school my friends went to, but I was raised in a Christian environment. Ultimately that spiritual environment, which included several years as a practicing Catholic—my wife was Catholic when we got married, so I converted and we raised our kids in the Church. That was a very substantial framework for my spiritual life in prison. Saying the rosary and going over the mass in my mind daily, as an example, as well as being close to God at that time. I'm not suggesting that you had to have that kind of a background to have a fulfilling spiritual experience in prison, either. It just happened to be the one that was unique to me and worked for me very well.

Wright

I'll bet you really stay tuned to the televisions and the newspapers now that North Korea is very much in the news.

Coffee

Oh, absolutely. I pride myself on staying current on most world issues. I write a weekly column for a newspaper here in Hawaii. Usually I write on current events and my perspective on things like North Korea. So, I have more than a passing interest in our nation's foreign policy and our military involvement and things like that. So, you're right. I do. I stay very closely apprised of those things.

Wright

Does the United States government, as far as you know, utilize some of this wisdom that people like you have in their policy making decisions now?

Coffee

Well, you know, relative to P.O.W. issues, they do. Several of my contemporaries are stationed in the Washington D.C. area. It's not uncommon for them to be called upon for opinions, advice or perspective, not only by the media but also by government officials as well. As far as other international relations issues, not specifically. Although, some of my contemporaries have gone onto achieve very high levels of involvement. My friend John McCain, of course he's a senator from Arizona, and he is very involved in making substantial decisions relative to our country's foreign policy and involvement. Orson Swindle is a commissioner on the Federal Trade Commission right now. He was a Marine colonel held almost seven years in Hanoi as well. Many of them have achieved flag rank in the military—admirals and generals and so on in decision making roles.

Wright

Give our readers some idea about your daily existence in the prison camp. Did you still consider yourself in a military situation?

Coffee

Absolutely, David. We were guided by a six-article code of conduct. It was designed specifically to give us guidance for those circumstances as P.O.W.s. We realized very early on that the North Vietnamese communists simply looked at us as resources to be exploited for military information early on before the information that we had became obsolete due to plan changes, and for propaganda purposes. When it became apparent to us that they intended to exploit us for everything that we were worth, it became our mission to thwart that effort. It was just combat on a different level. Although our code of conduct specified that we were only to give only our name, rank, serial number and date of birth, and to evade answering all further questions to the utmost of our ability. We began to realize early on with the isolation and torture that they imposed that that was not realistic and we ended up having to give something. Our mission became to minimize the net gain that communists could achieve by having us at their total mercy for such a long time. We realized that every man's ability to resist was different and as long as a man sincerely did his very, very best to minimize his value to them, that he was fulfilling his obligation to the code of conduct and his comrades. Consistent with this policy, we were kept in solitary confinement much of the time. In my case, I was probably in solitary confinement for about two-and-a-half out of the seven years. Fourteen months was the longest single time. We were fed twice a day and each feeding consisted of a bowl of rice, a bowl of thin soup made of whatever was in season—chopped up pumpkin or greens of some kind like chard or spinach. There were three kinds. We called them sour greens, slimy greens and sewer greens. That was about the extent of the variety. We had a lot of turnips. Then we also had a small side plate of whatever was in the soup but it was fried up with a little piece of pork fat.

That was our daily fare twice a day. Depending on what type of schedule you were on, if they were pressing you to get something for propaganda or make an audio tape or write a statement of some kind or to come clean in some type of interrogation, you might be in a punishment status and couldn't get out of your cell for an entire day for months. Other times you'd be allowed out maybe three times a week to bathe for 20 minutes and get a little bit of fresh air and sunshine and look at the sky. It wasn't until much later on that they perceived the Paris peace talks would become fruitful that they began loosening up and allowing us a little more leeway and outside time. Ultimately, just before we were released we were allowed to live together in cell bays of 20-30 men together and have maybe 4-5 hours a day outside. That is a nutshell version of what our treatment and circumstances were like.

Wright

I remember reading something years and years ago about the little tricks that some of the P.O.W.s had when they were forced to give false testimony on video camera. They would say things that were obviously ridiculous or give signals that were inappropriate to let the people in the United States know that they were being forced to do that. Did a lot of that go on?

Coffee

Oh, absolutely. Every opportunity that you had you tried to turn the tables on them. One guy, for example, was tortured into finally writing a statement about how all the people in his squadron were anti-war—of course none of them were. He wrote a statement saying that his commanding officer, *Clark Kent*, had vowed not to fly any more missions and the operations officer, *Ben Casey*, had refused to participate in any more operations. If you were forced to make a tape, for example. One guy had to make a tape extolling how great the food was for Thanksgiving. He said his Thanksgiving dinner was really a B.F.D. He said, "You know what that means mom, a Big Fine Dinner." If you're forced to read propaganda statements on the prison loudspeaker you'd mispronounce the words and just screw it up as much as you possibly could. Jeremiah Denton is a classic example. He was force to be televised reading a statement and as he was doing it he was blinking his eyes in Morse Code spelling out the word torture over and over. I mean, talk about presence of mind.

Wright

Oh, man.

Coffee

Jerry was on of the senior officers there. He is one of my living heroes.

Wright

What do you consider to have been the key to your survival there? Was it faith in yourself, your fellow captives, country, God?

Coffee

You hit it, David. All four of those. As a matter of fact, that's really the framework to the platform presentation that I've been giving over the last 18 years or so. I talk about going beyond survival. To do that, faith is key. Faith in myself there in prison to remember my responsibilities and obey the code of conduct to the best of my ability. To minimize my value to the enemy. To be there for my comrades. To fulfill the responsibility to encourage and comfort one another and, ultimately, to do my best and find my purpose in the whole ordeal. We had faith in one another because we continued to maintain our cohesion as a military unit. We organized ourselves along the military chain of command, of course. We had faith in one another and were there for one another when we could be. We communicated with each other by tapping on the walls from cell to cell and recognized that we could be far stronger as a unit. As a matter of fact, our motto was three words, *Unity Over Self*. So, we had faith in one another and of course I kept faith in my family a half a world away. I realized that they had to stay strong and keep faith in themselves and faith in me as well.

We had to keep faith in our country. We were overwhelmed everyday by negative propaganda about America's role in Southeast Asia. We heard every anti-war statement, about every anti-war riot, anti-war statements by celebrities and politicians, the same statements we were taking torture not to make. After four or five years of an overwhelming wave of negative propaganda, you have to remind yourself that you are an American, you live there, that is your home. This is not the place to change your mind. Keep faith. Honestly living there in that communist environment every single day my convictions were strengthened that we were right to be there in Vietnam in pursuit of that cause. I was able to see up close and personal on a daily basis who the enemy was and what we were fighting. I realize that the people on the outside of the prison walls in downtown Hanoi were no better off than I was inside of the prison walls. In fact, they were worse off because I still had hope of going home, but they had very little hope of a better tomorrow.

Then, of course, I had my faith in God. It is the foundation for all of my faith. Faith in God relative to realizing that He was the source of my strength. In fact, one of the early things that I saw scratched on the wall of a cell were two words with an equal sign: God = strength. For me, David, that really worked. I was never alone and I could always find a little bit more strength when I needed it. When you have time like that, when you are stripped of all the material trappings by which we sometimes identify ourselves and you've nothing left but your flesh and your bones and your soul and you have seven years to look inside and think about what you think, who you are, and where you came from you begin to realize that we are truly one family under God.

Wright

In context with what we've just been talking about, you use a strange word—purpose. Were you actually able to find any purpose in such an ordeal?

Coffee

I was, but this is where faith comes into play again. All those years in prison I never realized what the purpose was, but I simply had faith that there was one. This is kind of a metaphor for our daily lives. When we go through adversity or challenges or pain or sorrow, we may not understand it but everyone of those emotions or circumstances has a purpose and we simply need to keep faith that it's there. It wasn't until I returned home and began speaking in public that I realized that this is the purpose of my incarceration. If I didn't speak, I'd be blowing such a very strong responsibility to capitalize on the credibility that accrued from surviving my experience.

Wright

Did you come away from the experience with any hatred or bitterness?

Coffee

You know, I didn't. That was partly because of what I mentioned a moment ago about understanding that it doesn't matter the color of our skin or the shape of our eyes or the language that we speak we all laugh and cry and hunger and thirst the same way. We are all just brothers and sisters in God's family of humankind. I realize that my guards, jailers and torturers there were not that much different from me. The thing that divided us was ideology, not humanness or race— simply ideology. They were victims of a terrible, evil ideology. It taught me that there is indeed evil in the world and it is worth resisting at every turn, every place that we find it.

Wright

What was your relationship with your captors?

Coffee

It was, for the most part, very professional. One of the jailers that I had there for many years—his nickname was Sarge, which is a very respectful nickname considering some that we gave to the other guards—I realize that he got just as tired of my grubby face when he opened the door for me to set my bucket outside as I did looking at his. He was just trying to do his job. He did it very professionally. There was a kind of professional respect between us.

They feed you earlier on Sundays to get all of that out of the way. That way they can all go off on liberty or have their families come to the prison and spend time with them. But anyway, on a quiet Sunday afternoon the little peephole on my door opened up and I looked out. There was a guard that we called the Green Hornet, because he was always bouncing off the walls trying to catch us communicating. He looked at me very thoughtfully and looked up and down the passageway to his left and right to make sure that he was alone, motioned me over to the door, pulled the wallet out of his pocket, opened it up and showed me a picture of his girlfriend. I went, "Ooh, ahh, my, my," which is beautiful in Vietnamese. He smiled and was very proud of that. He looked at me and he pointed at me and with both hands made the shape of a woman, you know, the curves of a woman. He pointed at me and his question was, "How about you? You got a girlfriend?" I pointed to my ring finger, which had no ring, of course. I said, "Yes. I'm married." I motioned with my hand the stair step for my four children and gave him their ages in the Vietnamese numbers. Then I pointed to his ring finger and the picture of his girl and I said, "Are you guys going to get married?" He kind of threw his hands into the air as if to say, "Look what is going on. How could I possibly get married?" David, it was like I was having a conversation with a shipmate on the Kittyhawk. There was a human linkage there that reminded me that he didn't deserve my hatred. I came away from that experience without any hatred or bitterness about the experience or hatred towards the Vietnamese people. I came away hating communism, but I had no hatred for the people who kept me there. If for nothing else, I realized that if I continued to hate or feel bitter I would be allowing the object of my hatred to control me. So, intellectually hatred makes no sense. I know you can say to a person who is wallowing in hatred or bitterness to "get over it," but it's not that easy. For some of us the feelings go very deeply but I think that it is counterproductive.

Wright
Were you mistreated there?

Coffee
Yes.

Wright
How did you handle that?

Coffee
Well, torture was systemic. As I mentioned earlier, they looked at us as resources to be exploited and the prison authority was under a great deal of pressure to exploit us. Otherwise it was a waste of their time and resources to keep us alive. So, they would torture us for military information and to write propaganda statements. They tortured us to write letters requesting amnesty, which if you did was acknowledging that you were not a P.O.W. but a common criminal, which they called us. They didn't acknowledge our P.O.W. status or the Geneva Conventions on the treatment of P.O.W.s. They would try and get us to do what they wanted gently at first—which was by cajoling and chewing you out and sometimes some beatings and things like that, but ultimately they would torture us by using ropes tied very tightly on our upper arms. Ultimately they began using parachute nylon shroud lines because they slipped and could make a tighter knot. They would sit you down in the floor and put your ankles in stocks—big iron stocks—and tie your upper arms behind you

cutting off the circulation in each arm and binding them very tightly behind you. Then the torturer would put his foot in the back of your neck and pull very hard until your shoulders are practically touching behind you. It pulled the cartilage in your sternum and shoulders. Then after he got that as tight as he could, he would tie the rest of the nylon cord over your shoulders and down around your ankles and then cinch you up very tightly in a little ball until your ears were right between your big toes. It was like a portable rack. It would spread your legs apart at the hip and strain your back, shoulders and sternum. That was for starters, then they would take the rest of the rope and pull it over a hook in the ceiling and hoist you up off the floor until all your weight was on your arms. Then they would sort of play a tether ball game with their rifle butts and bamboo poles. Sometimes they would put you on top of a stool and cuff your ankles to the stool and make you sit there for two or three days. You'd become exhausted, delirious, pass out. That was when I began to realize that it was important for us to minimize our value to them by giving something before we became so incoherent and out of control that we would give them everything. So, we learned to pace ourselves and know when to give in and what to do so that you could be more wily and cunning and ultimately give them less than you might have given if you had tried to resist to the very max.

Wright
With that all going on, how did spiritual values come into play?

Coffee
I'll tell you, you could see Hoa Lo Prison glow from prayer. Every man had his own personal spiritual routine, but every Sunday morning the senior officer in each cell block would pass a certain signal on the wall "thump-thump, thump-thump," which was church call. Then he would wait a few minutes for that to circulate down from cell to cell to cell. Then every man would stand up in his own cell if he was able to, and in some semblance of togetherness, we would all recite, out loud, the pledge of allegiance to our flag and the Lord's Prayer. Frequently we also recited the 23rd Psalm, focusing on that part of the 23rd Psalm, as you might guess, that says, *"Thou preparest a table before me in the presence of mine enemies. Thou anointeth my head with oil; my cup runneth over."* As we looked at the officers and guards, the communists there that kept us, we realized that in spite of the fact that it was we who were incarcerated, it was our cup that

runneth over because we knew that some day, whenever, however, we would return to a beautiful and free country. We were able to keep our minds free, but they were doomed to live in their country for the rest of their lives. They were not likely to know much else—at least during their generation. We realized that in spite of our circumstances, it was our cup that runneth over.

Wright

How was your reintegration with your family after such a long separation?

Coffee

Well, you know, we came home and they used the term the *Rip Van Winkle Effect*. We had been out of circulation, out of society for so long—some as long as 8.5 years. My friend Everett Alvarez who was shot down in August of 1964 was the longest held P.O.W. in North Vietnam. We came back and, of course, a lot of things had changed. People sometimes ask, "What was the biggest technological change when you came back?" I kind of put them on and say, "Everybody's toilet water was blue!" But, in actuality, we had a lot of catching up to do. We had to catch up on our moon landing, for example. All of the advancements in technology in our military and our daily lives. We had to learn how to dial long distance direct, for example. Area codes were all new to us. It was little things like that. My wife, as you can imagine, being autonomous for seven years and having the benefit of all my pay and allowances and being able to live anywhere she wanted and do anything she wanted—nevertheless when I came home she said, "I'm so glad to have you home to take some responsibility and make some decisions." I said, "Well I'm really eager to do that." So I made a couple of decisions and she said, "We haven't been doing it that way." So there was some friction originally and it took some very hands-on intellectual analysis. I just couldn't come back and wade into the family as a big father figure. I had to take it easy and feel my way along gradually. For the most part, my integration was very easy because my wife had done such a good job of keeping my image alive and a part of the family all those years. I came back to four children, the fourth of which I had never known. My youngest son, Jerry, was born two months after I had been shot down. So he was seven years old when we first met.

Wright

Goodness gracious!

Coffee

I came home and my reintegration with my children was relatively easy because my wife had done such a great job. Ultimately, however, David, we weren't able to keep it together. Twelve years after I came home we were divorced. My friend Robinson Reisner, a devout Mormon man with a family of six kids, in his book, *The Passing of the Night*, said, "You know all those years I was in prison, my wife was in afterburner on maximum thrust, trying to be the best mother and father and all things to all people that she could be, while I was in idle. When I came home, I was ready for afterburner and she was ready for idle. There was an immediate disparity in pace and priorities, and ultimately the dynamics of that long separations undermined our marriage beyond repair." Many men kept it together and I admire them so much. On the other hand, many men didn't.

Wright

Did you stay in the military?

Coffee

David, I did. I stayed for another 12 years. I came back and took advantage of the opportunities. The military gave us every opportunity to do anything we wanted if it made any sense at all. You know, accept any assignment. I chose to go to post-graduate school on the Navy. That's how I got those two years at Berkeley and got the masters in political science. That was one of the best things I could have done. I can't take credit for it because I didn't know it was going to be so good, but as you can imagine being on campus at Berkeley I learned a lot between classes in 1973. As I say sometimes, I figured if I could survive seven years in a communist prison I could hack two years at Berkeley. Then I came to Hawaii and commanded an aviation squadron here for two years. I then went back to Washington D.C. to attend the one-year tour at the National War College at Fort McNair there. Then back to Hawaii to the staff of the commander of the Pacific fleet. I was the fleet air operations officer. I began getting more and more invitations to speak, so I spent the last three years on active duty as a public affairs officer and my job was to simply go out and speak full time. Most of my friends did stay in the military. As I mentioned earlier, several went on to make flag and move to general and admiral rank.

Wright

Boy that's really faith in your job. I would have thought that as soon as you got home you would never even think about the military again. But I guess I never thought about it as you have been describing it. I can see the camaraderie now.

Coffee

Yeah, and a couple of aspects. As I mentioned, having been in a communist prison for seven years, it gave me much deeper insight as to what kind of enemy we faced in the Cold War—Cold and Hot War years, I should say. And because I had survived the experience, I felt that the lessons I had learned there would make me that much better of a military officer. It would be a waste if I got out of the military when I first came back when I could stay in and feel I could make a greater contribution by staying in and continuing my military career. Up to a point, of course, when I finally got out after 28 years and began to realize that I could make more of an impact from a platform than I could as a Navy captain trying to make admiral.

Wright

Many people in this country have argued that since South Vietnam fell to communism anyway, the whole thing was really a big waste. Do you have any bitterness about sacrificing so much in what was considered to be a very unpopular war?

Coffee

I have no bitterness in that respect at all, David. As a matter of fact I am proud of my involvement. Polls have been taken of Vietnam veterans and contrary to popular belief, over 70-percent of Vietnam veterans are proud of their service and would go back and do it again if called upon. As I say frequently, we lost the battle for South Vietnam. There is no question about that. We had it won militarily, hands down. We never lost a battle, including the Tet Offensive, which was a huge defeat for the communists. But our political leaders snatched defeat from the jaws of victory. Our congress and our political leaders simply gave South Vietnam away to the communists after we withdrew our troops. But all of that doesn't change the fact that we won the war for Southeast Asia. Today, millions of people in those otherwise domino countries—you recall the *domino theory*?

Wright

Right.

Coffee

Thailand, Malaysia, Singapore, Indonesia, the Philippines and probably Taiwan as well, people are living in free, democratic, profitable societies because of the 10 years of holding action that we held against the momentum of Chinese and North Vietnamese communism from the northern part of South Asia. That part of the world looks entirely different today because we were there for 10 years. So, it wasn't all for naught and we should have been there. It was a gallant, noble effort. It's just a shame that we sold out on our South Vietnamese comrades and allies after we left.

Wright

I have one final question that I'd like to ask you. How are you a changed man because of the entire experience?

Coffee

David, I think I've changed in several ways. First of all, I think I've internalized my spiritual life more than I ever would have. I've seen first hand that God really does equal strength. I'm eager to turn to him when I feel like I need more strength still, just like I did in prison. That's certainly one way. I've learned that it is important to find the purpose in our adversities because it makes our pain and challenges so much more do-able and manageable if we can truly believe that there is a purpose for what we are going through at any given time.

I'm changed in that I feel that everyone has the capability to do the things they have to. There is certainly nothing extraordinary about me. I'm just a central California, San Juaqin Valley kid bopping out of UCLA into the Navy and not really having a firm grasp on what I was doing or where I was going. So, anybody in my audiences and anyone who reads this book can survive the same experience with the same reasons and the same orientation going in, of course. If I can plant that seed of belief in people's minds, then hopefully it does change their perspectives on the issues and challenges that they face on a daily basis. I say that we're all P.O.W.s at one time or another—

Prisoners of Woe. As in, "Woe is me." So we find ourselves in various kinds of prisons: physical situations, relationship prisons, financial prisons, health prisons, but we all have the capability to turn those situations around by finding the purpose and seeing how we can emerge from them better and tougher than we might have been.

I'm a changed man in that I don't have a lot of patience for boredom. When my grandkids say, "We're bored!" I say, "Wait a minute, how could you be bored?" I feel like it is important to utilize and appreciate every moment of everyday. We need to be conscious, be in the present and appreciate what God gives us on a daily basis. I'm a very grateful and happy man. One our contemporaries on the platform, Dennis Praeger, wrote a book called *Happiness is a Serious Problem*. His thesis says, "Happiness is directly proportional to gratitude." You know, that makes me a very, very happy man.

Wright

Well, you just don't know how much I have enjoyed this conversation with you. I really thank you and want you to know how much I appreciate you taking this much time. As we're speaking, just for our readers, you are at home in Hawaii and you speak mainly on the mainland. We were talking right before the interview started about the first time I ever heard you back in '83. You so inspired me and I want to thank you for doing that. I think you certainly did find your purpose.

Coffee

Well, I feel like it, David. I think it contributes to my sense of contentment and purpose and happiness. I think it would work for anybody. I'm sure you feel the same way relative to your path to where you are now and what you're doing and what you've been able to achieve with and for people. It seems to me that you're right on purpose as well.

Wright

Well, today we have been talking to Gerald Coffee who served our country as a Naval officer for over 28 years, much of that time as a P.O.W. To put his talent in perspective, there is one organization that he belongs to called the National Speakers Association, which has 4,000 members, and they name him as one of the top 10 speakers in the world today. We have found out today exactly why that distinction was given to him. Thank you so much, Gerald, for being with us today.

Coffee

David, you're sure welcome. My hope is that you and I can work together more in the future. Perhaps we can collaborate to satisfy the needs of your clients and just get together and be closer in the future.

Wright

Absolutely, I appreciate it.

Coffee

Alright, David.

Wright

Thank you.

Coffee

Listen, you have a beautiful day. Aloha.

About The Author

Named one of America's Top Ten Speakers, Gerald Coffee is considered by many clients as their most memorable speaker. Sharing insights derived from seven years as a P.O.W. in North Vietnam and his unique experiences since, he plants the seed of hope that we each can go beyond mere survival to emerge from our adversities and pain tougher and more capable than otherwise. His is not a story of Vietnam but a story of human survival; *a reaffirmation of the invincibility of the human spirit.*

Captain Gerald Coffee, US Navy (Ret.)

Coffee Enterprises, Inc.

99-905B Aiea Hts. Dr.

Aiea, Hawaii 96701

Phone: 808.488.1776

www.captaincoffee.com

Chapter 15

DR. TONY CAMPOLO

THE INTERVIEW

David E. Wright (Wright)

Today we're talking with Tony Campolo, Professor Emeritus of Sociology at Eastern University in Saint Davids, Pennsylvania. He previously served for 10 years on the faculty at the University of Pennsylvania. A graduate of Eastern University, he earned a Ph.D. from Temple University. As founder of the Evangelical Association for the Promotion of Education (EAPE), Dr. Campolo has provided the leadership to create, nurture and support programs for at-risk children in cities across the United States and Canada. He has also helped to establish schools and universities in several developing countries. Dr. Campolo is a media commentator on religious, social and political matters having appeared on such television programs as *Nightline, Crossfire, Politically Incorrect, The Charlie Rose Show* and *CNN News*. He currently hosts his own television series, *Hashing It Out* on the Odyssey Network and hosts *From Across the Pond*, a weekly program on the Premier Radio Network in England. The author of 28 books, his most recent titles are *Revolution and Renewal: How Churches are Saving Our Cities* and *Let Me Tell You a Story: Life Lessons from Unexpected Places and Unlikely People*. Dr. Campolo is an ordained minister, has served American Baptist Churches in New

Jersey and Pennsylvania and is presently recognized as an associate pastor of the Mt. Carmel Baptist Church in West Philadelphia. Dr. Campolo, welcome to *Conversations on Faith.*

Dr. Tony Campolo (Campolo)
Thank you.

Wright
I just finished reading your speaking itinerary for the next year. I'm out of breath just reading it. How do you fit 400 speaking engagements into your schedule and enjoy life at the same time?

Campolo
Well, the answer is quite simple. I enjoy speaking. So, having an intensive speaking engagement schedule is enjoying life for me. I thrive on it and it is a privilege and a joy. It is what gives me peace.

Wright
Does your wife generally travel with you?

Campolo
She travels with me about one-quarter of the time. She finds it difficult to keep the pace, so she'll go with me on a trip and be with me part of the time, then go home.

Wright
I was wondering how EAPA got started and what is its mission.

Campolo
Well, EAPA means the Evangelical Association for the Promotion of Education. It started when I was in my early days of teaching. I wanted to do two things. The first was to work among the poor in third world countries. The second was to work among the socially oppressed people of Philadelphia. In both cases, students who came from these area of the world about which I was deeply concerned prevailed on me to get involved in what was going on in their particular locations. Students in the Dominican Republic came to me and said that they had a desperate need for a university that was evangelical and asked me to help them. I did respond to that invitation and that started our (EAPA) work in the Dominican Republic. In Philadelphia, Youth for Christ wanted to start some work with at-risk young people

and asked me if I would head up an initiative. I did and we have since made that organization independent of Youth for Christ and it has now expanded into nine different cities across the United States.

Wright

Is it non-denominational?

Campolo

It is very much non-denominational. I don't think we have more than 4 or 5 people from the same denomination among the 300 that we have working with us.

Wright

That's great. You know, most of us have heard the term "at-risk" and I'm sure it must define a lot of different things. Could you give our readers your definition of "at-risk" children?

Campolo

In the United States, it generally refers to young people who are living in areas that sociologists say have a high propensity for turning out adults who will become criminal, who will find themselves unemployable, who will find themselves living below the poverty level and will end up in broken families. It is relatively easy to statistically evaluate a community and figure out which communities are most likely to generate an abundance of people who have these pathologies. Children growing up in those areas are, therefore, considered at-risk.

Wright

I was watching a television program recently about inner-city children. They were interviewing the children and one of them had a hopeless look in his eyes. He explained that the reason that he did a lot of the things he did was because he didn't really expect to live past 14 or 15 years with all of the shootings and things. Do you find that?

Campolo

I hear that often from young people in slum areas of the city. However, I don't think that boys and girls and teenagers comprehend what death is all about. They don't understand death because they haven't had enough time to reflect on its significance. They do not really understand the preciousness of life itself. The reality is that many young people deal with the whole question of dying in a very cavalier fashion. As they grow older, they may sense that they're treating this whole matter of dying a little too simply.

Wright

Let's talk about education for a minute. My Sunday school class has studied two of your tape series over a period of a few months and the consensus is that you take difficult Biblical stories, principles and concepts and apply them to everyday situations to facilitate understanding. Do you think ministers and church teachers should be more open to interpretation and application of the Bible in order to make scripture more understandable and meaningful?

Campolo

Of course they should. That is what preaching is all about, taking the general message of scripture and relating it to the time-bound existential situation in which we live. I would say that the reason it sounds as though I'm doing something unusual is that very often ministers in the church avoid preaching what Jesus really says because it would be too difficult for their people to live out. I think it's pretty clear that Jesus calls upon rich people to put aside all of the wealth they don't absolutely need and use it in ministry for other people. I think that he makes it clear that it will be hard for rich people to get into the Kingdom of Heaven. I think that ministers are afraid, especially in this time of the war with Iraq, to really go to what the scripture says about dealing with your enemies. It says to love them, do good for them, to overcome evil with good and be peace makers recognizing that those who live by the sword, die by the sword. It's very difficult for someone to go to the Sermon on the Mount without coming out passive. So, in times of national warfare, such as the one we're in now, ministers find it safest to avoid the sayings of Jesus on such things as war. Another issue would be dealing with the whole matter of social justice. Here we live in a society where there's two kinds of justice, one kind of justice for the rich and one kind of justice for the poor. Everybody knows this. If you don't believe it just watch the Kobe Bryant trial over the next few months and you'll get a pretty good idea that if you have enough money, you'll get a different kind of justice than the poor. I think that clergy are afraid to criticize American society because Evangelical churches, in particular, are so politically conservative and so loyal to America that they do not tolerate criticism of the American societal system. A good example would be the fact that we like to think we're a generous nation. That's the myth. Any study done on the 22 industrialized nations of the world will evidence that we are dead last in per capita giving to the poor in other countries. As a case in point, for every dollar that America provides for the poor in third world countries, the people of Norway, on a per capita basis, give 70. So, we're spending our money on things like a military machine and ignoring the poor. We are spending our money on building football stadiums instead of taking care of urban education. We have 44 million Americans who have no medical coverage whatsoever, 13 million children who have no medical coverage. Evangelical pastors are afraid to raise these issues for fear of angering the overly patriotic people in their congregations. I think that we, in America, are in danger of making patriotism into a form of idolatry. There's nothing wrong with being patriotic, but when your patriotism blinds you to the injustices being perpetrated by your own society, then you have moved beyond patriotism into a form of idolatry.

Wright

That's very interesting. It is almost the antithesis of what the prophets in the Old Testament went through.

Campolo

I think that's right. I think the church loses its prophetic edge. If you go to a Christian bookstore, you'll find that most of the books are of a pastoral nature. They are books that deal with how to be happy, solve your family problems, and overcome anxieties and fears. All of these things are essential when we preach the gospel. But, you will find very little on the shelves of the Christian bookstore that really has a prophetic edge.

Wright

I've been directing church music for about 47 years now and I cringe every time we do patriotic themes in our church. They always want me to do these great choir arrangements of *The Battle Hymn of the Republic.* These songs are not very scriptural, are they?

Campolo

When we are going to church, it is the one place where we should leave are nationalistic commitments behind because the early church affirmed the universal brotherhood and sisterhood of Christians and we don't do that. As a good example, right now we have no sense of affinity for the 15 percent of the Palestinian people who are incredibly oppressed in Palestine. Not only is the Israeli government, in many instances, exercising tyranny against them, but the United States supports that. We do not recognize that they are our brothers and sisters. I find that the Evangelical community is pro-Israel, which it should be, but it does so without much regard for their Palestinian brothers and sisters who are Christians. For that matter, they should be concerned about all people in terms of justice, but as it says in Galatians 6:9,10, *"Do good unto all men and women, but especially unto those who are of the household of faith."*

Wright

Speaking of books, you've written 28.

Campolo

Well, I think there are a couple more that have just come out. One is entitled, *Which Jesus.*

Wright

Oh, I know. I'm reading it now.

Campolo

Then there's another one called *Adventures in Missing the Point,* which I co-authored with Brian McLaren, perhaps the most prominent Evangelical post-modern preacher. He tries to talk about Christianity in terms of the post-modern era in which we live. I'm not as sold on the post-modern perspectives that he advocates so strongly. So, the book is a kind of dialogue between the two of us over the pros and cons of our respective positions.

Wright

I've been in the publishing business for many years and some of your titles that I've read are just wonderful: *Following Jesus Without Embarrassing God, Is Jesus a Republican or a Democrat, Everything You've Ever Heard is Wrong, How to be a Pentecostal Without Speaking in Tongues and Twenty Hot Potatoes Christians are Afraid to Touch.* Tell me, who dreams up these titles for you?

Campolo

Well, in almost every case I dream them up myself. In certain cases, the publisher suggests a title after reading the manuscript.

Almost all of the books have titles that I have given, but I can think of one publisher-created title right off the bat, *Twenty Hot Potatoes Christians are Afraid to Touch*. It was a good title and it helped sell the book.

Wright

It is good. I remember watching an episodic video series of yours where you and another gentleman are sitting in a diner in New York City and there is a lady there serving you.

Campolo

It wasn't so much a video series, it was a television series on the Odyssey Network and the show was entitled *From Across the Pond*. It was a commercially produced show funded by commercial sales that I did with a solid Evangelical Presbyterian preacher and teacher, Steve Brown, who is on the faculty of the Reform Seminary in Orlando, Florida.

Wright

Now I remember his name.

Campolo

We did that show for a couple of years. We committed ourselves to a form of television in which we could articulate beliefs about the scriptures, but we were committed to doing it in such an interesting way that we wouldn't have to raise money to keep the program on the air. We wanted to keep commercial sponsors interested in putting up the money. It worked very well. However, when you're not raising the money yourself you run into problems because when the Odyssey Network was sold to Hallmark Cards, Hallmark decided they didn't want to carry the show anymore. So, we were off the air after a couple of years. We enjoyed doing that show so very much.

Wright

I thought it was a great learning experience because both of you came at the same subject from different viewpoints.

Campolo

Both of us are committed Christians with deep commitments to the authority of scripture. What we were showing is how Christians have to wrestle with issues and there are no simplistic, easy answers to most of the issues that we have to face in life. There are two ways of looking at the thing, even if the people involved have the same commitments to Christ and the same commitments to the authority of scripture.

Wright

Your book titled *Everything You've Heard is Wrong* is about business with a twist. Did you use Biblical principles and character issues as a basis for building companies?

Campolo

Well, the reality is that I speak a good bit in the corporate community. I spend a great deal of time talking to corporate executives and business people. They have become very, very interested and very, very committed to changing the corporate behavioral patterns in America, so that they reflect a higher level of morality. The scandals, such as Arthur Anderson, Enron and Martha Stewart, combine to make America aware that there is just as much corruption among white collar people as there is among blue-collar people. The corporate community is beginning to realize that it is not only the right thing to do to restructure their businesses according to Biblical principles, but it is the only reasonable thing to do because if they don't people lose confidence in those businesses and negative economic consequences follow. So, corporate organizations are aware that if all you care about is the bottom line, it won't be long before that bottom line will be in serious red ink. Morality is a desirable business practice in today's world because businesses have been totally pragmatic without spiritual values for too long and the consequences have been horrendous, especially for the businesses themselves.

Wright

By the way, in your book titled *Is Jesus a Democrat or a Republican*, did you ever determine which he was?

Campolo

Yes, I did. He is an Independent. He finds things that are desirable and undesirable in both political parties. I believe that if Jesus was among us, and this is only my own evaluation, I think he would be angry with the Democratic party over its support of almost unrestrained abortion. I think he would be very upset with the Republican party over its obvious favoritism towards the rich and the powerful to the detriment of the poor and the oppressed. These are just two examples of how the Lord wouldn't be able to join either party. The book was written with the specific idea of showing that when a Christian is asked whether he or she is a Democrat or a Republican, the person ought to respond by asking a question in return, "On which issue?" On some issues we should be a Democrat and on others a Republican.

Wright

I noted that *Time Magazine* nominated you as one of the best preachers and speakers in America. After all the college classroom experience you've had and all the pulpits you've filled, what do you think it takes to be a great speaker or preacher?

Campolo

Well, I was very honored with that designation, but I've got to tell you that I'm not as impressed with my preaching as *Time Magazine* is. Let me say that what I think needs to be at the heart of preaching is a passionate concern. It's not enough just to give an interesting talk that is inspiring. A preacher, to really grab the audience, must be talking about something that is so important that he or she senses that if the congregation doesn't respond it will be an absolute tragedy. When I teach an evangelistic message, I must get up there with the sense that I'm not just laying out some good ideas that people can accept or reject. When I preach an evangelistic message, I do so with a deep sense that there are probably people in the congregation who have not surrendered their lives to Christ and if they do not do so tonight, they may be in mortal danger. It's that sense of urgency that makes for good preaching.

When I talk about the poor—I literally do this before I speak—I sit down and spend time thinking about the inner-city kids, the actual children that I know of who are being kicked around and abused, who are victims of poverty and mistreatment from the society in which they live. I think about children in places like Haiti. I think about dying children whom I have seen with swelled bellies and rust-colored hair from malnutrition and I put those images in my mind. When I go out to speak on behalf of the poor, it's not just an idea, I'm pleading on behalf of those children. I'm pleading on behalf of those suffering people that I firmly established in my consciousness before I spoke. I think that a good speaker has to very forthrightly relate the congregation to actual needs and those needs have to be very clear in his or her mind before he or she opens takes to the pulpit. Then the urgency of what that is all about has to come forth in the message. I hope that when I finish speaking that the humor and the information that I give that somebody in the audience is saying to his friend, "This man is almost fanatical about this stuff." And I am fanatical about the things that are of ultimate importance in life.

Wright

Through the International Speaker's Network I've been booking speakers for 13 years and down through the years probably the most frequently asked question has been, "What topic should I speak on to make a living in this business?" I always answer with the same answer, "Something about which you are passionate."

Campolo

I have to say that as a speaker I turn down a lot of engagements simply because they do not focus on the urgent issues that I want to address. In other words, I'm 68 years old and my time is short. If an insurance company says they'll give me $10,000 to come and really encourage people to sell a lot of insurance, I'll say I'm sorry because that's not important enough to me. Insurance can be a good thing if they will allow me to do one thing when I am with those workers—I want to communicate to insurance men and women that insurance is a necessary thing for people, therefore, they should seek out people who need insurance. Unfortunately, a lot of insurance people are just interested in selling a lot of insurance that people don't really need. If you're willing to let me speak about addressing needs rather than making profits, I'm going to be there for you.

Wright

I have just started reading your book that you published last year called *Which Jesus?* Can you tell our readers about the two men from Nazareth named Jesus?

Campolo

Yes. Ciprian in the first century, one of the early Church fathers, has uncovered for me the reality that Barabus, the man who was set free when Pilate gave the Jewish people the opportunity to release one of the prisoners, Jesus our Savior or Barabus. Barabus actually had a first name, Jesus. Jesus was a widely circulated first name in early history. As a matter of fact, it is estimated that 1 out of every 10 children born in Nazareth at that time was given the name Jesus. It was like the word John in our culture. So, here were these two young men growing up in this little village called Nazareth. There must have been, at most, about 300 people living there. They were probably the same age and had the same first name. The last name, Barabus, meaning son of Rabus. Whereas Jesus had a last name that we don't often think about, Bajoseph, son of Joseph. The two of them, obviously, wanted to change the world that is into the world that ought to be. Each of them had these visions of creating the Kingdom of God on earth. Jesus Barabus felt that the way to do it was by violence and creating an army that would destroy the enemies of Israel, driving out the Romans. He held up a guerilla warfare group known as the Sacari. This group was murderous. Much of what is going on in Iraq right now was the sort of thing that Sacari did. They were terrorists who saw the occupying army as one that needed to be destroyed. Every day they would kill one here or kill one there. I mean, the situations are almost parallel—as a matter of fact in the book I do share some parallels between what is going on in the Middle East today and what was going on there in Jesus' time.

So, these two men, Jesus Barabus and Jesus Bajoseph, both want to change the world. There are those who follow Jesus Barabus who believe that the way to change the world is through political power and military might. Then there is Jesus Barjospeph, who believes that the way to change the world is through sacrificial love, the ultimate expression of which is his own death on the cross to save us from our sins. In the end, and right now, we are all forced to make that choice. Who do we want to follow? Those who embrace the values of Jesus Barabus and say that America through military might and political power will be able to bring peace to the world and hence go the way that America is going right now believing that we are given the task of changing the world into what it ought to be through our power. Or, are we going to go the way of Jesus Barjoseph who calls upon us to look out to the rest of the world and instead of saying, "How can we force you to do what we believe is right?" Which is what we're doing in Iraq right now by imposing our form of society and government on those people. Or do we come and say, "We are here in the name of Jesus Barjoseph to lovingly sacrifice and help you to feed the hungry, clothe the naked, deliver the oppressed and bring joy to your lives even if it means we must sacrifice ourselves." There are the two ways of going into the future. Right now, as in every stage of history, we have to make decisions as to which mode of salvation we're going to adapt. It's always been that way. The most evil people in history have been people promising to make a better world through violence. Certainly Stalin, Hitler and Mao Tse-tung promised to create a better world, but they did it through violence. Only Jesus offers a better way.

Wright

In your books and presentations, you talk openly about the power of love as a guide for living. Do corporate audiences respond to this concept or is it too touchy-feely for them?

Campolo

Well, it has to be defined. If you're talking about love in terms of romanticism, they're too hard-nosed for that sort of thing. But, if you talk about love as a process by which you recognize the sacredness of other people and treat them as though each of them was Jesus, they are very responsive to that. Every business, in order to succeed, has to develop great human relationships. There's no better way to develop good relationships with people than to treat the people that you meet, day by day, in sales and in management as though each of them was Jesus. To treat each person as though he or she was Jesus is to insure that people will be treated with dignity and respect and caring. If that's what we mean when we're talking about love, then obviously the corporate community says, "We need our employees to do just that." I've had large department stores have me come in and talk to their salespeople. Whether the people are Christians or not they understand when I say, "Are you ready to treat the customer as though you are waiting on Jesus Christ himself?" Jewish people, Muslim people will say, "We understand what you are talking about." That's what we need to do if we are going to be good at what we are being employed to do.

Wright

Dr. Campolo, I've talked to many people from all walks of life that tell me your preaching, teaching and writings have made a positive impact on their lives. What are your plans and dreams for the future as you continue your ministry?

Campolo

I'm 68 years old. Most of my time and energy right now is spent on training up a new generation of preachers and teachers who will have a zeal for the things that burn within my heart. And to impart to them whatever resources I can to enable them to get going in developing the ministries that God has called them to develop. To put it in simple language, I'm going to spend the next few years of my life—as long as the Lord gives me—trying to empower the next generation, the Gen-Xer's as they're called, to be the spokespeople for salvation both on the personal level and the societal level. This new generation will speak words that will evangelize the lost and promote social justice in the world in which we live. I want to inspire young men and women to come along and take the baton I've been carrying and say, "It's our turn now." I want to empower, encourage, train them and get them on their way.

Wright

Well, what a wonderful goal and I certainly hope you reach it.

Campolo

I do too.

Wright

I really appreciate the time you've taken with us today, Dr. Campolo. It's been exciting and rewarding conversation for me. I've learned a lot and I really do appreciate you talking to me.

Campolo

Thank you.

About The Author

Dr. Anthony "Tony" Campolo is a professor of sociology and also director of the Urban Studies Program at Eastern College in St. Davids, Pa. For 10 years he was on the faculty at the University of Pennsylvania. He did his undergraduate work at Eastern College and earned his Ph.D. from Temple University.

He is the founder and president of the Evangelical Association for the Promotion of Education, an organization involved in educational, medical and economic development programs in various Third World countries including Haiti and the Dominican Republic. This organization also has done extensive work among at-risk young people in urban America. Campolo meets regularly with President Clinton to advise him on social policy and the problems affecting the nation's inner cities.

He is a best-selling author and has 25 books in print, including, *Twenty Hot Potatoes Christians Are Afraid to Touch, The Kingdom of God is a Party, Everything You've Heard is Wrong and Carpe Diem.* His weekly television program, *Hashing It Out,* is carried by the Odyssey cable television network into 22 million homes. Featuring Campolo and preacher Steve Brown of Orlando, Fla., the program the program is an extension of Campolo's book, *Is Jesus a Republican or Democrat?*—modeling how those from differing viewpoints can disagree, but still learn from each other and use the Bible in working through today's hot-button issues. Dr. Campolo is also an associate pastor of the Mount Carmel Baptist Church in West Philadelphia, and serves as an associate for international ministries of American Baptist Churches.

Dr. Campolo lives in St. Davids, Pa., with his wife, Margaret. They have two grown children, Lisa and Bart.

Dr. Tony Campolo
1300 Eagle Rd.
St. Davids, Pennsylvania 19087
Phone: 610.341.1722

Chapter 16

JANE BOUCHER, CSP

THE INTERVIEW

David E. Wright (Wright)

Today we are talking to Jane Boucher. Before owning her business, she was a counselor in Sarasota, Florida, working with at risk young people. She received her Bachelor of Science and Masters degrees from Ohio State University, and has done doctoral work at the University of South Florida. She has been an adjunct professor at the University of Dayton, Wright State University, and Sinclair Community College in Dayton, Ohio. Jane is a consultant, speaker, and author of six books including her latest, *How to Love the Job You Hate*. She is working on two new books, *Patients First,* written to remind medical professionals that in health care, the patient needs to come first. Her other book entitled, *Survival: How to Stay Out Once You Get Out,* is a guide on how to never go back to a toxic relationship. Jane's clients range from small businesses to Fortune 500 companies. Her client list includes GM, IBM, the United States Air Force, and INC. Magazine, where she has shared the platform with General Norman Schwarzkopf and Bernie Siegel, M.D. The National Speakers Association has awarded Jane the CSP designation, making her one of the few Certified Speaking Professionals in the United States. Fewer than 8% of all professional speakers hold this designation.

Jane, welcome to *Conversations of Faith*. Please tell us how you started in the speaking business and your inspiration to educate the adult learner.

Jane Boucher (Boucher)

I had just finished graduate school and I started working as a teacher/counselor in Sarasota, Florida, at an experimental school called New Directions. I was assigned a case load of students. My job was to help increase their self-esteem, teach them to read and write, learn personal hygiene, and help them become employable. My career was greatly shaped by the New Directions experience. I am a professional speaker today because of a student named, Debbie. She was 14 years old when I received her as a student. She had been kicked out of many Florida schools because she kept running away. I have always found it very strange that students in our country get expelled because they are not in school. It doesn't make sense. Debbie was one of my first inspirations. She was a very bright young woman. She could draw your portrait in five minutes and it would be worthy of framing even though she never had a day of art training. She also had very good reasons for why she kept running away. She had been living in an abusive home environment. No one ever thought to ask her why she kept running away. It took 5½ years, but she finally graduated. Today she owns her own art glass studio where she makes stained glass windows. Every Christmas and birthday, she still sends me another window...18 years later. This is really how Boucher Consultants was born. I hadn't heard of a professional speaking career. My intention was to continue to teach at a university. I didn't know that people could make a living conducting seminars, speaking, and consulting. It has been a very exciting career for me.

I decided to leave Florida and return to Dayton, Ohio, my childhood home to do more graduate work. When I returned, I decided to write articles on some of the experiences I'd had at New Directions. My boss, at New Directions, Chuck Eaton, was an incredible leader. I don't think he'd ever had a day of management or leadership training, but he just knew how to do it. I have known other people that have taken every seminar, but they still don't know how to manage or lead. Some people seem to have an instinct for managing and leading and Chuck was one of those people. He was my first boss out of college and I thought all bosses were like him. I found out later it wasn't true. He taught me a lot about bringing a group of very diverse people together and accomplishing a common goal. He taught us that every organization is the shadow of the leader. New Directions was successful because of Chuck's determination and leadership. The articles I wrote had a lot to do with *How to Build High Performance Work Teams* and *Team Self-Esteem*. Various Ohio newspapers decided to run my newspaper columns. I started receiving phone calls about my articles. People wondered if I would speak to their organizations on what I had written about. There is an assumption that if you can write, you can also speak. We know that isn't always true. I tell my Public Speaking classes that if they know what they're talking about and believe in what they are talking about, they will get over the fear of speaking in front of others.

An employee from Wright Patterson Air Force Base (WPAFB) in Dayton, Ohio, read one of my first articles. She was an upper level manager who needed a speaker for the Federally Employed Woman Program. She asked if I would speak about what I had written. I decided to accept her offer. Because of WPAFB and their belief in my work, I began a very successful speaking and consulting career.

Wright

Leadership is one of your main topics. What is different about your programs when you teach leadership?

Boucher

I think General Schwarzkopf said it all when he said, "Do the right thing." True leaders have integrity, are visionary, and see what needs to happen in their organizations. They are not stuck in the day to day trivia.

John Malloy (author of *Dress for Success*) said that the essence of being brilliant is taking a complicated subject and making it simple. I teach with a common sense, practical approach to some rather complicated subjects. We have hundreds of books on Leadership and Management. It's important to remember that they are very different. The key to a person's managerial success is their interpersonal skill, not their technical expertise. General Patton was a great leader, but history tells us that he was not always well-liked. He had a vision along with leadership excellence...very different from being a good manager. In leadership, one has to have a vision for the organization's future. A real leader has a good idea of where they want to be five years from now. It's about personal and professional vision. It's also about making a plan and sticking to it. Sometimes your direction may change and that's ok. But, a person needs to have a plan. My mother has always said that life is what happens to you when you're planning something else.

Wright

You have said that in these changing times, having management skill is not enough...and what is needed is leadership. What do you mean?

Boucher

Management skill is simply not enough to keep an organization alive today. We need people who are creative. The definition of creativity is to do old things new ways. Traditionally, managers have taken care of the more day to day activities of today's workforce. But today, with our shrinking workforce...our managers must become creative and develop leadership skills. There is a major difference between being a great manager and being a great leader. As I mentioned before, the key to a person's managerial success is their interpersonal skill. Leaders, on the other hand, may not be the best at interpersonal skill, but they are able to see into the future. Change is often met with resistance and so are leaders of change. However, if we are to survive, we must be prepared to follow visionary leaders.

Wright

Everyone talks about the importance of communication in personal and professional relationships. You give a lecture on the barriers to effective communication. Can you tell our readers what these barriers are and some examples of each?

Boucher

There are hundreds of barriers to communication, but I will focus on six of them. The first barrier is that people have very different expectations in both personal and professional relationships. One person expects one thing and the other person expects something else. Often, we don't discuss our expectations. In personal relationships, people often avoid discussing their most pertinent information like finances, having children, and religious preferences. They are suddenly surprised when the other person has a different expectation of their relationship. In professional relationships, I always advise my students to interview their possible employer. Often, they have a mind set that the employer is going to ask all the questions. I tell them to ask questions about the employer to avoid future surprises.

When we work for an organization, it's important that the communication go both ways.

The second barrier is that people often make assumptions about each other. My grandparents were married 60 years. They had a wonderful relationship. Every anniversary, my grandmother would take me to the ladies lounge at the restaurant and give me advice about men. She'd say, "You know, after all these years, you'd think I'd know your grandfather. I was walking around the house the other day and found Oreo cookies that your grandfather had hidden everywhere." He loved sweet things and knew he was not allowed to have them for health reasons. Then she would say, "Don't ever think because you've been married to somebody 60 years that you know everything about them. People change."

We assume a lot about people. We look at each other and size each other up. Rarely, do we know everything a person has gone through that has caused them to be or act as they do. During my lectures, I remind my adult students that just because someone is acting like a jerk towards you...it doesn't mean you have anything to do with their behavior. We often assume when someone we work or live with has "jerk behavior," that we are partially responsible. Often, it has nothing to do with us. Don't assume it has anything to do with you. People bring a lot of baggage to their personal and professional relationships. Try not to waste your energy getting defensive.

The third and fourth barriers are simple "one-worders." Most people do not know how to deal with anger and/or conflict. They learn how to deal with conflict or anger by what they experienced in their family of origin. If their mother or father was a screamer, they may think they are never going to scream. They may go completely the opposite direction and emotionally shut down. This is not a healthy way to handle conflict. If a person is uncomfortable with conflict, a natural response can be sarcasm. This is the first "one-worder" barrier to communication. Sarcasm can be a major barrier and entirely shut down all communication while putting the other person on the defensive.

The fourth barrier is inappropriate humor. When you are trying to be open and vulnerable with another human being and they turn it into a joke, it stops the communication. Everything is not funny.

The fifth barrier is the "That ain't my job syndrome." People with this syndrome need not say anything for another person to recognize this barrier. You can tell these people by their behavior. The way these people act speaks so loudly that you can not hear what they say.

The last barrier in this discussion has to do with a lack of feedback. People don't get enough feedback in the workplace or at home. Employee performance appraisals are typically not representative of how an employee is performing. People are not trained on how to give performance appraisals and no one really likes getting them. I was asked to write a seminar called Better Performance Appraisals and I've only taught it twice in 15 years.

In our personal relationships, it is crucial that we give consistent feedback to family members. Our spouses need to hear that we love them and our children need constant verbal encouragement. If a person does not receive positive feedback, human nature is to find acceptance somewhere else. There is a reason why 60% of all marriages in our countries end in divorce. When people stop encouraging each other, that is the beginning of the end.

Wright

Jane, you've talked and written about your concerns regarding our nation and how the public's confidence in its leaders has eroded. First, why do you think this attitude exist and what can the average person on the street do about it?

Boucher

I love our country and I am proud to be an American. This country has allowed my entrepreneurial spirit to thrive. At the same time, I talk to a lot of young adults who are confused about the leadership at work and in our government. They question their role models. They see major layoffs, economic scandals, unemployment, and a country at war. A lot of the students in my seminars are in their 20's and early 30's. They don't understand or have a lot of respect for the leadership in our country and government. They also have a completely different attitude about working. They value their "free" time and expect to be paid **well** by their employers. They want to know "why" they are doing whatever they are doing. They won't just take direction without understanding the process. They also change jobs often because they intend to go where they can get the best deal. Their employers complain because they don't stay in a job very long. The employers believe that the younger employee is not loyal.

It's hard to admit this, but our generation has created this phenomena. The younger generation knows that their financial security is their own responsibility. Their employer is not necessarily going to take care of them. They are educated and having trouble finding jobs. Many of them have returned to their parent's homes because they couldn't make it on their own. They resent this. They hear on the news that there is only one group of Americans getting a raise. In spite of major corporate scandals, CEO's are the only people in the United States last year that got a raise. And that was a 15% raise, while everybody else lost money! The younger generation is not stupid. They observe and become cynical. We wonder why they are not loyal, why they keep changing jobs, and why they seem to be so money-motivated. Our generation helped create their attitude. We have to stop blaming them and try to understand.

To the outsider, it looks like their mindset is "What's in it for me." However, their thought process says: "I'm going to take care of me, because no one else is going to take care of me." And then we somehow blame them for what we have created.

Wright

You have said that women bring special talents and viewpoints to management. Could you give us some examples?

Boucher

I believe women have learned a lot from men in business...and I think men can learn a lot from women in business. After men have an argument at work, they can shake hands, play golf, and have a beer. If women have that same argument, they never speak to each other again. I believe this behavior is a result of our socialization process. Women have been taught to be more relational and men are taught to be more goal-oriented.

Men can learn from women that it is a good thing to use the right part of their brain. Creativity and intuition are qualities in today's work environment. I've known successful men that are very right-brained. They allowed their intuition to help them make decisions. Men can also learn from women about interpersonal communications. Women tend to pick up on the small innuendoes and non-verbals better than men do. Let's say your husband has just answered the phone. You asked, "Honey, who was that?" "Oh, it was Betty." "What did she want?" "Nothing." The next time you go somewhere and you see Betty, she says "Well, did your husband tell you blah, blah, blah?" Women want all the details. Men just want to get to the bottom line. A man doesn't want to go into all that detail.

Often, women try to keep harmony in their relationships at work and at home. Men will more often say it like it is. Traditionally, women have learned to "make nice...not conflict." Women need to learn when to speak up and men need to learn more compassion and empathy. Of course, this a gross generalization. I have seen insensitive women. But in general, I believe the sexes have a lot they can learn from each other.

Wright

You work extensively in career development, and you have written a book entitled, *How to Love the Job You Hate.* Why do you think that two-thirds of today's workforce doesn't like their jobs?

Boucher

There are a lot of educated people today who are underemployed. They are not able to find work appropriate to their educational level. They are working just to have a job and a paycheck. After all, they need to feed their families. For men in our culture, their sense of identity is often defined by their work. Even though they know a person is not his or her job, men often define their worth by their work. Our job should be just one part of our life. Picture a pie with six pieces and identify each piece as one of the following components: emotional, social, spiritual, personal, physical, and financial. Notice that the financial piece is only one sixth of the pie. However, most Americans would admit that their one sixth is often five sixths or more. Clearly, most people are living lives that are out of balance. We spend out highest energy hours working and our families get what is left of us after we have given the best of ourselves away all day. Therefore, it's important to try to find a work environment that gives us meaning and satisfaction. In fact, Harvard studies state that there are three primary motivating factors for the American worker. First, we have the need for affiliation. We work with people we like. It's very difficult to spend our highest energy hours working with people we don't like. That is the number one reason why people quit or get terminated. If people do not like each other, it's very difficult to stay motivated.

The second motivating factor is that human beings need to feel a sense of purpose and meaning in their work. Most people do not work just for a paycheck. They want to feel as though they make a difference. I am blessed because my work is totally meaningful. I would hope that anyone involved in education would enjoy their work. But I know it isn't always true. I would hope that people in healthcare would be dedicated to their patients, but I know it isn't always true. We have lost our sense of purpose. Life is so short, I believe it behooves all of us to find our purpose.

The third Harvard motivating factor is "power." Some people like to be in charge and in control. Power can be used constructively if it is given away. That's where we get the word "empower." Too often, we have managers and leaders who micromanage. This stifles the employee's creativity. Does the manager and/or leader give the employee freedom to think for themselves? When they make a mistake, are they encouraged anyway? Creativity and vision have made America who she is. People often fail a lot before they succeed. Look at Thomas Edison and Abraham Lincoln. Both failed numerous times before they achieved success. People who use power destructively are not motivators. The only way to really have power is by giving it away.

An easy way to remember the Harvard motivating factors is that each factor begins with a "P"—People, Purpose, and Power. I remember this by the three "P's."

Wright

You've made some good points.

Boucher

We are the only country in the world that has a national slogan, "TGIF." Think about it. Most Americans are living for Saturday and Sunday. We're not saying, "TGIM" or "Thank God it's Monday."

Wright

Jane, "TGIF" confuses people like me who love their work and I do think "Thank God it's Monday." I guess most people don't run in every Monday morning, kiss their desk, and say, "I'm glad to be here!" But, those of us who really do love our jobs appreciate them more having been through the fires on some jobs that we hated. I worked on my first job for seven years and I really hated it.

Boucher

Wow!

Wright

The reason that I stayed is because I was so good at it that they kept giving me more and more money. I didn't know how to quit.

Boucher

The golden handcuffs.

Wright

By that time, I had two children. I knew how to work, but I didn't know how to quit.

Boucher

Exactly.

Wright

Jane, as you consider your life-long personal and professional decisions, has faith played an important role?

Boucher

It has played the most critical role in my life. I am blessed to have faith like a child. I remember having it as a little girl. When I was 15, I was sent to an Episcopalian girl's boarding school with a lot of strict nuns. With one exception, they were rigid and punitive. In my 15 year old mind, they represented God. The boarding school experience separated me from my earlier faith. After I graduated, I went to college and received a research scholarship to do my graduate work. I was extremely blessed without knowing that I was being blessed. Everything I touched seemed to work out. I received two degrees, got a four point average and was even chosen to represent Trans World Airlines as their campus sales representative at Ohio State University. This meant that I got all the free tickets I wanted to travel anywhere in the world. I couldn't believe it. I was a student traveling first class around the world. I had tremendous opportunities that most people didn't have at my age.

After graduate school, I was offered three fantastic jobs. Being the idealist that I continue to be, I took the job at New Directions thinking I could help young people change their lives for the better. I saw a lot of miracles happen with my students, but I thought it was only a result of our hard work. I now know that God was behind the success of our program. I am sure that people were praying for our student's lives.

There have been many experiences that have caused my spiritual growth. When I was a little girl, I remember reading my father's black Bible with his name engraved on the front cover. Years later, my father enjoyed taking me to the airport and picking me up after my many speeches and seminars. I remember telling his wife that one of my most important memories as a little girl was reading my dad's black Bible. I mentioned in passing that I would love to find it, but thought it was impossible. One cold winter night, my father picked me up at the airport and you could hardly see through the fog in the window. When we got into the car, he told me he had something for me. Between the seats, he slapped his black Bible. Seeing my dad's Bible, after so many years, caused something to happen that helped to restore my faith.

My eyes were opened to the spiritual world. I began meeting people whose faith touched my awakening spirit. Several of these people discipled me and for that...I am grateful. One of my first spiritual mentors was an inner-city missionary named LaVina Wilson. She recently died at age 90. For many years, I attended her Bible study on Saturday nights. We had great fellowship and learned how to apply Biblical principles to everyday life. Another spiritual mentor, Shirley Bliese, Ph.D., taught me about the power of the Holy Spirit. She taught me about the power of "the mouth." Our words influence our reality and can make or break our relationships. We have a society of children with low self-esteem. This is evident by the pervasive abuse of alcohol and drugs. I am shocked when I stand at the grocery line and hear how parents demean their children. If you call a child a "loser," they will begin to act like one. As Christians, we need to edify and encourage each other. We are too quick to judge those around us. Seldom do we take the time to really know what's going on with the other person. There's usually a lot more to a person than what meets the eye. The "world" often looks at the Christian and wonders where their Christian behavior is. One woman who truly exemplifies putting her faith into action is Dr. Jane Britt. She is the founder of Womanline and Caring Families in Dayton, Ohio. She has saved thousands of babies. I am sure there will be a special place in Heaven for her. I am proud to call her my friend.

My faith continues to grow. I thank God that He is very personal to me. I have seen major miracles in my life. One of them involved a serious car accident. A school bus hit our car, which quickly became an accordion. I was in the passenger side and dangerously injured. I had memory loss, ophthalmic headaches, and various other symptoms. It took me about two years to overcome most of the injuries.

Wright

That's a fantastic story.

Boucher

There's more to the story. On a beautiful fall afternoon, I was going to a doctor's appointment. This was about two years into my recovery. I really didn't feel like going and was very preoccupied. I was sitting in the car in my driveway, which lead out to a busy street. It was about 3 o'clock in the afternoon. I put my car in reverse and no matter how hard I tried, it would not budge out of my driveway. I decided to "gun it" and it still wouldn't move. Because of my preoccupation, I had not looked behind my car, as I normally do. Finally, I turned my head and to my amazement, I saw three teenagers behind my car walking home from school. There's no question in my mind that I would have hit them had my car not failed to work. The minute the three teenagers passed the back of my car, I put my car in reverse again and it went! What a moment! I praised God all the way to the doctor's office. After much reflection, I know that God has protected me throughout my life, sometimes more visibly than others. That's where my faith needs to come in. I have to remind myself that He's always taking care of me whether I see him or not.

Wright

Wow!

Boucher

The God I know is really personal. I don't make decisions without going to Him. If I don't feel at peace about something, I don't do it.

Wright

Recently, I read that the overall United States divorce rate is the same as that in the Christian community. Christians are not perceived by the public as being different. You know, being raised as a Christian, I was amazed. What do you think about this?

Boucher

First of all, I think that anybody can say they are a Christian. When I was new at my faith walk, I thought all Christians were devout and trustworthy. I was really surprised when I had some unfortunate business experiences with a Christian family from my church. They were financially desperate and I thought it was my Christian duty to help them out. We had a written agreement that they would begin to repay the debt after 12 months. That was five years ago. They have never made an attempt or even an offer to pay it back. In fact, they have hung up on me and ignored many written requests. This family was in leadership at our church and held in high regard. They had done this to other families in our church. I know they know the word of God. I do not understand how they can call themselves Christians. The secular world is confused when a Christian behaves this way. If there was any chance that an unbeliever was considering Christianity, this would certainly give them doubt. The bottom line is that there is a big difference between a person who **says** they believe and a person who really **acts** on their beliefs. You can tell a Christian by the way they live!

Wright

Right!

Boucher

You have to look at a man or a woman by the fruits they produce. How do they treat people? Do they treat some people as though they are important and others as unimportant? Or, do they treat everyone the same way? With dignity and compassion?

Wright

I like the words to the old song, "You will know them by their love."

Boucher

One of my favorites.

Wright

Real Christians who love each other don't take money and not attempt to repay it.

Boucher

That's my opinion.

Wright

People are motivated by good role models and mentors. Has there been anyone in your life that has made a profound difference and helped you to be a better, more effective person?

Boucher

There are many. I'll start with high school. My high school counselor told my parents that I would never make it through Ohio State University (OSU). She thought it was too big and I would get lost there. My parents didn't believe the counselor and sent me to OSU anyway. I had a wonderful educational experience. I did my undergraduate and graduate work there and have many beautiful memories. After receiving my degrees with a four point average, my father showed up at my high school and told the counselor, "I hope you never try to discourage another teenager again."

In spite of the counselor, I had a high school English teacher, Mr. Ron Price, who believed in my writing. Because of him, I was able to believe in my own ability to write. As a consequence, I have written six books...one a best-seller!

Later, I had a theater professor at OSU who knew that I was terrorized to get in front of people and give a speech. It's a miracle that I do what I do today. I make my living as a professional speaker, trainer, and consultant. It's because of Dr. Dorothy Laming (now deceased) that I can get up in front of large audiences and give a presentation with relative ease. I always tell my **Effective Presentation Skills** classes that if they believe in what they're talking about, they will get over the fear of being in front of people. She helped me learn this and I will forever be grateful.

Another person who had a major influence on my life was my grandmother, Margaret English. She had only one year of college, but she was one of the smartest people I've ever known. In those days, if you were a woman and decided to get married, you had to quit college. She was allowed to teach, so she supported my grandfather through college and law school. He became a banker and a lawyer. She was definitely the woman behind the man. She was a very practical person who had a lot of common sense. She was also highly intuitive. She was a practicing Christian who loved Billy Graham. I am sure that she prayed for me everyday. One of her sayings has been a primary inspiration for my work today—: "If you have knowledge, let other light their candles by it." I miss her wisdom and look forward to seeing her again someday in Heaven.

Today, I am more of a mentor than a mentee. I continue to be grateful to my strong Christian mentors, but the roles have now changed. I have chosen to be a yielding vessel of God's love. I want to help people in any way I can, however I can and I want God to use me.

Wright

What advice would you give our readers that would help them realize the importance of faith in their business and personal lives?

Boucher

When you have faith, you trust what you cannot see. If you are not sure where you are in terms of your faith walk, I ask people to explore that spiritual side of their life. The world is a lot more about what you **can not** see than what you **can** see. It is critical to open our hearts and minds to what God has for us. I recommend praying or meditating on the word every day. We need to treat people the way we want to be treated. We need to understand that bad things sometimes happen to God's people and we will not always understand why. But God says that His understanding is not our understanding. That's where faith comes in! Everyday, I pray for God's wisdom, discernment, and protection. When you are walking with Him, you don't have to wonder whether or not you are doing the right thing. He will gently nudge you and put you in places you never would have imagined. His plan is better for us than any plan we may have.

Wright

What a great conversation. I really appreciate you taking this time to discuss faith and how it manifests in your business. Thank you for being with us today.

Boucher

I would like to add one more thing. I've written a book about domestic violence. It's called: *Survival: How to Stay Out Once You Get Out*. It's important for us to address the terror that occurs in one out of four homes in our country. People don't want to talk about this topic. God told us to be peacemakers. Sadly, one out of four women is abused in our country and she goes back to the negative relationship eight to eleven times. My book addresses this issue so that she will never go back. We need to pray that there is healing in the American home and family. You mentioned earlier that Christian families look almost identical to secular families today. We need to do whatever it takes to rebuild our family structure. I don't think it can be done without faith, prayer, and action.

Wright

I totally agree. Today, we have been talking to Jane Boucher. She is an international professional speaker, seminar leader, consultant, and author of six books including: *How to Love the Job You Hate.* The revised version is being endorsed by Dr. Kenneth Blanchard and will be released in 2004. Please look for her book on domestic violence called: *Survival: How To Stay Out Once You Get Out.* The National Speakers Association awarded Jane the Certified Speaking Professional (CSP) designation. Less than 8% of all professional speakers hold this designation. Jane, thanks for being with us on *Conversations on Faith.*

Boucher

It was a real blessing to be here.

About The Author

Before owning her business, Jane Boucher was a counselor in Sarasota, Florida. She worked with chemically dependent young people. She has her BS and MA from Ohio State University and had done doctoral work at the University of South Florida. She is currently finishing her doctorate in natural medicine. She has been an adjunct professor ah the University of Dayton, Wright State University and Sinclair Community College in Dayton, Ohio.

Today she owns Boucher Consultants, a nationally recognized firm specializing in organizational effectiveness, professional growth and communications. She is a high energy consultant, professional speaker, author of four (4) books including her latest, *How to Love the Job you Hate*. She is currently working on tow new books, *Patients First*, to remind us that in health care the patient must come first. Another book entitled, *Surviving: How to Stay Out Once You Get Out*, deals with domestic violence.

She is also a weekly newspaper columnist. Her clients range from small businesses to Fortune 500 companies. Her client list includes GM, IBM, the United States Air Force, and *Inc.* Magazine—where she has shared the platform with General Norman Schwartzkopf and Bernard Siegel, M.D.

The National Speakers Association awarded the CSP designation to Jane. She is one of the few Certified Speaking Professionals in the United States.

Jane Boucher, CSP
PO Box 18368
Reno, Nevada 89511
Email: janeboucher@mail.com.
www.janeboucher.com
www.janeboucher.org

Chapter 17

Dr. Ray Charles

David E. Wright (Wright)

Today, we are talking to Dr. Ray Charles, pastor and founder of A Ray of Light Ministries. Dr. Charles is a Spiritual Coach, and a trusted advisor to an array of CEOs and pastors. His approach to Spiritual Coaching is grounded in the principle of "faith" and "faith for the whole man." Dr. Charles is well suited to influence and affect the belief system of both the corporate and spiritual aspects of leadership, having been successful in transitioning his career from business (as a Chemical Engineer & Risk Management Professional) to ministry (as an ordained pastor and Doctor of Philosophy). We are here to talk about faith as it relates to the whole man.

Dr. Charles, welcome to *Conversations On Faith*. As I examine your transition from business to ministry, I cannot help but notice that you risked it all. I mean you put it all on the line (your career, your degrees, and your reputation).

Dr. Ray Charles (Dr. Charles)

Dave, one thing I have come to realize is that exercising faith is neither a risk, a loss, nor a gain. It is moving into the continuous life-flow of God. Paul, the apostle, once said, "I count it all loss, that I may know Him." By this he meant, he counted everything before the call as simply preparation so that he may step into the new place in God—never looking back. Dave, I simply followed God's blueprint.

Wright

So, I'm curious. What exactly did you discover that caused you to make your transition from business to ministry?

Dr. Charles

In my role as a risk management consultant, I discovered the missing link to Risk Management. It was not another method or technique, but it was the Spirit of God, personified through spiritual coaching—extracting every form of toxicity in the heart of the leader.

Dave, it is critically important that I mention that the inertia I gained for my transition stemmed from the biblical principle which states *"If the first fruit is holy, then **the whole man** is holy."* The first fruit here is the leader. This was the birthing place for the concept of "faith for the whole man."

During my tenure as a risk management consultant, I was trained to identify and "cover" the risk (potential hazard) that companies were faced with through insurance or other alternative risk management techniques. I discovered that was God's way of using risk management as the foundation to transition me from a place where I was using insurance and other methods to cover the risk of organizational loss, to a place where I would be solely dependent upon His Spirit to impart righteous leadership into the heart of leaders—thereby, transforming the inner-structure of business.

Wright

I appreciate you sharing with me the genesis, or birthing place of the "faith for the whole man" concept. Can you elaborate further what exactly you mean by faith for the whole man?

Dr. Charles

In understanding faith for the whole man, we need to establish what we mean by "the whole man." He is a many-membered man. He crosses religious, racial, social, and all forms of territorial boundaries. He is unified in spirit with the other members of his body, and is built to walk in this "unity of spirit" experientially.

Whether we realize it or not, this man is already present in spirit form. We commonly know him as "all humanity." Dave, faith for the whole man begins by seeing all humanity as one. This type of faith is the substance that is required to breakthrough the position of deity that man has set up for himself. Without it, we would continue to experience individualism, denominationalism, secularism, and other bondages of corruption.

Dave, this man who has broken through must manifest himself in our homes, our businesses, our communities, and our nations. The sign of his appearing is that he gives life to every situation. The entryway to his appearing is that he "loves in the spirit."

Wright
What do you mean by love in the spirit?

Dr. Charles
To "love in the spirit" means to rightly discern the spiritual condition of your **neighbor** and make a conscious decision to make that person whole; not because you want to, but, rather, because of your direct acknowledgement of God, you know that it is His heart to make that person whole.

In my period of transition, for example, my decision to walk away from business and enter into the ministry to business, was not so much because of my desire, but because of the compelling force of compassion from the throne of God that was shed into my heart. Dave, you get to a point where it is beyond you; beyond the concealed purposes of your heart; beyond identifying yourself by your ethnic background, etc., and instead, you recognize that your neighbor is part of your own body. Dave, this concept of "faith for the whole man" is clearly illustrated in the biblical parable of "the Good Samaritan" in **Luke, Chapter 10.**

Wright
I can remember reading of a time when John the Baptist was in prison and, after being there for quite some time, he sent someone to Jesus to ask, "Are you really the one who has come?" This sounded strange since John was the one who baptized him. Was this an example of John missing the mark in this "faith for the whole man" concept?

Dr. Charles
Dave, this is an excellent example. What John was struggling with was double mindedness, which is one of the greatest adversaries to

"faith for the whole man." Why? The reason is that double-mindedness will always cause you to stop and think of yourself in the midst of challenging circumstances.

At first, John called Jesus "Lord." Well, the title "Lord" implicitly connects him to the head. When John's faith led to his imprisonment, his circumstantial condition shook his confidence in his connection to the head. He more or less said to himself "surely any real head would do something about my imprisonment." Dave, there is an order to this concept of "faith for the whole man." The key principle to this order is that you do not usurp the authority of the head. Double-mindedness caused John to feel somewhat disconnected to the head and caused him to miss the mark in appropriating "faith for the whole man."

Wright

So, why is it necessary to obtain faith for the whole man?

Dr. Charles

It is the one thing that will bring healing to the world system and to creation. Sure, I can have faith for the healing of my own body, my own finances, my own marriage, etc. But, what about laying down my life for my neighbor?

Dave, there is a corporate cry in the business world, and it is a cry for healing. Wounds have been left uncovered and unattended from acts of treachery, greed, non-disclosure, etc., leaving many without hope. The business world is awaiting the manifestation of this corporate man who demonstrates on a daily basis this "faith for the whole man."

Wright

But there are many who are achieving successes who are not so concerned with this faith of the whole man concept.

Dr. Charles

No argument there, Dave. But there is a vast difference between success in the eyes of God and success in the eyes of the world.

Wright

What's the difference?

Dr. Charles

The difference between success in the eyes of the world and success in the eyes of God is akin to the difference between growth and healthy or *wholesome* growth. Healthy growth is measured according to the degree to which the character of God is the pervasive influence in all we do.

Wright

Well, you've certainly described this refreshing concept of faith for the whole man. Is there a key principle here that you would like to leave with our readers?

Dr. Charles

Dave, the key principle here is "the wholeness of one is the strength of all."

Wright

Wow. What a message for today's leaders. So, what's the job of the CEO as he leads the ship in the sea of faith for the whole man?

Dr. Charles

Dave, the CEO's number one job is to bring life to his business "ecosystem." In the business setting, this business ecosystem (the employees, customers, vendors, neighboring community, etc.) is the whole man.

Wright

Can you provide me an example of a company or CEO that has practiced this concept of faith for the whole man?

Dr. Charles

Several of my clients comes to mind. However, a well-publicized case is the Malden Mills manufacturing plant in Northern Massachusetts. In 1995, when a massive fire nearly destroyed the plant, all the employees were certain they would be out of work. However, their CEO astonished them.

The CEO announced that he would keep all his employees on the payroll. This cost the CEO several million dollars. Dave, the significance of this is that his employees would have understood had he collected the insurance money and walked away.

When asked by the New York Times why he responded in such fashion, he responded: "I consider my workers an asset, not an expense. The quality of our product is paramount, and it's the employees who make that quality. I have a responsibility to the worker, both blue-collar and white collar. I have an equal responsibility to the community. It would have been unconscionable to put 3000 people on the street and deliver a **death** blow to the cities of Lawrence and Mathuen." Dave, this is such a classic example of faith for the whole man and a CEO that is singularly-minded on bringing life to "the whole man."

Well, the interesting thing is that his production volume doubled several weeks following the fire. According to the CEO, the people became very creative. Dave, creativity will always flow out of a demonstration of faith for the whole man by the leader.

The resulting debt eventually forced the company into bankruptcy. However, the company emerged from bankruptcy in late 2003. The seed of "**love in the spirit**" that was sown in 1995 brought forth a harvest of resurrection life in 2003.

Wright

Dr. Charles, as we close, there are many reasons why one may not be manifesting faith for the whole man in his business. Earlier in our interview, you mentioned double mindedness as a major adversary to this concept. If you were to pin point the missing link in producing this level of faith, what would it be?

Dr. Charles

Dave, the missing link would not be mission, vision, leadership, or any of those attributes that we normally hear in modern day business jargon. What it would be, without a doubt, is honor. Dave, we have lost our ability to honor or submit ourselves one to another. But honor is more than a core value. It is holding your neighbor (the other part of your many-membered body) in high esteem. When this is pervasive in the culture of the organization, the quality of life would be a high priority from the boardroom to the show-room.

Wright

Very interesting. Very interesting concept indeed. Is there anything that you can tell our readers that they can do as they go about there daily lives to facilitate this system of faith for the whole man, and create the attitude of honor in their lives?

Dr. Charles

Take heed to the first commandment that had a promise associated with an interpersonal relationship, which was, *"Honor your mother and your father that you may have **long life**."* Now the words mother and father can be viewed both literally and figuratively. In the case of a company, for example, the mother is the many-membered body of employees that is giving birth to the corporate vision. So, if you look at it figuratively, the commandment is saying honor your mother and your father (the source of all wisdom, almighty God) so that your company may have long life.

Wright

Wow! What a great conversation on faith. Dr. Charles, I want you to know how much I appreciate you spending this much time with me and answering these very difficult questions. I really think you helped me today, and I know you will help our readers.

Dr. Charles

Dave, I have seen this concept transform companies and families. I strongly believe that with adaptation of this concept, we will witness **a ray of light**, enhanced quality of life, and a more trusting workplace environment. I certainly have seen significant and positive enhancement, coupled with increased productivity among the CEOs that I have coached who have embraced this concept of "faith for the whole man."

Wright

Today we have been talking to Dr. A. Ray Charles, spiritual coach and trusted advisor to many of today's leaders. He is the pastor and founder of A Ray of Light Ministries—a company that is dedicated to "Transforming the Inner-Structure of Business." Dr. Charles, thank you so much for being with us.

Dr. Charles

Dave, it was indeed my pleasure.

About The Author

Dr. Ray Charles is a Spiritual Coach and trusted advisor to many CEOs and pastors. He is the pastor and founder of A Ray of Light Ministries—a company that is dedicated to "Transforming the Inner-Structure of Business." His corporate philosophy is rooted in the proverb, *"When the righteous are in authority, the people rejoice."*

Dr. Ray Charles
A Ray of Light Ministries
PO Box 1206
Matteson, Illinois 60443
Phone: 443.250.8455
Fax: 802.609.0883
Email: spiritualcoach@arayoflight.com
www.arayoflight.com